Patent
and
Antitrust Law

Patent and Antitrust Law

A Legal and Economic Appraisal

Ward S. Bowman, Jr.

THE UNIVERSITY OF CHICAGO PRESS
CHICAGO AND LONDON

The University of Chicago Press, Chicago 60637
The University of Chicago Press, Ltd., London

International Standard Book Number: 0–226–06925–7
Library of Congress Catalog Card Number: 72–90910

Contents

Preface

The compatibility or the conflict between patent and antitrust law has been a subject of controversy since the Sherman Act was passed in 1890. This book attempts, by applying economic analysis to cases, to critically appraise the relationships between the fields and to determine the appropriate spheres for the exercise of monopoly under patents and for competition under antitrust.

Both economists and lawyers have increasingly recognized that work in each field leads to a better understanding of the other. This is especially, although by no means uniquely, true of public policy issues concerning competition and monopoly. Here these issues are purposely exposed and critically analyzed according to economic premises which, although they are controversial in law and to a lesser extent in economics, may increase the relevance of future discourse in this important subject area.

The analysis on which the conclusions of this work are based is derived from years of association with colleagues, from whose oral and written contributions I have long borrowed heavily. Although I have no intention of slighting others, including past and present students who have made stimulating observations, I am especially indebted to professors Aaron Director, Robert H. Bork, John S. McGee, and Ralph K. Winter. My very competent secretary, Miss Sadie Dziadik, has been indispensable.

A research grant provided by the General Electric Company to Yale Law School is gratefully acknowledged. It has supported research for this undertaking.

Introduction

The principal subject of this book is the agreements that owners of patents make with others who wish to use them. The title, *Patent and Antitrust Law*, reflects the importance of antitrust law, a general law favoring competition, in determining the permissible conditions which patentees with limited monopoly, long exempt from rules applicable to nonpatented products or processes, may include in agreements with their licensees. What constitutes patent misuse has been interpreted by courts so as to severely contract the permissible use of patents in resolving supposed conflicts between patent and antitrust law. The central purpose of this study is to assess this conflict by evaluating the various forms of licensing.

A principal conclusion is that the antitrust/patent conflict, as courts have assessed it, is to a large extent illusory. It is based on a long-accepted but mistaken notion that a legal monopoly, a patent, may be used as a lever to monopolize the unpatented. In addition, courts seem oblivious, whether or not patents are involved, to the consumer-benefiting efficiencies derivable from agreements sellers make with buyers concerning how, when, where, and under what conditions a licensee may use information.

Included among those licensing arrangements that will be found *not* to be means of creating new and broader monopoly are: agreements requiring that products used with a patented product be purchased from the patentee (tie-ins); sale or resale at a stipulated price (price-restrictive licensing); sale or use confined to a particular area (territorial licensing); use for a particular purpose (functional division of use); pricing of a final product of which only one of the essential components is patented (end-product pricing); and licensing multiple patents in blocks (all-or-none offers).

To evaluate the foregoing examples of patentee-licensee contracts in terms of whether they "extend monopoly" is to apply a test that assumes the propriety of allowing a patentee to use any method of charging what the traffic will bear if, but only if, the reward to the patentee arising from the conditional use measures the patented product's competitive superiority over substitutes. Profit maximization—charging what the traffic will bear—it will be shown, is consistent with the patent law and is the main test the courts have assigned themselves. This profit maximization test does not depend upon whether a particular contractual arrangement restricts or expands the use of the particular innovation given patent protection. That is a test appropriate in the absence of a legally sanctioned monopoly. Allowing maximization of the return ascribable to a valid patent need not involve assessing whether the reward arises from efficiency (resulting in output expansion) or trade restraint (resulting in output contraction). This latter efficiency/trade restraint trade-off analysis is appropriate under antitrust laws, where the desirability of a legal monopoly such as a patent is not countenanced. However, it will be demonstrated that many of the licensing arrangements judicially condemned should be permissible even under appropriate antitrust standards in the absence of patent protection because they are means of expanding rather than contracting output.

Of course an antitrust test (output effect) is much more rigorous than a patent-extension test. It does not require the assumption either that some monopoly such as a patent is desirable or that, if it is, its full exploitation is necessarily in the public interest. Patent law, however, assumes that a time-limited patent, giving patentees the right to exclude others from making, using, or vending that which is patented, is an important and necessary incentive for incurring the necessary costs of producing useful inventions. The reward depends upon providing competitive advantage to users. It is market oriented. Without patent protection, patent law assumes, rapid copying by others (who have not incurred the cost) would greatly diminish wealth-creating activity, to the detriment of the community. Invention would be underrewarded.

The first three chapters of the book may be viewed as providing the economic rationale for the existing patent system; they explain the propriety of assessing patent-licensing contracts in terms of whether they maximize reward attributable to that which is patented or whether monopoly is extended to broader areas. Insofar as one's interest is centered on how well this judicially accepted task of assessing monopoly extension is performed, this study is a self-contained unit beginning with chapter 4. The purpose, however, is broader. Public policy considerations involve not only interpretation of patent law, antitrust law, and possible conflicts between them, but also an evaluation of the goals sought and the alternative means of achieving these goals. Chapter 1 therefore attempts to explain why the long-run aims of patent law and antitrust law are the same. Both seek better allocation of scarce resources in the interest of consumers by utilizing the pricing system as a principal regulator. Chapter 2 evaluates the patent reward system in terms of whether it is likely to underreward or overreward invention, thereby misdirecting resources away from more valuable use. The conclusion is that departure from optimality is predictable, but that suggested alternatives, including no patent system at all, are worse. This problem is particularly difficult to prove empirically. It rests upon the plausibility of the contrasting theories compared. Chapter 3 supplements chapter 2 by analyzing the standards for patenting inventions. The question here concerns whether monopoly rewards are likely to be given for routine improvements which the community would soon receive from others without cost.

The general conclusion of the first three chapters is that a patent reward system, allowing patentees the right to maximize the reward ascribable to the differential advantage different users find worth paying for, deserves continued support.

Beginning with chapter 4, which explains the economic standards upon which monopoly extension analysis is based, the analysis assumes that patent rights are given and granted under valid legislation in pursuit of social policies thought to be desirable.

The correct economic evaluation of patent-licensing arrangements under patent law or antitrust law, as with similar arrangements when patents are not involved, is a complicated process and deserves careful analysis not only in terms of monopoly extension, but also because of the efficiency aspects of such arrangements. They are often, if not usually, means by which the community is able to get more of what it wants at lower prices. For purposes of either monopoly extension or efficiency analysis it is useful to distinguish vertical arrangements involving the coordination of complementary aspects of the productive process from horizontal arrangements involving unified control of competing aspects of the productive process (e.g., pooling of competing patents or agreements between a patentee and makers of unpatented substitutes).

It will be shown that courts, blinded by the monopoly-extension fallacy, have failed to see the efficiency-facilitating role of vertical agreements. Also, but to a lesser degree, they misconceive or are insensitive to the different efficiency implications of horizontal arrangements.

Beginning with chapter 5 and continuing in chapter 6 the focus turns to an analysis of the efficiency of numerous vertical arrangements. Then attention is directed to the history of the judicial treatment of such arrangements (chapters 7, 8, and 9). Next is an analysis of horizontal arrangements (chapter 10) and the development of the judicial treatment of these (chapter 11). The failure to prescribe effective relief is the principal subject matter of the last chapter, which in its final pages contrasts the findings of this study with the ad hoc patent-licensing conclusions of the 1968 Report of the White House Task Force on Antitrust Policy (the Neal Report).

1

The Compatibility of Antitrust and Patent Law Goals

Antitrust law and patent law are frequently viewed as standing in diametric opposition. How can there be compatibility between antitrust law, which promotes competition, and patent law, which promotes monopoly? In terms of the economic goals sought, the supposed opposition between these laws is lacking. Both antitrust law and patent law have a common central economic goal: *to maximize wealth by producing what consumers want at the lowest cost*. In serving this common goal, reconciliation between patent and antitrust law involves serious problems of assessing effects, but not conflicting purposes. Antitrust law does not demand competition under all circumstances. Quite properly, it permits monopoly when monopoly makes for greater output than would the alternative of an artificially fragmented (inefficient) industry. The patent monopoly fits directly into this scheme insofar as its central aim is achieved. It is designed to provide something which consumers value and which they could not have at all or have as abundantly were no patent protection afforded.

Antitrust Law

Under the Sherman Act agreements in restraint of trade (section 1) and monopolization or an attempt to monopolize (section 2) are condemned as illegal. The economic rationale for this condemnation is that monopoly makes it possible to restrict output and raise prices so that consumers pay more for and get less of the things they want most. The output restriction made possible by monopoly idles, or transfers to less urgent uses, those resources which but for the monopolistic restriction would be more efficiently employed. Conversely, a competitive market process allocates scarce resources to those uses

1

the community values most highly. Insofar as the antitrust laws are successful, they promote a market-oriented, profit-incentive process unimpeded by artificial roadblocks to efficiency. Such is the rationale of market competition and the antitrust laws that support it.

Patent Law

Patent law, thought by some to be an exception to a general rule in favor of competition, shares with antitrust law its central purpose—efficiently providing those things consumers value. But the means are different. Patent law pursues this goal by encouraging the invention of new and better products. Invention, like other forms of productive activity, is not costless. Those who undertake it, therefore, must be rewarded. And so elusive a commodity as an idea which qualifies as invention is peculiarly susceptible to being freely appropriated by others. A patent is a legal device to insure that there can be a property right in certain ideas. Thus the temporary right of a patentee to exclude others is a means of preventing "free riding" so that the employment of useful private resources may be remunerated. Without a patent system, prevention of "free riding" would be severely limited. Ability to keep secrets and to enforce private "know-how" contracts would, without patent law, provide inventors very limited protection from rapid and widespread copying by others. Central to the economic justification of a patent system is the presumption that without the patent right, too few resources would be devoted to invention.

The "exclusive right to make, use and vend the invention or discovery," which Congress has long granted patentees,[1] is thus a legal monopoly exempt from the more general proscription of trade restraints and monopolization under early common law and more recent antitrust statutes.

Goal Evaluation

The goal of both antitrust law and patent law is to maximize allocative efficiency (making what consumers want) and productive efficiency

---

1. Rev. Stat. § 4884 (act of 8 July 1870). Invention has long been recognized as a productive activity requiring special protection. Article I, section 8 of the Constitution empowered Congress "To promote the Progress of Science and the useful Arts by securing for limited Times to Authors and Inventors the exclusive Right to their respective Writings and Discoveries."

(making these goods with the fewest scarce resources). In achieving this goal under either antitrust or patent law the detriment to be avoided is output restriction. This may arise from monopolization which diverts production from more urgent to less urgent use or from legal rules requiring inefficient methods of production. The evil, then, may be viewed as net output restriction after efficiency increases are accounted for. Both antitrust and patent law seek output expansion, not output restriction. Competition deserves support insofar as it brings about this result. And so it is with patents. The temporary monopoly afforded by a patent, once a particular invention has come into being, will have all the output-restrictive disabilities of any monopoly. The argument for patents is that without this temporary monopoly there would be insufficient profit incentives to produce the invention, and that because an invention is profitable only if consumers are willing to pay what the patentee charges, the consumers are therefore better off than they would be without the invention, even if they are charged "monopoly" prices. If this is so, a trade-off (some monopoly restraint for greater output in the long run) is in the interest of socially desirable resource allocation.[2] An appraisal of alleged conflicts between antitrust law and patent law depends upon understanding the role of profits in providing the incentive for undertaking efficient production of those things consumers value.

The Role of Profits

In economic analysis, monopoly and competition are opposing concepts. Their greatest usefulness is in predicting how individuals, alone or in firms or associations, will use scarce resources to expand or contract the production of goods and services according to what consumers want. In the United States the basic (although not exclusive) method of organizing production is private enterprise under a price system. In such a system, the motivation for producing what con-

2. If this is so, it is not because the trade-restraining effect is beneficial; rather, it is because correcting the restraint would involve greater cost (in the form of misdirected resources elsewhere) than would be saved by eliminating the particular restraint (see Williamson, "Economies as an Antitrust Defense: The Welfare Trade-offs," 58 *Am. Econ. Rev.* 18 (March 1968). This is an example of what antitrust law recognizes as an "ancillary restraint"—one *necessary* to the achievement of a greater gain elsewhere. Even with trade-offs, however, economic assessment is in terms of output—a search for more output, overall, of the things consumers prefer.

sumers want is search for profit. Sole control (monopoly) of any resource which is scarce and for which substitutes are few or distant will, to reemphasize a central proposition, make for less output and higher prices for that resource than would be the case if the substitutes were close and numerous (competition).

Private enterprises, whether conducted under competitive or monopolistic conditions, are motivated by search for profit. Obtaining profits, or avoiding losses, is an objective of all market participants. Both antitrust law and patent law, insofar as they are directed toward achieving community welfare through an allocative process beneficial to consumers, seek this end by making this profit system work, or work better. Profits, it must be emphasized, provide motivation both for the social efficiency of resource allocation (output expansion) and for social inefficiency (output restriction) under monopoly. A central policy goal of both antitrust law and patent law is resolving this efficiency/trade restraint trade-off.[3]

Under a market system, productive resources are directed to their most valued private use. As consumers' preferences change, or as improved production techniques occur, new outputs and different quantities of existing outputs are called for. Changing combinations of resource inputs are also required. Thus a continuous reshuffling process is occasioned, all in the search for profit. The process by which each productive resource is directed to its most valued use involves a successive appraisal (marginal analysis) of alternative uses.

The profit-maximizing process also involves minimizing costs, under either competition or monopoly. The relevant costs are the alternatives forsaken (opportunity cost). Cost reduction (a form of productive efficiency) is thus consistent with profit maximization for both competitors and monopolists. And all such cost reduction, whoever achieves it, is wealth-increasing to consumers. It is socially as well as privately efficient. It is a popular and serious mistake to presume that because profits arise from monopoly profits and productivity necessarily diverge. Profits can and do signify productive efficiency —lower costs or new and improved products.

---

3. This "trade-off" method of welfare assessment is applicable to many situations in which productive efficiency and trade-restriction are involved. See, for example, Professor Williamson's "trade-off" analysis of mergers in "Economies as an Antitrust Defense."

Allocative Efficiency and the Competitive Model

A model of "perfect competition" is a useful conceptual device in economic analysis, but departure from its static assumptions in which marginal costs are equated with prices is not, never has been, and cannot be a workable standard for judging legality under antitrust law. Perfect competition is a conception of an extreme (and unrealistic) degree of competition in which all the productive resources are so efficiently utilized that not a single resource can be induced to move from one use to another. To achieve such an equilibrium there would have to be complete mobility of resources among uses. In addition, of course, the owners of the resources would have to have full knowledge of their alternative uses. Perfect competition would also require that the participating firms be so numerous that each would act independently. This means that each would be so small relatively that the action of any one would not have a retaliatory impact on the action of any of the others. Any central control over an industry's action either from concert among participants or from outsiders would have to be eliminated. In addition, the various products and services would have to be finely divisible, or the resources could be moved from one use to a better use only when incremental advantage reached a critical size. Given all these preconditions to perfection, profits in the economic sense (rewards in the form of "rents" to fixed, immovable, or lumped factors of production) would disappear as fast as they arose.

This concept of perfection, externalities apart, provides a model of allocative efficiency. It describes a condition in which no change is desirable on grounds of resource allocation. Needless to say, there is nothing even closely approximating perfect competition in the real world. Its principal relevance is in the analytical base it provides, not the utopian state it conjures up. Its value lies in the central focus it places on competitive forces leading, impersonally and selfishly, to the solution of that immensely complicated and important social problem—Who should produce how much of what, when, how, and for whom? But when perfect competition is used as a goal rather than as an analytic tool, either for restructuring the number of market participants in any activity or for proscribing their activities, it can lead to worse rather than better resource allocation. Given the imperfect conditions all markets share to a greater or lesser degree, public policy requires the assessment of the alternatives available in an uncertain world, not the pursuit of a textbook model.

As a public policy tool perfect competition does provide useful insights into the equilibrating forces of a competitive process unencumbered by either external or internal impediments to the flow of resources responding to price and profit signals. Monopoly and agreements in restraint of trade are such impediments, and, as has been stressed, they are condemned for this reason. This does not mean, however, and the antitrust laws have never been interpreted to mean, that every departure from the perfect competitive model becomes illegal. Rather, these laws, when consistently and rationally applied, view competition as a process designed to work for the benefit of consumers. They take the world as it is and evaluate available alternatives. And the allocation of resources cannot be fully evaluated unless productive efficiencies (cost savings or better products) are assessed along with restraints. Stressing perfect competition as an ideal involves the danger of underplaying the importance of productive efficiencies: savings arising from large size and efficiencies arising from innovation in manufacturing and from company organization and management, as well as from dissemination of knowledge through sales effort and advertising. Employee relations and myriad other activities also are sources of productive efficiency. None of these commonplace examples would exist if competition were perfect. These examples, moreover, are not output restricting. Imperfect competition is not monopoly. Dealing with imperfections is what competition as a process rather than a static model is all about.

Undertaking the uncertainties and risks of entering into or expanding productive endeavor in search of profit is a central economic problem. This is always a game of chance in which odds of gain or loss are crucial. As Professor Hayek has emphasized, "The solution of the economic problem of society is in this respect always a voyage of exploration into the unknown, an attempt to discover new ways of doing things better than they have been done before."[4] The purpose of patent laws is to facilitate this process. No less is it the function of antitrust.

A consumer welfare test, applied to antitrust law, patent law, or conflicts between them, constitutes a central criterion for making decisions and appraising them. To admit the central importance of resource allocation—what consumers want at the lowest cost—is to

4. Friedrich A. Hayek, *Individualism and Economic Order* (Chicago: University of Chicago Press, 1948), p. 101.

recognize that the analysis of competition under antitrust law or of temporary monopoly under patent law permits the conclusion that both are means and not ends. Under such an approach the productive and allocative efficiencies associated with particular industry structures or particular trade practices are exposed and given their appropriate weight.

Efficiency and Antitrust

The relevance of productive efficiency to the resolution of antitrust cases is illustrated by contrasting the way the law treats horizontal mergers of competing firms with the way it treats contractual associations in price-fixing cartels. The latter—a typical case being a conspiracy among competitors to fix prices—has come to be judged illegal per se. Although this per se doctrine is not without exceptions, its rationale under antitrust law is clearly grounded in notions of consumer welfare. The only purpose or predictable effect of such an agreement is restraint, not expansion, of trade. Moreover, even though common selling agencies which arguably increase efficiency by lowering selling cost are found in some price-fixing cases, a per se rule is applied and justified by the argument that such efficiency is so rare, or so minor, that it would be a pointless waste of judicial effort to make the trade restraint/efficiency assessment.

Experience has thus led to a satisfactory general conclusion. Price-fixing conspiracies face an almost conclusive presumption that they do what they are meant to do—raise prices. This is a conclusion that their predictable effect is output restrictive. In contrast, if the very firms which were party to the illegal price agreement merged their companies, their ability to fix prices and restrict output would be no less. Indeed, it probably would be greater because control over independent action would be enhanced. But mergers are not automatically illegal, as are cartels, and for good reason. The combined facilities may be intended to create, and may actually result in, greater productive efficiencies. Costs may be reduced, resulting in more rather than less output. If two small firms with many competitors merge, the predictive effect is efficiency and output expansion, not restraint and output restriction.

The difficult efficiency/trade restraint assessments arise in mergers among few sellers when market percentages are high. Some argue that such mergers should be prohibited because of the alleged monopolistic effects (output-restricting ability) of oligopoly even in the absence of collusion. The restrictive or the potentially restrictive result of mutual reaction among few competitors is the basis for condemnation of oligopoly. In the absence of agreement, express or tacit, however, antitrust law does not automatically condemn oligopoly unless it is achieved by merger. Under merger, as contrasted to oligopoly achieved by internal growth, the restrictive effects are simply assumed to outweigh the efficiency effects of larger-scale operations. That this assumption is often more heroic than rational does not detract from the importance of this trade-off assessment.

Similar problems of assessment are involved in vertical and conglomerate mergers; but here the analysis becomes more complicated, because the premerger and postmerger market shares are not directly affected. The efficiency effect may be presumed to be relatively greater here, if only because a different and even more elusive theory of trade restraint is required—so elusive, indeed, that its proponents are still awaiting its discovery. What there is is largely mythology, equally applicable to vertical contracts (tie-in sales, exclusive franchising, vertical price fixing, and so on) as well as to vertical mergers.

Efficiency and Patents

If the temporary monopoly afforded to inventors is to be justified as on balance desirable, as chapters 2 and 3 seek to establish, its existence and the uses to which it is put must face up to the kind of restraint/efficiency assessment applied under antitrust law. Analytically, the combination of two competing patents raises the same questions as the merger of two competing companies; both combine competing assets. That the productive efficiencies predictable from a patent pool may seem *de minimis* does not change the nature of the analysis. It may, however, seem more analogous to the antitrust cartel rule than to the rule on mergers. And, of course, jointly fixing the price to be charged for competing patents is an even more obvious analogy.

The problem of assessing permissible output restriction under patent law is, in one important sense, different from that under antitrust law. The legal propriety of a basic patent monopoly has to be recognized.[5] Consequently, evaluating whether certain patent licensing practices should be sanctioned will involve the proper scope of the legal

5. 35 U.S.C. § 154 (1952 codification). In the United States the right to exclude is for seventeen years from the date of the patent grant.

monopoly. Is more being monopolized than what the patent grants, or is the practice merely maximizing the reward attributable to the competitive advantage afforded by a patent? In the example—pooling competing patents—the *something more* was the issue, and efficiency was at least not obvious. But many cases of alleged patent misuse— many, indeed, which are said to violate antitrust law—involve vertical contract relationships between patentee and licensee in which, it will be argued in subsequent chapters, no such extension of scope is explicable. Many such contracts between patentees and licensees, moreover, lead to productive efficiencies unattainable if the practices are prohibited. Given a legal patent monopoly, it is important not only to appraise whether the monopoly has been broadened—scope extension—but also to insure that prohibiting alleged misuses does not leave the holder of the patent a permissible alternative which, although less profitable, is more restrictive than the alleged misuse. The "misuse" may actually be the most efficient use of the patent from the social as well as the private point of view. It pays monopolists as well as competitors to be efficient, as has been stressed.

Alternative Goals

Many view a single-dimensional assessment of antitrust and patent law as misleadingly one-sided.[6] I do not purport to join the debate over this issue. Although it is deliberately assumed that economic efficiency in serving consumers is the goal of antitrust and patent law, whether or not that is the *sole* purpose of these legal systems, no serious student of the issue has ever contended that it is not a *major* purpose, and one worthy of careful appraisal. The most persistent hostility to patents, moreover, is based on their characterization as "monopoly." And output restriction is what monopoly is about.

However, other supposed goals of these statutory schemes have achieved prominence in the literature, and it is useful to classify them: (1) goals which are important but not effectively achievable through application of antitrust or patent law; (2) goals which are either illusory or subsumed under the goal of consumer satisfaction; and (3) goals which conflict with consumer satisfaction.

6. See, for example, Blake and Jones, "Toward a Three-Dimensional Antitrust Policy," 65 *Colum. L. Rev.* 422 (March 1965).

1. *Important but Inappropriate Goals*

There is general consensus that the efficient allocation of resources is not the only important function of an economic system. Two other functions are generally accorded a prominent role. Equitable distribution of income is one, and a rising growth rate is another. Neither, however, necessarily conflicts with economic efficiency in satisfying consumers.

If the community feels that the distribution of wealth under the prevailing reward system leaves some too poor and others too rich, a more progressive tax system (including a negative income tax) may be employed. Of course, tax policy should insure that the equalization does not destroy the sources of the prosperity being apportioned. Achieving equalization by indiscriminately taxing all sources of income or wealth minimizes the distortion of otherwise desirable resource allocation. In contrast, deciding antitrust or patent suits on the basis of which party is richer, or larger, would not only misdirect the efficient use of resources but would also set courts, administrators, and legal participants adrift on a sea of doubt and confusion by abandoning the obvious goals of the antitrust and patent systems for a cynical egalitarianism. Attempting to ration the myriad goods of the economy by deciding such cases "fairly" would surely qualify as highest in cost and lowest in efficiency as a means of reducing income inequality. It is summarily concluded, therefore, that only the most naive, to put it politely, would openly recommend that income inequality be redressed on such a haphazard basis.

Growth makes an economy richer in successive years. Achieving continuously more efficient resource allocation is not only compatible with growth but is an essential aspect of it. But economic growth is more often associated with a decision to produce more and newer products for tomorrow by foregoing consumption today. This may be done by voluntary savings and investment or by a centralized decision about what should be growing. In neither case, however, is there any compelling reason to believe that tomorrow is necessarily more important than today. And this, as I will indicate in a subsequent section, is as true for that unique commodity information, the subject matter of patent law, as it is for other unpatentable commodities. Thus, even though the patent legislation looks to the promotion of the progress of science and useful arts, and the antitrust law prohibits artificial barriers to the entry of new products or new production methods, neither need favor or disfavor investment over current consumption, and neither need favor particular forms of investment. The allocative function which antitrust law should support and patent law should supplement is market motivation, making it profitable to produce the wide variety of things that people choose. Free exercise of choice is not limited to choices among goods, or choices between goods and services, or choices between either of these and leisure. Timing—the choice between having now and having later—is also involved.

The patent law is often described as a special inducement to growth. But, as has been indicated, the patent law, like antitrust law, does not foster growth for growth's sake. Rather, it is designed to make possible those new products and new production methods which customers deem worth paying for. Promoting science and the useful arts, as the next chapter attempts to explain, is not to be viewed as a reasonably exact facsimile of a crop-support program for the over-production of invention. If the patent system works as it is designed to work, growth can be expected to be fostered. Scarce resources are diverted from current consumption to better products for tomorrow. Growth under a patent system is thus not a separate goal competing with consumer choice. It is a result of it.

2. *Illusory Goals*

The term "illusory" may be attached to two different problems. The first relates to so-called collective demands—those products and services which consumers do not buy individually. The second relates particularly to patents: Is it not a goal of patent law to encourage the divulging of secrets?

First, the notion of "consumer sovereignty" assumes that consumers do better when voting their own dollars than when somebody else votes for them. This "buyers know best" assumption is, of course, not uniformly or generally accepted. Few recommend it for minors or mental defectives. Others find, even for competent adults, a general need to protect "gullible" or "unwise" consumers from their own judgment. Assessment of alternatives to individual choice as a measure of welfare is not a purpose of antitrust law or of patent law. So-called collective decisions—the imposition by some person or group of persons (including political majorities) of its will on the rest—are presumed necessary to those transactions in which there is a "spill-over" of benefit or detriment to those other than the individual market participants. These are cases in which private cost or benefit can be said to diverge from social cost or benefit.[7] Examples include schools, highways, national defense, police protection, court administration, space exploration, and certain kinds of parks and recreational facilities.

Efficient allocation of scarce resources to particular ends is an important problem irrespective of how these ends are determined. Although collective decisions override the market vote of the individual consumer and direct the community's resources otherwise, the central authority—once it decides how much of what it wants—has, and should have, the same interest as individual consumers in getting these items supplied as efficiently as possible. The government often, if not usually, goes to the market to have these services supplied. When it does, its interests, like those of individual consumers, are furthered by effective antitrust law and effective patent law. For example, antitrust law's stress on competitive performance is no less relevant for government purchases than for individual purchases, even though the political majority which wants them has imposed them upon the minority which does not. And the interest of the government as a consumer is correspondingly similar to individual consumers when a patent system fosters useful production.

Second, the patent system is sometimes described as a public contract with an inventor for the disclosure of his secrets. In exchange

7. Social cost problems signal no automatic call either for relaxation of antitrust or patent law or necessarily for other government action. See Coase, "The Problem of Social Cost," 3 *J. L. Econ.* (1960). Divergence between private cost and social cost, or private benefit and social benefit, sometimes identified as neighborhood effect, is often weighted in terms of one's political preference for or against collective action. Libertarians perceive it as an unusual exception to a general rule stressing the benefits of the impersonal market process in an exchange economy. Others, including those especially dubious of the social effectiveness of the competitive process, tend to view the social cost problem as so widespread as to rationalize almost any attempt to overrule "dollar rationing." Thus, from the obvious fact that private lighthouses cannot be supported because of the "free riders" who cannot be made to pay, or that dirty factories can impose the cost of their soot-creation upon the community as a whole, it has come to be suggested that most activities of life, commercial and noncommercial, are reasonably exact facsimiles of lighthouses or dirty incinerators. On the other side, all actions and transactions have side effects: street parkers gain from the building of garages; a neighbor benefits from a good gardener next door; a local community suffers when a major firm fails or moves away. The list is endless. If the existence of any "social effect" (an effect on those not bearing the cost of the action) were to call for recalculating the desirability of all transactions having such effects, most of the scarce resources of the nation could be expected to be spent on calculation.

for temporary monopoly over a product, the argument goes, the public gets the benefit of information on how to make it. Thus one goal of patent policy seems to many to be the broad dissemination of knowledge. An alternative to the patent monopoly, therefore, is the private means of keeping the invention secret. Keeping secrets is not costless to inventors, however, and secrecy costs can be expected to differ with different kinds of invention. For some kinds of invention, private secrecy costs may be so high as to foreclose invention. On the other hand, the cost of secrecy may be so low that public disclosure of the invention at the price of a seventeen-year monopoly will be more costly than secrecy. Moreover, the costs of secrecy vary not only with the nature of the invention, but also with who does the inventing, the breadth and scale of participation through which the invention can be most efficiently exploited, and the amount of special know-how required for its practice. And of course, the longer the time span covered by the patent, the greater the reward available from disclosure. It also should be evident that inventions, especially processes, whose efficient exploitation requires production and therefore knowledge by a large number of firms, will have higher secrecy cost than those whose exploitation can be confined to a single firm. And even within those single firms capable of exploiting an invention internally, the cost of secrecy will be lower the fewer the persons who must know the secret.

Public revelation of the secrets of invention, however, is not the primary function of patent law. Patent law insures that those who incur the costs of inventing will reap its reward if users find the result worth paying for. This cannot occur if others reap where the investor has sown. The patent system is thus designed to stop "free riding" so that the profit-incentive system may operate in the interest of the patentee and in the interest of consumers. Without patent protection, secrecy provides the principal means by which "free riding" may be avoided. In such circumstances, inventive resources would be directed toward invention having high secrecy potential. There are not obvious reasons to believe either that significant inventive results would occur or that those inventions which were brought forth would be valued more highly by consumers than those susceptible to easy copying. Avoidance of secrecy seems, therefore, clearly subordinate to that basic goal which antitrust and patent law share: the efficient allocation of scarce resources for those products and services consumers value.

3. A Conflicting Goal: The Limitist or Populist Contention

Court opinions and commentaries discussing the purpose of antitrust law often state that it is more than a law in favor of competition; also, they claim, it is a law against bigness. The suggestion is that efficiency is not enough, that small business as a way of life is desirable, and that antitrust law not only does, but should, embody this notion. To a lesser degree, the same kind of contention is made with respect to patent law. Here the purpose is said to be to aid individual inventors (ideally, one working alone in an attic by the light of an oil lamp) rather than to aid large industrial or research organizations which seem able to protect themselves without the aid of patent monopoly.

Were protection of an individual or particular competitors an ultimate goal of patent law, it would indeed be in basic conflict with consumer interest. If, on the other hand, concern for competitors, or particular competitors, is not viewed as a purposive subsidy to inefficiency, but only as a declaration of faith about a precondition to efficient resource allocation, no policy conflict need arise. The analysis here assumes that there is no legislative purpose in either antitrust or patent law to protect particular competitors unless their protection is a means of promoting consumer interest. And although it is not my purpose to establish this consumer interest primacy, proceeding upon this assumption is not only a requisite of rational antitrust and patent analysis but is also consistent with the numerous judicial decisions to be reviewed.[8]

In the next two chapters attention is directed to the question whether patent law is likely to be an effective means of achieving better allocation of the nation's scarce resources in the public interest.

---

8. A convincing case has been made that the primacy of the goal adopted here represents the intent of the legislature in passing the Sherman Act. See Robert H. Bork, "Legislative Intent and the Policy of the Sherman Act," 9 *J. L. Econ.* 7 (Oct. 1966).

2

Economic Evaluation of Patents

There is considerable divergence of opinion about whether a patent system, or more particularly the patent law in the United States, is an appropriate means of achieving the "right" amount of investment in innovation. The preceding chapter described the purpose of the temporary patent monopoly—the right to exclude others from making, using, or vending the product of invention—as being the creation of a profit incentive for allocating resources to the production of a special kind of knowledge in order to insure the economical provision of those things consumers value most highly.

Whether the allocation of resources to the production of that knowledge which qualifies as an "invention" deserves special inducement has been thoughtfully appraised by many competent economists. Their conclusions differ in a number of ways. In one respect, however, there is substantial consensus: the effect of a patent monopoly, like any monopoly, is that too little of the monopolized product is produced. All agree (perfect discrimination apart) that once a patent has been granted it will be underutilized by competitive standards. As a result, even many of those who recognize the need for special incentive for invention have sought alternative forms of reward.

An economic appraisal of a patent system must resolve three basic problems. The first is the incentive question itself. Some have argued that invention is simply not profit motivated or is motivated by profit in so small a degree that a special reward is not needed. If invention is generated by such motives as instinct for contrivance or creative curiosity rather than by a search for profit, any patent monopoly will be hard to justify. Second, the amount of innovation is not solely a function of either pecuniary incentive or instinctive curiosity. It also depends upon the availability of previously accumulated knowledge.

Whether a patent reward system deters this accumulation or facilitates it will also determine whether it deserves support as an efficient resource allocator. Third, appraisal of a patent system must also take into account the standards applied to determine which inventions qualify for the monopoly and make a judgment whether these inventions are, as a result, overrewarded or underrewarded. The ultimate purpose of pursuing these three lines of inquiry is to determine whether a patent system aids consumers in achieving more of what they want at the lowest cost. Obviously this cannot easily be appraised with precision, and "on balance" judgments will be necessary.

The first two questions concern what governs the amount of innovation generated by an economy. They are dealt with in this chapter. The third, what constitute appropriate standards for invention, is the subject of the next chapter.

The discussion here is not a comprehensive survey of the literature on the subject. Rather, this chapter will analyze the contrasting opinions of three economists who have been principal contributors to the discussion of how a patent system relates to desirable resource allocation: professors Arnold Plant, Kenneth Arrow, and Frank Knight.

One of the most articulate economic arguments against a patent monopoly has been made by Plant, who takes the position that a patent system misdirects resources by overrewarding innovative ideas. Arrow, on the other hand, stresses the peculiar and unique economic characteristics of ideas in general and innovation in particular and concludes that such activity is underrewarded. An analysis of the conflicting theses of these well-recognized economists is an efficient way to expose and assess the incentive-reward problem in terms of too little or too much. The other question—what is it that is deserving of reward—has been raised by Knight, whose position is that rewards go to last-step routinizers rather than to true innovators. This kind of question, of course, involves appraisal of the standards for invention and is the subject of chapter 3.

Limits of Reward from Patent Monopoly

The revenue obtainable from the right granted an inventor depends ultimately upon how users evaluate the benefits of the invention. Informed users can be expected to pay no more than the added value the invention makes possible. The limitation of the user's willingness to pay is, of course, applicable to all monopolies, whether condemned by the antitrust laws or permissible under the patent system. The benefits of a patent system, if they exist, must be assessed in terms of what alternatives consumers have with or without the disadvantage of the temporary monopoly a patent system imposes upon them. The most obvious case of net social advantage of a patent system arises when except for the patent protection the product of the invention would not be available. In such a case anything users would be willing to pay would be an improvement (wealth increasing) over not having the product. If, however, to take an opposite extreme case, a patent monopoly were granted for a product which would have been forthcoming anyway, then the restricted output caused by the patent monopoly leads to a net social loss to the community.

There is considerable divergence of opinion about whether on balance a patent system makes for better or worse resource allocation. The product of a patent is information. Information lacks one aspect of scarceness which other economic goods share. Most goods are exhaustible; they can be used up. When one person gets a unit of physical product another gives up a unit. Not so with information. Requisition of information by a second person leaves the first with the same information he had. This is not to say that keeping information to oneself would not make it more valuable to that one person, but it raises marketability problems. In terms of either private interest or community interest, there is optimal utilization when a commodity with such properties is distributed to everybody who has use for it, so long as the value of that use is greater than the cost of its distribution. Because a rational patent monopolist can be expected in his own interest to exploit a wide use pattern, this minimizes the output-restrictive effects of the legalized monopoly. Insofar as secrecy is a practicable alternative to a patent system, it also results in output restriction by deliberately not taking advantage of the widespread uses to which information can be put. The problem should thus be recognized as involving a trade-off between the short-run disadvantages of monopoly on already granted patents and the possibly greater advantages of having new or better products not otherwise available.

Investment in Innovation and the Misallocation Problem: Overrewarding Innovation

The right amount of investment in a new steel plant, in an advertising campaign, or in a college education is not economically different from

investment in a new idea for a method to develop films rapidly inside
a camera, or an idea that significantly cuts the cost of producing steel
sheets in volume by a method of continuous rolling, or a cure for the
common cold. All investments are uncertain, all involve risks, and
all would be increased if they were made more remunerative. A rational patent system should be able to identify the unique attributes
of investment in ideas which qualify them for special treatment as
opposed to investment in alternatives.

In a thoughtful discussion of the effects of a patent system on the
amount of inventive activity, Plant noted the considerable differences
in opinion among economists in this respect, as well as the scanty
evidence available at the time he wrote (1934).[1] Professor J. B.
Clark, referred to by Plant as representative of economists who viewed
a patent system as a desirable stimulus to innovation, had earlier
called specific attention to the importance of avoiding the drying up
of useful productive activity by a "rivalry in waiting." The ability to
free ride at the expense of others, Clark suggested, might well bring
costly inventive activity to a halt. "If an invention became public
property the moment that it was made, there would be small profit accruing to anyone from the use of it and smaller ones from making it."

Plant went on to point out that the early nineteenth-century economists were as definite as Clark that inventions would actually cease
if the patent system were abandoned. Jeremy Bentham and John Stuart
Mill had justified a patent system in the same manner as Clark. As
Bentham put it: "an exclusive privilege is absolutely necessary in
order that what is sown may be reaped."

For the expression of a very different view, Plant noted Professor
F. W. Taussig's doubt about what Taussig characterized as the view
of the older utilitarians. The utilitarians assumed that the patent system was responsible for the greater part of inventive activity, whereas
Taussig had suggested, in contrast, that invention may arise mainly
as a spontaneous manifestation of a human instinct for contrivance.
But more specifically, Taussig pointed out that the question the utilitarians failed to ask was what these people would otherwise be doing
if the patent system were not diverting their attention to the task of
inventing by the offer of monopolistic profits. Taussig asked, and
Plant stressed with approval, the question: "By what system of economic calculus were they [the utilitarians] able to conclude so definitely that the gain of any inventions that they might make would not

1. Arnold Plant, "The Economic Theory of Patents for Inventions," 1 *Economica* (*n.s.*) 30 (Feb. 1934).

be offset by the loss of other output? By no stretch of the imagination can the inventing class be assumed to be otherwise unemployable. Other product which is foregone when scarce factors are diverted in this way completely escaped their attention."

For Plant the temporary patent monopoly entails a subsidy for invention, causing overinvestment in this form of economic activity. Since economic resources are scarce, overinvestment in invention leads to underinvestment in other forms of activity. As Plant says, "It enables those who have monopoly of the right to use a patented invention to raise the price of using it for the whole term of the patent within the limits fixed by the elasticity of demand, and in that way derive a larger profit from invention than they could otherwise obtain. The effect must surely be to induce a considerable volume of activity to be diverted from other spheres to the attempt to make inventions of a patentable type." Without the patent laws, according to Plant, people who spend their time inventing would serve the community better by doing something else. If Plant is correct, a patent system has misallocative results not unlike those of an acreage allotment program where the subsidy involved causes too much fertilizer to be put on too little land.

Plant criticized Clark for holding, as late as the beginning of the twentieth century, that (quoting Clark) "If the patented article is something which society without a patent system would not have secured at all—the inventor's monopoly hurts nobody. . . . His gains consist in something which no one loses, even while he enjoys them." Plant's objection is double-edged: (1) As to inducement for new innovation, there is, he says, "no inkling here that the patent inducement to invent diverts scarce human effort from other production," and (2) "that the subsequent exploitation of patents again interferes with the disposition of scarce factors which would obtain under competitive conditions."

1. *Resource Diversion*

Plant was most dubious about the allegation that the *amount* of inventive activity is in the main unaffected by the inducement offered by patent monopolies. He recognized that such a position challenged traditional profit-maximizing theory[2] but stressed that overinducement

---

2. Absence of profit-induced innovation is also belied by a more recent empirical study regarding industrial research and technological innovation. See Mansfield, *Industrial Research and Technological Innovation* (New York: W. W. Norton, 1968).

results from luring away resources more appropriately utilized else-where. The "nobody is hurt" conclusion rests on the stated premise that what the patent protects is something society would not have had at all but for the patent system. Clark's omission of specific reference to the doctrine of opportunity cost as relevant, as Plant stressed, to any "how much" question in economics, including innovation, there-fore need not adversely affect his argument. It is the property right (temporary monopoly) in the product of an invention that makes possible the production of things consumers value. If no invention facilitating this production would be forthcoming because no return is available to cover the costs of research leading to the invention, then Clark's conclusion follows. In all cases the expected value of market-oriented invention must be greater than the expected costs (opportunity costs) of invention. Plant's analysis, with its stress on alternative use of resources in the absence of patent protection, merely made explicit, as Clark did not, that true costs of investing in inven-tion, as in other investment, include the cost of alternatives foresaken.

As is so often true of apparent disagreements among competent economists, the difference arises from the preconditions which are assumed. Plant implicitly acknowledges this when he later says, "The only conceivable line for such an argument [that granting a monopoly can achieve greater general usefulness—better resource allocation] would seem to be that *ultimately* the inventions of a patentable type which will be made in response to the grant of a temporary monopoly will possess a sufficiently greater general usefulness than would result from the other inventions or other output immediately foregone to outweigh the immediate loss." But that is the argument made by Clark. But for the patent system, the argument goes, there would not be the products of invention—which reflect opportunity costs—re-strictions on whose use, however certain, could never outweigh the greater restriction of not having them at all.

Whether a patent system in general can be justified on incentive-for-invention grounds is, indeed, related to alternative uses of re-sources, as Plant stressed. But Plant believed that free copying by others was not a sufficient deterrent to innovation to justify granting a monopoly which would draw too many resources to a less socially important use. Plant thus rather casually dismissed "free riding" in his analysis. There is, however, no obvious reason to believe that an arbitrary monopoly for any specified period of time will accurately accommodate differing kinds of inventive activity. An "on balance" judgment seems called for. Is an imperfect patent system worse than no patent system at all? Or should an alternative system be employed?

An economic system utilizing profit incentives based on property rights performs acceptably from society's viewpoint when costs as perceived by those incurring them are tolerably consistent with the total real costs. Plant's "Economic Theory of Patents for Inventions" places principal focus on the dangers of departing from the competitive ideal. He viewed the patent system as providing an undesirable subsidy. And this subsidy overrewards innovation so that the marginal rates of return to producers of new methods and new products are relatively too great while these rates to producers of existing products and methods are too small. Essentially, Plant viewed investment in invention as much like investment in a farm. Competitive forces bring about better allocation of materials and effort than would a system of farm subsidies. Clark's model of a patent system, on the other hand, is not a farm to which property rights attach and the output of which can be sold. Clark's justification for a patent system suggests analogy to a lighthouse rather than a farm. What private investor in his right mind would ever build one, no matter how useful, if he could not charge anyone for its services and thus receive a return on the costs incurred?

2. *The Patent Reward System*

The second basis for Plant's criticism of patents relates to the system of reward itself. Here the argument is closely related to, and in some respects is a part of, the incentive problem just discussed. For example, the problem of almost simultaneous discovery is set forth as an example of how the patent system rewards the "first inventor" with a monopoly and renders almost nugatory the labors of all the rest. And the existence of the first monopoly diverts the efforts of the losers (and nonparticipants) in this race away from what might well be the most fruitful field for further invention. Except for the winner of the first patent, Plant suggests, efforts are diverted from the most socially useful activity—improving the best—to finding possibly inferior alternatives to circumvent the original patent monopoly.

Whether socially wasteful "inventing around" will take place depends upon an assumption that the private costs undertaken in this activity will lead to products or processes which users will judge inferior to those covered by the existing patent. "Inventing around" may lead to better products or better processes than those covered by previous patents. It seems reasonable, moreover, to assume that one incurring the cost of "inventing around" would expect to invent a superior rather than an inferior substitute for the existing patent. One contemplating entering any economic endeavor can be expected to assess his competition. This involves a price/cost assessment. The relevant calculation is the cost of "inventing around" as contrasted with the price of the existing invention. And the relevant price to a potential competitor for this existing invention is not its current price but rather its future price after the new invention is available.

Whether or how much the existence of a patent monopoly causes wasteful "inventing around" depends upon a number of imponderables. It also depends upon the patentee's licensing policy—number of licensees, license-back provisions on improvements, royalty rates, and related factors. Irrespective of how these are determined, however, once a patent has been issued the patentee can be expected to utilize the exclusive rights he has been granted to maximize his reward. In this process he can be expected, subject to the legal restraints of the patent grant, to act like the monopolist he is. And, of course, as far as *existing* patents are concerned this means restricting output of the patented product or process by producing less than the amount that would have been produced in the absence of a patent, and less than the amount that would be most desirable to prospective users. But this is a short-run evaluation, equally applicable to monopoly of farms, lighthouses, or invention. A relevant question about a monopoly of any of these is whether the costs they entail in the form of under-production of existing commodities are essential to the achievement of greater future benefits from new or better products not obtainable without monopoly incentive.[3]

Plant's example of almost-simultaneous discovery is not evidence that a patent system is unnecessary or that it overrewards useful invention. It seems reasonable to expect, for example, that there could be a similar waste if there were no patent system. Almost-simultaneous discovery without patents also involves wasted effort. Here the discoverer who comes in second could have saved his cost of discovery by waiting to copy the first.

There is no second prize in a patent race; the winner gets the entire reward. Still, none of the contestants might have been in the contest

3. In terms of this kind of trade-off assessment the propriety of granting patents as contrasted to the combination of competing patents can, of course, lead to very different conclusions.

were not the chance of the reward available. And each contestant presumably knew and calculated as part of his cost of investment in innovation that another contestant might win the prize.[4] Who, Clark might have asked, would enter a race to build a lighthouse if no toll could be collected? If, on the other hand, monopolies of long duration were to be given for chance discoveries or routine improvements— instead of the mere advantage of a head start in producing a new product, or even a short-run advantage in adopting a more efficient means of production—the patent grant would indeed impose a net burden to the community. Whether a patent system, to repeat the analogy, directs productive resources more in the manner of a farm than a lighthouse is thus not easily determined.

Investment in Innovation and the Misallocation Problem: Underrewarding Innovation

The special nature of information as a commodity, although thought by Clark to justify the patent system, was not confronted directly by Plant's critical evaluation of the system. Professor Arrow, writing a quarter of a century later, focused directly upon the special nature of information in a provocative theoretical probe of market allocation of this unique commodity.[5] His conclusion, in contrast to Plant's, is that innovation is underrewarded rather than overrewarded.[6]

4. An incentive system providing for production under conditions of uncertainty is not justifiably condemned unless the total costs incurred by the successful and the unsuccessful are greater than the value of the product of the successful. But even this is not a *sufficient* reason for condemnation, which would assume that all benefit is measured by the value of the product (output times price). All benefits net of cost deserve assessment. Important among these is investors' free choice. Since investors do not steal the resources they use, why should they be stopped even if on balance their failures outweigh their successes?

5. Kenneth J. Arrow, "Economic Welfare and the Allocation of Resources for Invention," in *The Rate and Direction of Inventive Activity: Economic and Social Factors*, edited by the National Bureau Committee for Economic Research (Princeton, N.J.: Princeton University Press, 1962), p. 609.

6. It should be noted, however, that in part Arrow's conclusion of "too little" rather than "too much" innovation rests on his evaluation of uncertainty. This is a general conclusion not unique to innovation. Uncertainty, he contends, leads to less than optimal allocation to activities which are chancy, and where risk-bearing is unmarketable (uninsurable). Hence he finds that any unwillingness or inability to bear risks discriminates against risky enterprises. Although recognizing that a preference for risk might give rise to misallocation in the opposite direction, he does not believe that these balance out. His reason for this conclusion is brief and rather dogmatic (p. 612): "the limitations of financial

A unique aspect of information as a commodity, Arrow noted, is the nature of its marketability: "In the absence of special legal protection, the owner cannot . . . sell information in the open market. Any one purchaser can destroy the monopoly, since he can reproduce the information at little or no cost."[7] Arrow stressed the high cost of secrecy. Not only is there high and increasing mobility of personnel among firms, as Arrow indicated, but in addition and perhaps more important, one might add, embodying information in a product will often provide information freely without its direct sale.[8] Because of the "enormous difficulties in defining in any sharp way an item of information and differentiating it from other similar sounding items,"[9] he concluded that only legal property rights in information can provide a partial barrier to appropriation by others. Legal property rights in information are not completely lacking without a patent system, but Arrow's "appropriability" conclusion is especially relevant to such nonpatent contracts as covenants not to disclose contained in know-how licenses which in the absence of patents can be protected only by private contracts. But according to Arrow, even with a patent system there is likely to be a substantial amount of what has previously been identified as "free riding."[10]

Arrow also stressed the unique aspects of the demand for information. First, the use of information is subject to indivisibilities: "Use of information about production possibilities, for example, need not depend on rate of production."[11] Although this "indivisibility" conclusion is plausible as a characteristic of information which is sold or otherwise disposed of unconditionally—for example, the outright sale of a process patent—there are, depending upon the kind of licensing arrangement permissible under patent law, means of achieving

---

resources are likely to make underinvestment in risky enterprises more likely than the opposite." Why the availability of limited financial resources should be positively correlated with risk aversion needs further explanation. But Arrow's case, nevertheless, need not rest on this uneasy assumption about imperfect capital markets or internal financing.

7. Arrow, "Economic Welfare," p. 615.
8. See chapter 1 regarding patents as a means of overcoming secrecy.
9. Arrow, "Economic Welfare," p. 615.
10. This "free ride" effect, sometimes referred to as "spillover" effect and more generally an "externality," is a matter of degree. All market transactions have some beneficial or adverse effects on others who are not parties to the transaction. Here, however, the point deserves special emphasis because of the inherent elusiveness of that to which the property right attaches.
11. Arrow, "Economic Welfare," p. 615.

the equivalent of divisibility for the use of patentable information under license. In fact, contractual arrangements by which intensity of patent use is measured are a principal function of patent tie-ins.[12] License restriction by field of use is also a device for achieving far more divisibility by means of contract than Arrow's example exposes. So is end-product pricing.[13]

A second characteristic of demand for information emphasized by Arrow is that its value cannot be known until the user has acquired it, but that then he has in effect acquired it without cost. Here, unlike the foregoing example, Arrow acknowledges that this problem is diminished by the existence of patent law "if the seller can retain property rights in the use of the information."[14] But again stressing incomplete appropriability of so elusive a commodity as information, he stresses the nonoptimal purchase of information at any given price and the nonoptimal allocation of information purchased.

Again, Arrow, by ignoring the possibility of overcoming these difficulties through carefully tailoring patent-licensing practice, and by stressing departures from an optimality, a departure which all actual markets share, perhaps substantially exaggerated the disabilities of "ownership" of innovative information. Most patent licensees are able to find rather decisively, if not precisely, the use value of information before they purchase it; and although discovering infringement is not costless, probably few users of valuable patented information "in effect acquired it without cost." Neither is the "nonoptimal purchase of information at any given price" or the "nonoptimal allocation of information purchased" so much more beyond the range of a revenue-maximizing patentee than it is for the vendors of other commodities as the Arrow analysis implies.[15]

Appropriability of information (a patent system) provides significantly better inducement to produce special information than Arrow suggests. The inducement provided by a patent market, like other

---

12. See, for example, Bowman, "Tying Arrangements and the Leverage Problem," 67 *Yale L. J.* 19 (Nov. 1957). It should be noted that a per se rule against patent tie-ins may have more to do with the indivisibility of patent information than with the intrinsic nature of the information product.
13. See chapter 4.
14. Arrow, "Economic Welfare," p. 615.
15. Succeeding chapters will reveal that it is the court-imposed law, rather than the uniqueness of information, that has the greatest effect on appropriability. This is particularly true of the increasingly stringent proscriptions courts have imposed on patentees' use-restrictive licensing.

markets, is far from perfect—perhaps less perfect than other markets. But its inducement potential for better allocating the production of information (as contrasted with the restrictive effect of allocating existing information), at least until alternatives are evaluated,[16] leaves room for reasonable dissent from Arrow's conclusion that "There is strong case for centralized decision-making under these circumstances."[17]

Arrow's analysis of information accentuates the conditions of uncertainty under which it is produced, its lack of appropriability by its producer, and its indivisibility for purposes of commercial transfer. A patent system, for Arrow, is only a partial corrective for the deficiencies he sees. But to agree that a patent system is an especially deficient instrument for inducing basic research is not to condemn it. It is an incentive system which is not necessarily appropriate to basic research, having only tenuous or remote connection to prospective commercial value accruing to the individuals or the firms which undertake it. One may agree, therefore, that the more general or basic the research undertaken, or the earlier the stage of research, even research directed at a particular goal, the more likely it is, even with a patent system, that such research will be inadequately remunerated by a market system. A patent system, being market oriented, is appropriate where private benefit bears a calculable relationship to the costs incurred. Arrow convincingly argues that basic research typically requires a wide variety of studies to begin with, the less promising being eliminated as information is accumulated.[18] Consequently, "At each stage the decisions about the next step should be based on all available information." And, "This would require an unrestricted flow of information among different projects which is incompatible with the complete decentralization of a free enterprise system."[19] Arrow did not evaluate the compatibility of the substantial economies of scale in the integrated production of information with the size of the relevant information market in order to determine whether competitive information production would be more workable than nonmarket public

16. See the similar criticism of the Knight analysis, infra at note 31.

17. Arrow, "Economic Welfare," p. 616. Centralization of what, by whom, and for whose benefit is left unanswered and necessarily untested in the "optimality" terms applied to the market. If by "centralization" Arrow means merely centralization in a large and possibly widely diversified firm, one of many such firms, rather than "centralization" in a public authority, the implications for patent policy would, of course, be very different.

18. Ibid., p. 618.

19. Ibid.

regulation of research. Rather, he reached the more modest conclusion that underinvestment in research will be greater for more basic research. All along the line, however, we can expect in a free-enterprise economy less than ideal investment in invention and research. It is risky, the product can be appropriated only to a limited extent, and it has increasing returns in use. Furthermore, even if a firm succeeds in engrossing the economic value of this activity, there will be (as with all monopoly, as previously indicated) an underutilization of that information as compared with an ideal allocation.[20]

Arrow does not directly relate his information analysis to an assessment of the patent system, although his conclusion that "there is a strong case for centralized decision-making"[21] suggests that it is a very imperfect legal instrument for optimizing the production and distribution of a unique commodity. But his basic conclusion, that innovation tends to be underrewarded by the market, is far more tenable for basic research than for the "later-stage" research a patent system seeks to induce. Insofar as innovation leading to patentable invention is market induced and leads to investment which is expected to be recovered by returns that could not exist without a patent system, then even with high uncertainty there is strong reason for concluding that a patent system is an important implement for correcting the underrewarding of innovation which Arrow exposed.[22] But this assumes

20. Ibid., p. 619. And see also id., p. 623: "for optimal allocation to invention it would be necessary for the government or some other agency not governed by profit-and-loss criteria to finance research and invention." This conclusion, widely suggested but too often unanalyzed, overlooks or forgets the high cost of benefit identification when the government displaces the market. The potentially high costs of political decision-making (as contrasted to even an imperfect market system) include both the cost of paying for nonexisting benefits and the cost of making those pay who do not benefit.

21. See note 17, supra.

22. But see Hirshleifer, "The Private and Social Value of Information and the Reward to Inventive Activity," 61 *Am. Econ. Rev.* 561 (Sept. 1971). He states that (p. 573) "The standard literature on the economics of research and invention argues that there tends to be private underinvestment in inventive activity, due mainly to the imperfect appropriability of knowledge. The contention made is that, even with a patent system, the inventor can only hope to capture some fraction of the technological benefits due to his discovery. This *literature overlooks the consideration that there will be, aside from the technological benefits,* pecuniary effects (wealth redistributions due to price revaluations) *from the release of the new information.* The innovator, first in the field with the information, is able through speculation or resale of the information to capture a portion of these pecuniary effects" (emphasis added).

An example of the kind of pecuniary reward (leading to possible overrewarding of invention) described by Hirshleifer is his example (his n. 20): "A rela-

that patentable invention is a consumer-benefiting activity. The patent system has been criticized because it emphasizes gadgeteering or mere routinizing. Frank Knight's position regarding patents exemplifies the dangers of misplaced reward.

Patent Reward for the Inconsequential

According to Knight the patent reward system is undesirable not because it overrewards innovation but because it underrewards true innovators and gives an undeserved monopoly to the last-step routinizers. To him, investing in some form of innovation is what the profit system is all about. In his classic work *Risk, Uncertainty and Profit*,[23] Knight emphasizes that incurring uninsurable risks—specializing in uncertainty—is the economic service provided by entrepreneurship, the reward for which is the chance of acquiring what economists define as profit.[24] Business judgment is uninsurable because it is unmeasurable and unclassifiable. Odds for success do not fall into categories within which actuaries can predict that fluctuations will cancel out. The measurability is only after the fact. There is also a peculiarly persistent preserve of what Knight calls a *moral hazard* with this sort of undertaking. "The decisive factors in the case are so largely on the inside of the person making the decisions that the 'instances' are not amenable to objective description and external control."[25] These problems fall away, according to Knight, insofar as consolidation can be expected within the scale of operation of a single

---

tively minor shift in locomotive technology, for example, might lead railroad planners to select an entirely different route for a new line, with drastic upward and downward shifts in land values." The suggestion is, of course, that if one with "inside" information could forecast these results he could greatly increase his "reward" by land purchase. Hirshleifer recognizes the limitations on the feasibility of such speculation by innovators. The contingencies are inconceivably vast. It would be interesting to know, for example, if any patentees, even among those who turned out inventions that are extremely valuable technologically, were ever able to realize any significant speculative gains of the kind that Hirshleifer hypothesizes. And even if such pecuniary gains could be forecast, an interesting question remains. Would they not be more likely under a secrecy-incentive system than under the kind of disclosure required under a patent system?

23. Frank H. Knight, *Risk, Uncertainty and Profit* (Boston: Houghton Mifflin Co., 8th impression, 1957).

24. This is not accounting profit. Normal return is an opportunity cost under this meaning.

25. Knight, *Risk, Uncertainty and Profit*, p. 251.

individual or in an organization where responsibility can be centralized efficiently and unity of interest secured. This, of course, as far
as self-insurance of business uncertainties is concerned, involves economy of scale. Knight says that investing in some form of innovation
is the heart of the entrepreneurial function. Offsetting good and bad
judgments over a large number of decisions involves a form of self-
insurance when outside insurance is unavailable. Knight points to a
twofold estimate of the future, involving both technological and price
uncertainties. He stresses the latter: "The responsible decisions in
organized economic life are price decisions; others can be reduced
to routine and men are hired to make them."[26] And as to invention:
"Though we cannot describe a new invention in advance without
making it, nor say what quantity and quality of new natural productive capacity will be developed and where, yet it is possible in a large
degree to offset ignorance with knowledge, and behave intelligently
with regard to the future. *These changes are in large part the result
of deliberate application of resources to bring them about,* and in the
large if not in a particular instance, the results of such activity can
be so far foreseen that it is even possible to hire men and borrow
capital at fixed remunerations for the purpose of carrying it on."[27]

Knight emphasized that investment in invention is different from
investment in material things. Owing to the low cost of indefinitely
multiplying an idea, he stressed the difficulty of capitalizing an increase
in its productive power. And although he acknowledged the inventor's
right to keep his secret as long as possible in order to safeguard it, he
stressed the impracticability of this procedure in the usual case. But,
interestingly enough, Knight, immediately after pointing out how
manifestly beneficial new inventions are to society (a justification for
a patent system?) and after acknowledging the "fairness" of consumers' paying for them, then stressed the ill effects on those who are
prevented from using the invention by the "artificially high" monopoly
price. His principal criticism of the patent system, which he characterized as "this exceedingly crude way of rewarding invention,"[28]
however, was that "it is undoubtedly a very rare and exceptional case
where the really deserving inventor gets anything like a fair reward."[29]

26. Ibid., p. 317.
27. Ibid., p. 318 (emphasis added).
28. Ibid., p. 372.
29. Ibid.

Knight viewed the patent system as a means of misdirecting rewards for innovation. Patent reward, he contended, went to the one who puts on the "finishing touch." The routinizer thus gets the reward while the *real* pioneering and exploration are done by others. He thus concluded: "It would seem to be a matter of political intelligence and administrative capacity to replace artificial monopoly with some direct method of stimulating and rewarding research."[30] What he had in mind as that *direct* method which would improve upon "artificial monopoly" as a means of stimulating and rewarding research was not revealed. The "direct" method suggests the need for a direction of rewards. If this is so it has the inherent difficulty of choosing a rewarder who would predictably be better than the consumers, even those too few who participate in a monopolized market. To use Knight against himself: one who thinks dollar voting by consumers a mistake might well say so clearly; and it would be in order for him to describe the alternative he advocates, including the name and address of the proposed rewarder![31] And who knows? Knight's unidentified "rewarders" might favor popular baby doctors, penurious university professors, or putting the first man on the sun.

Moreover, if invention is the end product of investment in producing salable ideas or embodied in salable products (and patents are denied the work of those merely skilled in the art, contrary to Knight's assumption), hired inventors or independent inventors working in attics would presumably be rewarded with no more or less "fairness" than any other paid or independent workers. The demand for inventive services, derived as it is from the salable products created by their efforts, should be considered no more "unfair" than that obtained by workers in any endeavor. Tinkering with rewards to productive factors may achieve neither equity nor good resource allocation.

Professor Knight's criticism of the patent reward system is compelling on the single assumption that what is rewarded is costless. It is not that the inventive process is costless, or that its results are not desirable, but rather that the whole reward goes to that last party in the inventive process—the one who drives the last and easiest mile

---

30. Ibid.
31. See Frank H. Knight, "An Answer to, 'Is Group Choice a Part of Economics?'" 67 *Q. J. Econ.* (1953) 608, as follows: "One who thinks liberal civilization a mistake might say so clearly; and it would be in order for him to describe the alternative he advocates, including the name and address of the proposed dictator." See also infra at note 32.

in the long race to marketability. And should this wrong-reward characterization turn out to be incorrect, or even exceptional rather than general, so that by and large the reward for invention goes to those who incurred the innovating cost, then a market-oriented reward system may well be substantially superior to one depending upon "political intelligence and administrative capacity to replace artificial monopoly with some *direct method* of stimulating reward for research."[32]

Professor Knight's analysis of the role of profits in directing and rewarding entrepreneurial activity under conditions of uncertainty is concerned with the normative aspects of economic theory as well as its explanatory value. Knight, indeed, has a reputation as an "effective demolisher" of those who generally reject consumer sovereignty, which his "direct method" of rewarding seems to overlook in his patent prescription. In another context he is more convincing: "A large part of the critics' strictures on the existing system [a competitive order] come down to protests against the individual wanting what he wants instead of what is good for him, of which the critic is to be the judge; and the critic does not feel himself called upon even to outline any standards other than his own preferences upon a basis of which judgment is to be passed."[33] He then goes on to suggest a remedy which seems applicable to his own patent prescription: "It would be well for the progress of science if we had less of this sort of thing and more serious effort to formulate standards and to determine the conditions under which free contract does or does not promote individual interests harmoniously and realize social ideals."[34]

An alternative reward system to supplant consumer judgment as the ultimate determinant of the value of patentable invention is not necessarily superior merely because a patent provides some monopoly power. It should be recognized, however, that if the standards for invention are as low as Knight characterizes them, the real cost to the community occasioned by the restrictive effect of patent monopoly might well be greater than the meager benefits provided by routine improvements. The applicable standards of invention thus deserve careful appraisal, along with the feasibility of raising them, before a judgment is made that a more "direct" way of stimulating and rewarding research would be desirable.

32. See supra at note 31.
33. Knight, *Risk, Uncertainty and Profit,* p. 182.
34. Ibid.

A patent system increases the incentive for, and thus the production of, patentable invention. The production of knowledge in general (especially basic research) as Arrow stresses, tends to be substantially underrewarded in a market system unless special provisions are made for its production. Whether the specific form of knowledge qualifying for patentability would also be underrewarded without protection depends upon what it is that is patentable. But given appropriate standards for invention—the subject of the following chapter—there is good reason for supporting the long-standing legislative judgment that a consumer-oriented reward system, granting a patentee the temporary right to exclude others from "free riding," is in the social interest because resources are thereby better allocated.

3

Standards for Patenting
an Invention

The principal justification for patents, as I stressed in the last chapter, is the need to foreclose rapid copying by others. Thus, a patent system is a corrective for underinvestment in innovation. This inducement to invention is supportable in the public interest only if the invention induced gives the community something more useful than the alternatives the community would have were these inventions not protected by patents. The alleged likelihood that a patent system would over-promote rather than redress underproduction of invention was the basis of Plant's criticism. Patentable inventions should, net of their costs, make for increased consumer welfare. This occurs, of course, only if the inventive process stimulates "useful" invention.[1]

This has suggested to some that one precondition to patentability might be "usefulness." The suggestion is rejected in spite of numerous early cases to the contrary, and including more recently Justice Fortas's 1966 opinion in *Brenner* v. *Manson*.[2] Usefulness is a proper precondition for *reward*, but not for *patentability*. The market performs more reliably than patent examiners in determining usefulness in a price-oriented patent system.

An invention worthy of patent protection is presumed to entail something not already available. Novelty is a prerequisite to patentability. Were reward given for information previously available (a part of the prior art), the whole purpose of sponsoring new and better products and processes would be subverted and the community would then needlessly pay for what it already has. The importance of novelty

---

1. See for example, Kitch, Graham v. John Deere Co.: New Standards for Patents, 1966 *Supreme Court Rev.* 293, at pp. 330–35.
2. 383 U.S. 519 (1966).

is assumed. But novelty alone is not enough. That which is novel should also not be obvious, even to one skilled in the art. Nonobviousness is an important standard for invention. But this is true only insofar as it can be a means of withholding a patent's temporary monopoly from those "inventions" which predictably would quickly be available even without the special inducement patents provide. Here, one object is to insure against Knight's concern that patent monopoly not be provided for "last-step routinizing." There is need for careful application of a nonobviousness test. This is generally recognized by courts and by commentators. But the proper application of the test in particular cases is not as obvious as its desirability in the abstract. Hindsight of the critics is more likely to involve twenty-twenty vision than the foresight of the patent office.

A patent system rewards only the nonobvious invention so as to reserve "monopoly" solely for cost-incurring activities giving rise to services which are worth the cost of the monopoly. But to conclude from this that particular costs incurred by an inventor should be a precondition to patentability, or a measure of proper reward, would be most delusive. A "cost plus" patent reward system, it is contended, would be a wanton subsidy to inefficiency.

A seventeen-year term for patents is arbitrary. Undoubtedly it provides more than enough incentive for some kinds of inventions and less than enough for others. But tailoring the term of the patent grant to particular inventions is not recommended as an avenue to improvement. Patent standards, unfortunately, elude precise evaluation.

Inducement for Invention

A conclusion that a "temporary monopoly" patent system will on balance be in the public interest depends both upon what it is that qualifies as invention and upon how profit incentives operate to produce a "product" which qualifies for patentability. Unless the production of patentable information shared with other forms of production the fact that it is profit motivated, the case for the existing patent system would be substantially weakened or destroyed. But a profit-motivation system is not disabled by recognition that individuals are also motivated by stimuli other than the cash register. Were market analysis incapable of accommodating preferences expressed in non-dollar terms its usefulness would be greatly impaired. Nonprofit motivation affects the supply of and the demand for all forms of production, including those affected by joy of work, guilt from not working, service to mankind, sheer habit, instinctive urges to gamble, or propensity for contrivance. Just as some inventors would undoubtedly invent if the rewards were much less, so would some teachers teach, preachers preach, and businessmen venture were they paid less. But the propriety or the impropriety of price incentives is not usefully judged by the existence of nonprice incentives.

The efficient apportioning of production or of consumption (priced or unpriced) involves incremental valuation—marginal cost of production and marginal usefulness in consumption. Market pricing is a useful and efficient means of apportioning resources in this manner. Marginal analysis is often misunderstood or ignored in discussions of production. It is as relevant and important in understanding and evaluating the production of invention as the production of other things. Thus, to take an extreme example, if three equally adept inventors would be willing to work at inventing for nothing, but a fourth could not be employed at less than one hundred dollars, then, if the value of the product of an equally adept fourth added four hundred dollars to the product of the other three workers, all four are efficiently utilized even if each now must be paid one hundred dollars. Not hiring the fourth inventor, and continuing to pay nothing to the other three, would be less profitable to the enterprise and more costly to the community. Not hiring the fourth, even though three are paid nothing, would impoverish the community by giving customers less of what they want most.

The question of profit motivation as an incentive to invention, as profit incentive for the production of anything else, then, is not usefully evaluated by evidence that does not face up to the importance of *incremental* analysis. In spite of the great quantities of ink and paper spent in describing the undeniable dedication of many famous inventors, and the statements of numerous experts from private research laboratories, the business community, the government, or academic institutions to the effect that they all would continue research, development, and the search for knowledge whether or not a patent system existed,[3] the fact remains that this tells nobody anything about

3. Floyd Vaughan, in chapter 1 of his *United States Patent System* (Norman: University of Oklahoma Press, 1956), lists numerous instances. For example, on p. 12, "People of ancient times had such inventions as the wheeled vehicle, the needle, the loom, the potter's wheel, metal working, the plow . . . . By the end of the fifteenth century . . . the mariner's compass, paper and print-

what must be known to evaluate the need for patents: Does the community get more of what it wants at lower cost with or without a patent system?

The production of invention, like that of other things, is often accomplished jointly with other productive activity. That invention may be a joint product does not disable a patent system. Whether invention is more cheaply carried on by those working on the products, or with the processes to which invention applies, or whether it is more efficiently done as a specialized activity in a separate establishment is immaterial to the efficiency of a price-incentive market system. A principal advantage of that system is that it sponsors the low-cost method and eliminates the high-cost method. Thus, if invention of a machine process—for example, to produce a product more cheaply by a new method—is a predictable by-product of the efforts of those involved in an existing production process, incentive reward draws useful resources to the joint activity in the same manner as if it were separately induced. Joint product involves the same kind of marginal analysis as a single-product analysis. Essentially, the invention case is not different from that of sheep-raising. Sheep-raising involves the production of both mutton and wool. Similarly, the production of gasoline involves a wide range of other outputs. Market motivation and the social advantages it makes possible, with or without a patent system, do not depend upon the jointness or the separability of either the inputs or the outputs.

Research policy cannot be as readily related to particular products or processes as, for example, price and output policy on an existing product. And, as has been indicated, the more basic the research, the less particularized is the product focus. But this only changes the calculation about where rewards may arise, it provides no reason for casting doubt that the profit motive operates in the research and development aspect of business. Recent studies of profits expectation

----

ing press, the mechanical clock . . . . *There is no evidence of patent grants anywhere which might have fostered them.*" Again (p. 12), "The presidents of three automobile companies . . . along with other business executives have testified that *their research would continue even though they could not take out patents on their inventions.*" And again (p. 6), "Thomas Jefferson refused to take out patents on his inventions. Benjamin Franklin . . . 'never deigned to patent any of his inventions' " (emphasis added).

related to research support market-motivation theory.[4] In fact, it is so generally recognized that it is scarcely discussed as a debatable issue. Although it is reported that more than half of the nation's scientists and engineers are supported directly or indirectly by federal research and development expenditures,[5] this evidences no absence of a need for incentive. Hired research undertakers, no less than those working on a "commission" provided by the "patent market," must be paid. Moreover, it is far from clear that the case for a patent system would be weakened even if the government supported still higher proportions of the nation's scientists and engineers. The role of the government in supporting research is in no small measure directed toward basic research. This is a kind of research which gives rise to "spillover" benefits—benefits which individual purchasers of the knowledge cannot be expected to support adequately. Here, as the analysis by Arrow in the preceding chapter stressed, beneficiaries are not solely, or even primarily, those who could be expected to purchase the information. A patent market is likely to be a particularly inefficient resource allocator for basic research.[6] This is not the kind of information a patent system fosters. Furthermore, the relevance of either the actual or the proportionate amount of private or government-sponsored research depends upon whether each serves the same or competing ends. Even if the ends are noncompeting, however, whether or not a wide and rapidly expanding amount of general scientific knowledge tends

4. See Edwin Mansfield, *The Economics of Technological Change* (New York: W. W. Norton Co., 1968) (particularly chap. 3, "Industrial Research and Development," pp. 43–98, with many citations). See also Dean Worcester, *Monopoly, Big Business and Welfare in Postwar United States* (Seattle: University of Washington Press, 1967), p. 157; Zvi Griliches, "Research Costs and Social Returns: Hybrid Corn and Related Innovations" 66 *J.P.E.* 419 (Oct. 1958).
5. Mansfield, *Economics of Technological Change*, p. 206, n. 1.
6. The government's role in supporting general or basic research can be analogized to its support of general education. The benefit rebounds not only to those educated but in a large measure to the entire community. And such educational support does not preclude the propriety of private educational institutions designed to train people for particular tasks where the increase in earnings is more directly related to the costs incurred in the specific training. And, of course, even in this latter area where individual and public benefit do not diverge widely the government may be operating its own facilities for its own use. In occupational training, the service academies provide examples. The space program provides an example in research.

to make superfluous the more specific "consumer-oriented" research which a patent system is designed to accommodate depends upon the *additional* real costs of achieving this more particular customer-oriented result. To put the question as Knight asked it: Does this make a patentee's reward more likely to arise from mere routinizing?

That the patent system is an important instrument of national policy regarding technology, and that it is a market-oriented system depending upon commercial reward, does not, of course, eliminate the appropriateness of alternative systems if they too provide the means of recovering the costs incurred. But there is neither theory nor evidence to suggest the view that no form of financial inducement is required or that any particular form meets all the community's requirements for differing sorts of knowledge or information. The patent system has an advantage over a system of government grants in that it is consumer oriented. There is no payoff unless consumers deem the invention worth paying for. That there are types of information, as with other productive services, where social and private product diverge is hardly better grounds for condemning a patent system than for condemning the entire competitive system on these grounds.

In the preceding chapter I discussed the likelihood of overrewarding or underrewarding, and the conclusion was imprecise in terms of optimality; but no alternative was exposed which was *less* arbitrary or did not have unfortunate resource allocation consequences. This conclusion, however, was not directly related to that particular kind of innovation qualifying for a patent. Specifically, Knight's contention that patents reward mere routinizing of a kind which others might well make without the special inducement afforded the patentee was not directly confronted. Neither was any basis given for a specific length of time for which the exclusionary right should extend.

Prerequisites for Invention

The United States patent laws grant the inventor control over the use of his invention for seventeen years from the time the patent is granted. It must contain some minimal degree of novelty—a new principle or mode of operation having as its subject a physical result or a physical means of attaining a result which is supposed to be beyond what could be expected of one merely skilled in the art.[7]

7. 35 U.S.C. § 103 (the 1952 act).

Knight's point was that much of what is patentable is almost cost-less. Why not then reward only costly patents? Only the costlier kind presumably would be retarded by the absence of patents. How, if at all, can cost of invention be estimated so as to induce only that inventive production which would otherwise not be forthcoming? And how can one know whether seventeen years is "right," or whether a patent for one year or one for perpetuity would be better?

Cost of Invention

A production system that based its reward on the particular costs a particular producer incurred for a particular purpose would be a subsidy to inefficiency. And the production of invention is no exception. Moreover, in any highly uncertain activity where odds of success are low and odds of failure high, even the relatively high indirect costs of mistakes should be added to the possibly low direct costs of success.[8] It is not promising to try to judge in terms of the cost of particular inventions. An ideal reward system covers the costs of the efficient; and since the relevant costs are those not yet incurred rather than those sunk, even the most efficient get no assurance of profit under a price system. The correct appraisal of "cost-covering" in the production of anything, as Plant emphasized in his patent appraisal, is the benefit foregone. If this opportunistic cost process is to work for community advantage, it must lead to greater output of the things the community values.

Insofar as investment in invention is motivated by reward, as it surely must be at the margin, it matters little in terms of socially efficient cost coverage that in particular instances it occurs from luck, plodding human effort, flashes of genius, idle contemplation, or a sensitively wired electronic inventing machine. Judged by the irrele-

8. How, for example, should the cost of the discovery of so vital a product as Teflon be assessed? A *Wall Street Journal* report (18 July 1968) by John Prestbo ascribes it to sheer luck. Chemist Roy Plunkett was trying to make an improved refrigerant for Du Pont. He filled cylinders with various mixtures of gases and stored them in dry ice. In one of the cylinders a waxy substance formed which did not dissolve in conventional solvents or react to extreme temperatures. It was no refrigerant. It was the nonstick coating now used on more than 100 million pots and pans. Surely this invention was not costless because it was accidental. Of course it was an unexpected windfall. The result was also nonobvious, but it did derive from a "costly" research program. If this makes a significant "cost" difference, would anyone seriously contend that such a patent should not be issued if it were developed by a hobbyist rather than a paid researcher? Such are the problems of "cost-finding."

vant standard of costs historically incurred, overrewarding or under-rewarding can exist irrespective of how an invention comes about.

What the patent system rewards, how much, and for how long deserves most careful assessment. How rigorous are the standards for either getting or keeping patent protection? Should the patent statute be construed to cut down the flow of patents issued each year or to expand this flow? And what of the role of the courts in maintaining or canceling a patent once issued?

The Patent Act of 1952, section 103, sets forth a precondition for invention which potentially, at least, could add rigor to the standard:

> A patent may not be obtained though the invention is not identically disclosed or described as set forth in section 102 of this title, if the differences between the subject matter sought to be patented and the prior art are such that the subject matter as a whole would have been obvious at the time the invention was made to a person having ordinary skill in the art to which said subject matter pertains. Patentability should not be negatived by the manner in which the invention was made.[9]

The nonobviousness test makes an effort to meet the kind of economic problem with which this chapter is concerned. As Kitch says:

9. 35 U.S.C. § 103 (the 1952 act). Other requirements for patentability are to be found in sections 101 and 102:

§ 101. *Inventions patentable*

Whoever invents or discovers any new and useful process, machine, manufacture, or composition of matter, or any new and useful improvement thereof, may obtain a patent therefor, subject to the conditions and requirements of this title.

§ 102. *Conditions for patentability; novelty and loss of right to patent*

A person shall be entitled to a patent unless—

(a) the invention was known or used by others in this country, or patented or described in a printed publication in this or a foreign country, before the invention thereof by the applicant for patent, or

(b) the invention was patented or described in a printed publication in this or a foreign country or in public use or on sale in this country, more than one year prior to the date of the application for patent in the United States, or

(c) he has abandoned the invention, or

(d) the invention was first patented or caused to be patented by the applicant or his legal representatives or assigns in a foreign country prior to the date of the application for patent in this country on an application filed more than twelve months before the filing of the application in the United States, or

(e) the invention was described in a patent granted on an application for patent by another filed in the United States before the invention thereof by the applicant for patent, or

(f) he did not himself invent the subject matter sought to be patented, or

(g) before the applicant's invention thereof the invention was made in this country by another who had not abandoned, suppressed, or concealed it. In

"The non-obviousness test makes an effort, necessarily an awkward one, to sort out those innovations that would not be developed absent a patent system. Through the years the test has been variously phrased, but the focus has always been on the question whether the innovation could have been achieved by one of ordinary skill in the art, or whether its achievement is of a greater degree of difficulty."[10]

Kitch recommends that it would be a significant step in improving the patent system if the courts would focus on the single inquiry of nonobviousness.[11] This is because the idea behind this test "is to evaluate the magnitude of the costs involved in a given innovation."[12] Kitch's conclusion has much to recommend it if it provides a means of identifying *kinds* of innovation which would not be made but for the patent system. But evaluating sunken accounting costs of particular inventions is likely to lead to a sort of public utility cost-finding technique for which even regulatory commissions are not extremely proficient—much less so a patent office and even less so the courts. And judging patentability by how much a particular invention costs could give rise to a kind of cost-justification defense which has been the subject of serious criticism of the Robinson-Patman Act.[13] The problem is not to disinter and measure. Rather, it is the much more difficult task of determining whether inventing is a cost-incurring process depending upon the patent reward, or whether without the reward another would have done it quickly anyway. Such is the economic rationale of an obviousness test.

An obviousness test is at best a very rough standard. Objective criteria are hard to come by; and subjectively, after the fact, nonobvious innovations have a tendency to become obvious—more or less obvious, of course, depending upon the education, accumulated knowledge, and particular expertise of those making the "obviousness"

---

determining priority of invention there shall be considered not only the respective dates of conception and reduction to practice of the invention, but also the reasonable diligence of one who was first to conceive and last to reduce the practice, from a time prior to conception by the other.

The precursors of these sections can be found in the act of 21 February 1793, c. 11, 1 stat. 318; act of 4 July 1836, c. 357, 5 stat. 117; act of 8 July 1870, c. 230, 16 stat. 198; rev. stat. § 4886 (1874).

10. Kitch, Graham v. John Deere Co.: New Standards for Patents, 1966 *Supreme Court Rev.* 293, at p. 301.

11. Ibid., p. 346.

12. Ibid., p. 338.

13. See for example: Bowman "Restraint of Trade by the Supreme Court: The Utah Pie Case," 77 *Yale L. J.* 70 (November 1967).

judgment. Whether or not a court or the patent office, or a separate body of experts, is likely to carry out this important task efficiently needs careful appraisal. One should not be quick to conclude that the task would be better or more economically achieved by a non-expert court (through an adversary process) than by more specific attention in the first instance at the patent office, by examiners who are, or could be, especially skilled in the patent art of the field under review.

The Supreme Court and Patentability

The Supreme Court does not decide a large volume of cases involving the issue of invention. In 1966, however, the Court decided four cases[14] involving the effect of the standard of nonobviousness imposed by section 103 of the Patent Act of 1952. Not since the *Supermarket* case[15] in 1950, before the passage of the 1952 act, had the Court had before it a case turning on the issue of patentability. In this earlier case, especially in the concurring opinion of Justice Douglas, there was direct and scathing comment directed at too-low standards for invention.

This *Supermarket* case involved a patent issued for a cashier's counter and a movable frame useful for expediting the checking-out process in a supermarket. The Supreme Court, without dissent, decided that the mere combination of several old and well-recognized parts or elements producing no new or different kinds of function or operation was not patentable invention. The Court held invalid the patent claims in this very useful and widely used device even though the two courts below held to the contrary. Stress was placed on the more exacting standards required for patents involving combinations made up entirely of old components. The language of the opinion, however, gave clear notice that exacting standards for patentability were not to be viewed as uniquely related to combination patents.

Justice Jackson, who delivered the opinion of the Court, stressed that in a case of this kind, in contrast to such fields as chemistry or electronics where a combination of elements "take on some new

14. Graham v. John Deere Co., 383 U.S. 1 (1966); U.S. v. Adams, 383 U.S. 39 (1966); Calmar, Inc., v. Cook Chemical Co., 383 U.S. 1 (1966); and Colgate-Palmolive Co. v. Cook Chemical Co., 383 U.S. 1 (1966).
15. Great Atlantic and Pacific Tea Co. v. Supermarket Equipment Corp., 340 U.S. 147 (1950).

quality or function from being brought into concert,"[16] there are no unusual or surprising consequences from the unification of elements concerned. No new and different functions came from the combination than they performed without it. "The three-sided rack will draw or push goods put within it . . . just what any rack would do on a smooth surface. . . . Two and two have been added together and they still make four."[17]

Justice Douglas, in a concurring opinion in which he was joined by Justice Black, went much further. His was a general condemnation of all patents involving gadgeteering as well as a condemnation of the patent office for issuing them. His characterization of the cashier-counter patent was one in a long list of "incredible patents which the Patent Office has spawned."[18] The Douglas appraisal of the *Super-market* patent went considerably beyond a test for nonobviousness—whether a three-sided rack to push groceries through a check-out counter was "routinizing" of a type for which no special reward was required to induce the invention cost. "The question of invention," Douglas wrote, "goes back to the constitutional standard in every case."[19] The constitutional question for Douglas was that every patent is the grant of "a privilege of exacting tolls from the public,"[20] and to justify this privilege was to make a distinct contribution to scientific knowledge. For Douglas inventive genius and social usefulness are both presumed to provide useful tests for patentability.

The Douglas opinion listed some twenty early patents which "extend monopoly to the simplest of devices."[21] His criticism of the Patent Office made disdainful reference to the issuance of patents for a list of "trivia" ranging from rubber grips for bicycle handlebars to a revolving cue rack. Douglas did not explain how his "trivial" patents signaled "nonobvious" invention. Inventive "genius" for "important" breakthroughs is Douglas's patent model. There are surely "useful arts" requiring substantial outlay of productive effort even though not undertaken by geniuses or in a very flashy manner. Nor is there apparent correlation between the means by which an invention is achieved and its production in the absence of a patent. In any event,

16. Ibid., p. 152.
17. Ibid.
18. Ibid., p. 158.
19. Ibid., p. 156.
20. Ibid., p. 154.
21. Ibid., p. 156.

the legislature in 1952 seemed to be answering Douglas directly on this issue when it provided in section 103: "Patentability shall not be negatived by the manner in which the invention was made."[22]

Among the four cases accepted by the Supreme Court for review fifteen years later were a combination of old mechanical elements for a device to absorb shock from plow shanks in rocky soil[23] and a combination involving a plastic finger sprayer with a hold-down cap used as a built-in dispenser for liquids. Both were held to be devices *obvious* at the time of invention to a person having ordinary skill in the art.[24] The determination of "nonobviousness," according to the Court, is made after determining the scope and content of the prior art, the difference between the prior art and the claims at issue, and the level of ordinary skill in the pertinent art.

The opinion in *Graham* v. *John Deere* clearly supports and strengthens a long line of case precedents that preclude patentability for mere routinizing. Although it does not articulate an unequivocal standard for the single purpose of insuring that patent monopoly does no more than make possible the production of those things which but for the system would not be available, it does recognize the "obviousness" question in reaching this goal. The goal is not a new one. Indeed, it was understood and specified in the constitutional grant making a patent statute possible. Justice Clark quotes that well-known economist, Thomas Jefferson, who, clearly recognizing the social and economic rationale of the patent system,[25] put the issue simply and directly: "the things which are worth to the public the embarrassment of an exclusive patent must outweigh the restrictive effect of the limited patent monopoly. The inherent problem was to develop some means of weeding out those inventions which would not be disclosed or devised but for the inducement of the patent."[26]

Whereas the principal focus of the opinion was an appropriate standard to be applied by the courts, specific comment was also directed to the area of *primary responsibility*, the Patent Office. "To

22. 35 U.S.C. § 103 (the 1952 act).
23. Graham v. John Deere Co., 383 U.S. 1.
24. Ibid., p. 26. In U.S. v. Adams, 383 U.S. 39 (1966), a wet-battery combination patent was held valid under the nonobviousness test. In view of the Court's long-standing "antipatent" reputation, this case is notably indicative that nonobviousness is a genuine test and not just another peg on which to hang the Court's "invalidity" hat.
25. Ibid., p. 9.
26. Ibid., p. 10.

await litigation," Clark stressed, "is—for all practical purposes—to debilitate the patent system."[27]

Justice Clark in *Graham* v. *John Deere* also observed, but in a somewhat more restrained manner than had Justice Douglas in the *Supermarket* case, "a notorious difference between the standards applied by the Patent Office and the courts."[28] Recognizing the difficulty of the task with which the Patent Office is confronted—about 50,000 patents are granted from almost 100,000 applications filed each year with a 200,000 backlog in 1965—the Patent Office is criticized for "the free rein often exercised by Examiners in their use of the concept of 'invention.' " Greater intensity must be concentrated on the requirements of section 103. This is not, however, because the court found a change in the strictness with which the legal test must be applied: "The standard has remained invariable in this Court."[29] Technological change is stressed: "The ambit of applicable art given fields has widened by disciplines unheard of a half century ago."[30] Consequently, it "is but an evenhanded application to require that those persons granted patent monopoly be charged with awareness of these changed conditions. The same is true of the less technical, but still useful arts." Those concerned that a patent system might reward mere "routinizing" or "the last and easiest mile in the long race to marketability" have substantial support on the Supreme Court.

The Supreme Court opinion in *Graham* v. *John Deere*, although it stresses the importance of not rewarding that which is so obvious that those skilled in the art could be expected to produce it without the incentive of a patent, does not spell out, except in most general terms, how this advice is to be carried out.[31] The particulars of nonobviousness in widely varying situations, of course, cannot be expected to be foretold by courts; but case-by-case analysis can place primary focus on the general state of knowledge in the field where the validity of the patent is being tested. On the other hand, attempts to evaluate such patent attributes as "novelty" and "usefulness" may be unpromising if not detracting in achieving this standard for invention. As Kitch has indicated, by adding nonobviousness to other tests, some

27. Ibid., p. 19.
28. Ibid., p. 18.
29. Ibid., p. 19.
30. Ibid.
31. Kitch, Graham v. John Deere Co.: New Standards for Patents, 1966 *Supreme Court Rev.* 293, at p. 341.

redundant and others in conflict, the Court has left it possible to
continue a mythology which Justice Clark did not dispel.[32]

More important, however, is the unmistakable direction the Court
has pointed. Neither inventors, patent counsel, lower courts, nor the
Patent Office now has, if indeed it ever had, reason to doubt the position of the Supreme Court on the validity of patents involving "routinizing."

The Patent Office Role in Standards for Patentability

Cases reaching the courts, especially those reaching the higher courts,
usually involve products or processes of substantial value to users.
This is to say that the "monopoly" value of these patents—the differential advantage to consumers over alternative products or methods—
is likely to be much higher than for patents as a whole. That high
litigation costs are borne by the parties to the action is strong testimony to their usefulness. This, of course, is not characteristic of the
de novo cases with which the Patent Office deals. Consequently, it is
most misleading to conclude that there are high "monopoly" costs
because a high proportion of applications result in patent grants by
the Patent Office. A very large percentage of patents granted, even
those which involve nonobvious invention and result from substantial
investment in innovative activity, may be in fields where substitute
patents or nonpatented substitutes are so close that in economic terms
the "patent monopoly" may be very limited or even nonexistent. There
are also, unquestionably, numerous patented products for which there
is no demand. The fact that payoff under the patent system is possible
only for inventions which customers are willing to pay for leaves the
real burden of predicting utility to the users. A patent office cannot
be expected to perform very well if it attempts to take over this function of making such perilous economic forecasts. That there may be
a rough correlation between nonobviousness and utility provides no
obvious justification for using predictions about the latter as a standard
for invention. The market is a stern taskmaster in this respect.

The Patent Office, as the Supreme Court has emphasized, could
be more active in raising standards of patentability. This is desirable
not as an end in itself but only if it effectively insures against long-run

32. Nonobviousness is sufficient. Other tests obscure or are in conflict with the
achievement of the proper goal of a nonobviousness test: "to induce innovations that would not otherwise appear in a competitive system." Ibid.

output restriction. Easy patentability can foster a wider variety of products and processes which consumers find useful. Some of these are much more costly than others—costly in the relevant sense of deserving scarce (costly) resources devoted to their production.

Skepticism about either the courts' or the Patent Office's taking on the task of predicting usefulness or attempting to judge and reward relative merit is reinforced by the judgment that the market, imperfect as it is, is a better assessor of usefulness. Judging patentability in terms of actual costs incurred by prospective patentees has also been described as a dangerous policy because it misconceives the true role of costs in a market system. Rather, it focuses on the irrelevant costs —the sunken costs. Moreover, rewarding specific cost outlays is a means of sponsoring wastefulness. Nonobviousness as a test for patentability is properly assessed in terms of how good a proxy it is for measuring inducement cost. It seems reasonable to assume that obviousness is a means of predicting that no special inducement is required—others could be expected to do the same rapidly and without patent protection.[33] The nature of the invention as contrasted to the state of the arts in the field, and the degree of skill required, are means by which patent examination might be used to overcome the possibility of awarding monopoly for the routine; but it is easier to recommend a nonobviousness test than to apply it and relate it to real costs without destroying incentives for investing in research where payoff odds are low and risks are high. The "obviousness" of a checkout device in the *Supermarket* case provides an example of the difficulty. After the device had been put into use it seemed "obvious" to the Supreme Court that one skilled in the art should have brought it out shortly without any need for special inducement. And this was to the Supreme Court still "obvious" even though self-service stores had been in existence long before this device occurred to anyone. What better evidence is there of nonobviousness than that those myriad

---

33. In economic terms there is thus no alternative or opportunity cost in bringing the idea into existence. And with respect to specific inventions which are not in the least obvious, there are numerous examples which seem unrelated to a particular cost-incurring process designed to achieve a particular result. Undoubtedly "flashes of genius" do occur, and there is no denying the existence of what some have described as an "instinct for contrivance." Were such "inventions" separable and identifiable in terms of costlessness, then whether obvious or nonobvious, they would seem to need no special reward. But when the true nature of economic costs requiring identification in order to make such a judgment is understood, the *costliness* of *cost-finding* becomes of overriding importance. Screening for nonobviousness avoids this difficulty.

persons "skilled in the art" of checking out groceries had for so long not brought this "invention" into existence?

Carefully assessing patent applications, only a small percentage of which may turn out to be commercially feasible, is, of course, a costly process. Time costs are also involved. From patent application to patent issuance is a slow process.[34] Very stringent patent review could be expected to increase both time lag and Patent Office costs. And although alternatively, court determination of validity through an adversary system is far more costly *per patent*, it does have the advantage of incurring these costs only on patents whose economic importance has been established. Prospective litigants cannot be expected to ignore revenue-cost relationships.

All this is not to resolve how far it would be appropriate for the Patent Office to go in making patents more difficult to obtain. Recommending how much a Patent Office should spend doing what, including the admirable objective of screening patent applications to eliminate "obvious" inventions, does not evolve from the limited observations contained in this chapter. The relevance of two important issues, however, should emerge. The first—should the Patent Office attempt to determine a patent's usefulness? involves an evaluation which is not dependent upon, and does not require, any special information about Patent Office practice. This relates to consumer-sovereignty, a central assumption of this entire discourse. No one should be led to the delusive conclusion that a patent office can be converted into a sort of institutional divining rod for finding worthwhile and rejecting nonworthwhile patents.

The second issue, nonobviousness as a standard for invention, is extremely important. Rewarding "last-step routinizers" as Knight has convincingly argued, can seriously misallocate resources. The Supreme Court strongly concurs that patents should not reward routinizing.

The Term of the Patent Grant

The question of how long a patent grants the right to exclude others from making, using, or selling a product or a process has been, still is, and will undoubtedly continue to be imprecise if not downright arbitrary. Of course, the longer the life of the patent the greater the

---

34. "In recent years, the average patent is issued after 3.5 years before the Patent Office." Mansfield, *Economics of Technological Change*, p. 211.

potential income from the exclusive grant, the greater the incentive for costlier and riskier investment in innovation, and the less attractive the secrecy alternative. But lengthening the term of a patent provides no guarantee of long-continued profitable exploitation. In industries where technological change is rapid and competitive invention is effective, reward can be eroded or eliminated long before a patent with a substantial life has expired. And, in the absence of collusion among competing patentees, "inventing around" of the sort Plant condemned as potentially wasteful of resources can provide a useful brake on the exploitive possibility of existing patents. With patent claims narrowly defined and open to contest by rivals or public authorities, a patent monopoly could be monopoly in name only after a few years even if the patent grant were in perpetuity rather than for seventeen years. The drug and chemical industries in particular provide numerous examples of patent obsolescence because of rapid technological change.

But to encourage the most expensive innovations by promising very long patent "monopolies" for *all* innovations would, it has been argued, involve an indefensibly high social cost. This is Professor Machlup's conclusion.[35] Even though he recognizes that "there will always be the possibility of very expensive developments that cannot be profitable even if a 30- or 50-year monopoly grant were promised," he finds it equally likely that "there will be innovations that can pay for themselves in less than a year; and there will be a spectrum of possibilities between these extremes."[36]

Of course the range of these possibilities and the likelihood of their occurrence depend upon, in addition to the competition among patents and the rate of technological advance, the strictness with which the standards for patentability are applied. And the lower the standard of nonobviousness, the more mere routinizing may be rewarded and the stronger is the case for a shorter rather than a longer period.

Because of the wide variations in the costs of achieving different sorts of useful innovative activity from the profit-motivated private sector, some have suggested that it might be desirable to vary the term of the patent grant for different kinds of inventions, giving long grants to inventions involving expensive technological breakthroughs and graduating the patent period downward to a very short period of pro-

35. See Fritz Machlup, *An Economic Review of the Patent System*, Study of the Senate Subcommittee on Patents, Trademarks, and Copyrights, study no. 15 (1958) 85th Cong. 2d Sess. at p. 39.
36. Ibid.

tection for routine invention.[37] This suggestion would indeed be appealing if foresight were anything like hindsight. But the kind of imponderables which have been shown to be needed even for an assessment of nonobviousness by the Patent Office should be a warning of the far greater dangers of imposing on that office this extravagantly more complicated responsibility. The Patent Office, like the New York Giants, appears to be fair game for Monday-morning quarterbacks.

The case for a uniform patent period for all eligible invention, although it falls far short of an optimality standard, does provide a modicum of certainty for a very uncertain form of enterprise (shooting at a fixed target usually makes for better aim); and although it is arbitrary, it is probably far less so than one measured with the kind of uncalibrated yardsticks available to the Patent Office.

Whether a seventeen-year period, arbitrary as it is, is too long or too short is perhaps best judged by whether in general the production of patentable information is overrewarded or underrewarded. The case is peculiarly unsusceptible to empirical proof.[38] The discussion in these last three chapters (especially that of Arrow), suggests that

37. Mansfield, *Economics of Technological Change*, p. 210.
38. With a perpetual rather than a limited-time patent system, the prospects of monopoly pricing, it is typically contended, will lead to such a scale of investment in producing knowledge that too many resources would go to this activity. This was Plant's argument against even a time-limited patent.

Professor George Stigler has commented on this overinvestment problem: "too many resources would go into research and innovation in this sense: the monopolistic sale of new knowledge would yield the same rate of return on resources as the competitive sale of other investment goods . . . . The fixed term of 17 years, then, operates to reduce the rewards of a patent system more nearly to those of a competitive exploitation of new knowledge. If we use a 10 percent interest rate, a 17-year annuity is worth 80 percent of a perpetuity, *so implicitly* our patent system assesses the overstimulation of perpetual patents at about 25 percent (that is 2.5 percent on capital) above the competitive rate of return" (George J. Stigler, "A note on Patents," in *The Organization of Industry* [Homewood, Illinois: Richard D. Irwin, 1968], p. 125).

But this implicit assessment, it should be stressed, is heavily dependent upon the interest rate chosen. Its usefulness, therefore, depends on the predictability of the appropriate rate, even when the average degree of monopoly from patents can be assumed. If, for example, the interest rate should drop from 10 to 5 percent, then ten and one-half years would be the approximate equivalent of seventeen-year patent life at 10 percent. Conversely, should the interest rate rise from 10 to 15 percent, then a patent in perpetuity would be considerably less rewarding than a seventeen-year patent at the 10 percent rate. Stating this same proposition in different terms, the differential rate of return, comparing perpetuity with seventeen years, varies inversely with the interest rate.

the latter is more likely than the former. But many useful patents "for mere routinizing" would detract from this effect, and attempting to weigh these adverse tendencies does not seem promising.[39]

Alternatives to Length of Term for Correcting Underrewarding or Overrewarding

Underrewarding or overrewarding is as much affected by legal restrictions on the exploitation of the patent monopoly as by the term of the patent grant. What constitutes patent misuse or patent abuse and what antitrust standards are applied when patent law and antitrust law collide have a direct bearing on the potential profitability of the production of invention. But using abuse or misuse standards liberally or strictly in an attempt to countervail underrewarding or overrewarding would be both arbitrary and improper—arbitrary because the higher or lower court-imposed standards would be applicable only to litigated patents, and improper because of the legislative function the courts would necessarily be undertaking if they were to pass judgment on this basis. Thus, for example, if in a case in which an abuse of the patent privilege were alleged it were determined that the patent period was in effect extended from seventeen to twenty years, finding the alleged abuse legal because the invention deserved greater reward would be most improper. Equally improper would be a holding that the alleged extension did not take place but that the patent was abused anyhow because fourteen years provided sufficient reward. The same would be true for other criteria of misuse or abuse. If, for example, competing patents could be pooled, eliminating competition between them and thus violating antitrust law, the greater reward from the pool would be no proper occasion for relaxing antitrust standards.[40] And, on the other hand, if two patents were mutually blocking, preventing their joint exploitation on grounds that that would make more reward possible, that would be equally bad.

These examples have not been of a kind that either the legislature

---

39. Fritz Machlup has contended that "neither the *theoretical* nor the empirical evidence thus far presented can support the claims frequently made for the patent system as an important or even the chief factor in technological and economic progress." See Fritz Machlup, *The Production and Distribution of Knowledge in the United States* (Princeton, N.J.: Princeton University Press, 1962), p. 176.

40. Neither, of course, would collusive elimination of competing claims before issuance of a patent.

or the courts have found appealing. But in succeeding chapters it will be shown that much of what has been determined to be abuse or misuse has related to an analysis of scope extension. Patent tie-ins, for example, have come to be almost automatically illegal because of the erroneous notion that they provide a means of leveraging a legal patent monopoly into an additional second monopoly over what is unpatented. An opposite example involves upholding pools of competing process patents because outside of the pool there were remote or inferior substitutes—as if a cellophane cartel's legality hinged on the existence of old newspapers in which fish might be wrapped.[41] As I will attempt to show in succeeding chapters, these results arise whether courts purposely "legislate" or whether they do so as a result of applying economic standards which they seem not to comprehend. Leveraging to new monopoly, the subject of the next chapter, is a basic source of judicial confusion.

Lengthening or shortening the patent period seems a far better solution to the rewarding problem than is manipulating patent exploitation standards. Analysis of those standards make up the remaining and major part of this analysis, for which the foregoing material may be considered either a long introduction or a supplement.[42]

---

41. The analogy is not imaginary. See McGee's analysis of the gasoline cracking case reproduced in chapter 10 at n. 23.
42. See the Introduction.

4

Standards for Limiting the Means by Which a Patentee May Exploit Temporary Monopoly

The essence of the patent privilege is the right to exclude others from making, using, or selling that which is covered by the patent during its life. The value of this right depends upon how valuable the patented product or process is to users. This in turn depends upon the closeness of substitute products or processes, patented or unpatented, which are available. When a patented product or process is not "better" in this sense no return to the patentee is possible. Many patents are economically useless. On the other hand, when a patent is "good enough," and when its substitutes are remote, it may provide the patentee a very substantial return. It may give the patent holder enough economic power to substantially "control the market" in the field in which the patent applies. But "control of the market," an invidious description in the absence of a legal monopoly, when a patent is involved, is merely a description of the patent's value. And, of course, any patent worth paying anything for would be used more extensively if less were charged for it, and even more extensively were it free, as it would be were there no patent protection. In this sense, then, any return to the patentee no matter what form the charge takes (short of perfect discrimination) makes for less use of the patented product or process than would be the case were no protection afforded patentees. The basic conception of a market-oriented patent reward system, as I stressed in the first chapter, is to provide protection from this "free" use by others so that incentive is provided for new and better products. As a necessary cost of this socially desirable result, under American patent law, it is assumed that some temporary monopoly consequently restricting output and raising prices—that being what monopoly is about—can hardly be the useful criterion for judging legality of patent licensing contracts.

The law concerning patent licensing agreements, unlike that in other fields in which monopoly pricing is prohibited and competitive results are sought in order to achieve scale efficiencies without output restriction, has not called for rate regulation or the fixing of "fair" prices. Patent reward, rather, allows the market to be the rate regulator. Patent reward under this conception is purposely regulated by what the market will bear for incentive reasons—the "better" the patent the higher the reward.

Patent law contains no provisions concerning the level of permissible reward or fair rate of return; and courts, except in attempting relief when patents have been found to have been misused (see chap. 12 concerning compulsory licensing at reasonable rates) do not, with few exceptions, attempt to assess fair return as the determinative consideration in deciding the legality of agreements between patentees and licensees. Principal judicial concern, rather, is directed to whether the reward to the patentee comes from advantage ascribable to the patent rather than from another source not deserving of monopoly protection. This is the "scope" problem. And monopoly beyond the patent's proper scope, being subject to antitrust law and not patent law, is of course not deemed deserving of patent protection. Consequently, the legality of contracts that patentees make with licensees is judged in terms of whether or not monopoly is extended. If the proper scope of the patent privilege (the legal rights conferred by the patent) is measured by competitive superiority of a patented product or process over substitutes, as the analysis in succeeding chapters assumes and the court decisions confirm, then the most pertinent question involves whether patentee-licensee agreements are profit-maximizing or are monopoly-extending.

Monopoly Extension or Profit Maximization

In large measure an analysis of the misuse of licensing agreements involves an assessment of patent extending. How are patentees able to achieve monopolies which extend longer or are broader in scope than that differential advantage properly ascribable to the invention for which the patent has been granted? The law has come to condemn two principal forms of patent misuse in which patent extension has been thought to exist. The first involves agreements with competitors producing products or processes that are close substitutes for those covered by the patent. The pooling of competing patents provides an example of this kind. Here broader monopoly is obtainable. These are monopoly-extending. In contrast, those agreements—vertical contracts —which patentees make with licensees for the purpose of "restricting" the use licensees may make of the patent under the terms of the license, as the subsequent analysis demonstrates, are not monopoly-extending. Ascribing to these vertical contracts a monopoly-extending effect is indulging in the "leverage fallacy." Such arrangements are profit-maximization devices.

An example of the monopoly-extension fallacy in the patent context is the way courts have come to judge tie-in cases. A typical case (detailed in chap. 8) is exemplified by a patented salt-dispensing machine sold or leased on condition that all salt dispensed by it be purchased from the patentee. Such a tying contract, it has come to be presumed conclusively, is illegal because a monopoly of the tied product (unpatented salt) is created. In this by no means untypical example it is held that new monopoly is an additional monopoly not ascribable to the advantage provided by the superiority of the patented salt-dispensing machine. Actually it is not that at all. This tie-in, like many other contractual restrictions upon use, is a means of measuring the value of the patent to the user. In the salt-dispensing example, sale of salt by the patentee allows him to measure the intensity of the machine's use and charge users accordingly, just as if the machine were metered. And metering, an economic equivalent in this situation, has not been proscribed—at least not yet. Other forms of restrictions upon conditions of use, it will be demonstrated, are similarly not means by which a patentee can extract more from his licensees than the differential advantage the patent itself affords. Patent leveraging, in a word, is no more plausible than lifting oneself by one's bootstraps. And this "patent-extending" conclusion which courts have found in vertical contracts between buyers and sellers, it will be shown, is not only theoretically implausible but also empirically unsupported.

As a prerequisite to judging the various contractual arrangements patentees make with their licensees we must understand why they might be used and to what effect. Why, it is appropriate to ask, if no leveraging to new monopoly is involved, do patentees voluntarily not set a single nondiscriminatory royalty rate for all licensees and thereby foster competition among them?

The answer is that conditioning the sale or lease of patented products or processes upon territories or types of use, or upon use with particular products or services, or upon amounts of final product sold, or upon the prices at which final products are sold, are all means not of creating monopoly, but rather of maximizing the return the patent affords. These contractual techniques, in the absence of collusion with competitors, as has been emphasized, are to be explained as profit-maximizing techniques, not as leveraging devices.

A patentee in attempting to achieve the full differential advantage his patent provides over competing substitutes, especially when fields of use are diverse and where competitive advantage varies, will often find that setting a single royalty rate will result in his charging some customers less than the patent is worth to them. (Tying the sale of salt to a patented salt machine is such an example.) At a single price some users who would like to participate if the price were lower are denied the use of the invention. A single royalty rate, with no conditions of use attached, may also force the patentee into a kind of price averaging which either denies him the ability to enforce most efficient production and distribution methods in the use of the patent or the right to exploit the differential advantages the patent provides in different fields or areas of use. Moreover, because the law regarding the permissibility of such practices is applied most unevenly to differing types of use restriction in license contracts, and hardly at all to situations in which the patentee exploits his invention without licensing others, even though the economic purposes and effects in these alternative situations are indistinguishable, special penalties attach to patents whose efficient exploitation is not susceptible to large economies of scale. This, of course, means that arbitrary disadvantage is imposed upon those patentees who do not or cannot efficiently produce those goods in which the patented information is embodied. Efficient specialization in production of patentable ideas by independent inventors is also inhibited. Inefficient integration is sponsored to the detriment of more efficient smaller firms.[1]

Similarly, special penalties attach to patents in which the divisibilities of use are measurable by use with other products rather than, for example, by the legally permissible divisibility of use based upon geographic area. Without an economic rationale for these distinctions, substantial misallocation of resources is predictable.

---

1. Patent misuse or antitrust standards which force decisions to turn on whether the patentee practices the patent art himself or licenses others are the equivalent of a tax on going to the market and are a subsidy to integration. This "protecting large business" result is indeed an anomalous application of an antitrust law under which decisions in other areas reflect a populist bias toward the protection of small business.

The risk of unlawful patent misuse or antitrust violation is substantially increased when a patentee licenses others. And as more complicated licensing schemes are undertaken to improve upon the limited profit afforded by a uniform royalty rate to all prospective users (see chap. 5) the legal risks increase greatly. These legal risks are not unique to patentees, however. They derive in large measure from antitrust doctrine diametrically opposed to the consumer-welfare goal previously outlined.

Effects of Misdirected Antitrust Law

Much of what has come to be patent misuse stems directly from fallacious antitrust theory concerned with exclusionary practice and foreclosure. Here adverse effect on competitors has come to be assimilated with an adverse effect upon the competitive process. Thus buyer-seller contracts—vertical arrangements with noncompeting parties—have come to be illegal, just as the tying of salt sales to the patented salt machine has been found to be illegal. The existence of a patent does not provide immunity. On the contrary, a rationale for finding additional and improper monopoly by patentees is afforded, and the leveraging fallacy becomes supported in a wide variety of antitrust contexts under sections 3 and 7 of the Clayton Act, the Robinson-Patman Act, and the Federal Trade Commission Act, as well as the Sherman Act. Recent decisions based on this "foreclosure" theory proscribe certain trade arrangements, even when the parties are noncompeting, because they "tend toward monopoly" under antitrust law or allow "leveraging to new monopoly" under patent misuse law. Equally adept outsiders are, the advocates of foreclosure theory claim, excluded from the contract in question. This explanation, it will be shown, is not explicable unless they are less efficient than those foreclosed. Arbitrary foreclosure is no obvious means for either maximizing patent reward or leveraging to additional monopoly.

"Tending toward monopoly" under antitrust law and "leveraging to additional monopoly" under patent misuse law are conceptually indistinguishable. Leveraging a legitimate patent monopoly into an additional or broader monopoly, the basis of much if not most of patent misuse doctrine, is a mythology derived directly from erroneous antitrust doctrine long familiar to students of Aaron Director. Widely ignored by antitrust enforcement agencies and by courts are the fallacies in the argument that monopoly may be achieved by such "coer-

cive" tactics as vertical integration with suppliers or outlets, territorial
allocation among customers, franchising arrangements, noncollusive
resale price maintenance, discriminatory pricing contracts, tie-in sales,
full-line forcing, and exclusive dealing contracts among others. There
are grave deficiencies in the legal hypotheses that (1) monopoly can
be either achieved or extended by exclusionary practices or (2) that
potentially restrictive activities may be nipped in the bud before they
reach substantial proportions—the doctrine of incipient monopoly.
Neither has been shown to be a useful means of achieving the aims
of antitrust or patent law.

1. *Exclusionary Practices*[2]

Economic theory indicates that present notions of the exclusionary
practices are fallacious. This was first perceived by Professor Aaron
Director, of the University of Chicago Law School, who noted that
practices conventionally labeled "exclusionary"—notably, price discrimination, vertical mergers, exclusive dealing contracts, and the
like—appeared to be either competitive tactics equally available to all
firms or means of maximizing the returns from a market position
already held. Director's analysis indicates that, absent special factors
that have not been shown to exist, so-called exclusionary practices
are not means of injuring the competitive process. The example of
requirements contracts illustrates the point. The theory of exclusionary
tactics underlying the law appears to be that firm X, which already
has ten percent of the market, can sign up more than ten percent of
the retailers, perhaps twenty percent, and, by thus "foreclosing" rivals
from retail outlets, obtain a larger share of the market. But one must
then ask why so many retailers are willing to limit themselves to selling
X's product. Why do not ninety percent of them turn to X's rivals?
Because X has greater market acceptance? But then X's share of the
market would grow for that reason and the requirements contracts
have nothing to do with it. Because X offers them some extra inducement? But that sounds like competition. It is equivalent to a price cut,
and surely X's competitors can be relied upon to meet competition.

---

2. Reproduced from Bork and Bowman, "The Goals of Antitrust: A Dialogue
on Antitrust Policy," 65 *Colum. L. Rev.* 363 (March 1965) p. 366 (footnotes omitted). But one general reference deserves special citation: Director
and Levi, "Law and the Future: Trade Regulation," 51 *Nw. U. L. Rev.*, 281
(May-June 1956). See also Peltzman, "Issues in Vertical Integration Policy,"
in *Public Policy towards Merger,* ed. Weston and Peltzman (Pacific Palisades,
Calif.: Goodyear Publishing Co., 1969), p. 167.

The theory of exclusionary practices, here exemplified in the use of requirements contracts, is in need of one of two additional assumptions to be theoretically plausible. One is the assumption that there are practices by which a competitor can impose greater costs upon his rivals than upon himself. That would mean that X could somehow make it more expensive for his rivals to sign retailers to requirements contracts than it is for X to do so. It would be as though X could offer a retailer a one dollar price reduction and it would cost any rival two dollars to match the offer. It is difficult to imagine that such a mechanism exists in the case of requirements contracts, price cutting, or the usual examples of predatory or exclusionary practices, but it is perhaps conceivable.

The other assumption upon which the theory of exclusionary practices might rest is that there are imperfections in or difficulties of access to the capital market that enable X to offer a one dollar inducement (it has a bankroll) and prevent its rivals from responding (they have no bankroll and, though the offering of the inducement is a responsible business tactic, for some reason cannot borrow the money). But it has yet to be demonstrated that imperfections of this type exist in the capital market.

Professor Director's reasoning applies to all practices thought to be exclusionary or monopoly gaining. A moment's thought indicates, moreover, that the notion of exclusionary practices is not merely theoretically weak but is, for such a widely accepted idea, remarkably lacking in factual support. Has anybody ever seen a firm gain a monopoly or anything like one through the use of requirements contracts? Or through price discrimination? One may begin to suspect that antitrust is less a science than an elaborate mythology, that it has operated for years on hearsay and legends rather than on reality. The few supposedly verified cases of the successful use of exclusionary tactics to achieve monopoly are primarily in the early history of antitrust. The story of the old Standard Oil trust is probably the classic example. The Supreme Court's 1911 *Standard Oil* opinion is pivotal not merely because it is thought to have launched the famous "rule of reason," nor because it decreed a dissolution that made the oil industry more competitive. Its greatest significance is that it gave substance and seeming historical veracity to the whole theory of exclusionary and monopoly-gaining techniques. It thus provided much of the impetus for the passage of the Clayton and Federal Trade Commission acts in 1914. Such intellectual support as can be mustered for the law against price discrimination derives from the lessons supposedly taught by that case. The factual accuracy of the *Standard Oil* legend is under attack and is coming to seem as dubious as the theory that it is thought to support. Professor John McGee has reviewed the entire case record of the *Standard Oil* litigation and reported that there is not one clear episode of the successful use by Standard Oil of local price cutting or other predatory practices. The other supposed instances of monopolies gained through such tactics deserve similar investigation.

It would be claiming too much to assert that there is no merit to the theory of exclusionary practices, but it is fair to say that that theory has been seriously challenged at both the theoretical and the empirical levels. Perhaps a sound theoretical base can be constructed. The law could then be directed at those practices that in particular settings may be exclusionary. So far as is known, however, this task has not been undertaken or even recognized by the Antitrust Division, the Federal Trade Commission, or any court.[3]

2. *Incipiency*[4]

The incipiency theory starts from the idea that it is possible to nip restraints of trade and monopolies in the bud before they blossom to Sherman Act proportions. It underlies the Clayton Act, the Robinson-Patman Act, and the Federal Trade Commission Act. Though the idea initially sounds plausible, its consequences have proved calamitous. The courts have used the incipiency notion as a license for almost unlimited extrapolation, reasoning from any trend toward concentration in an industry that there is an incipient lessening of competition. The difficulty with stopping a trend toward a more concentrated condition at a very early stage is that the existence of the trend is prima facie evidence that greater concentration is socially desirable. The trend indicates that there are emerging efficiencies or economies of

---

3. The foregoing analysis relating to the way monopoly is allegedly achieved by exclusionary practices is as applicable to keeping a monopoly as to achieving one. In either case barriers to new competition must be erected. And a theory of how entry may be barred by arrangements buyers make with sellers, whether or not coercively imposed, in the absence of consumer-benefiting efficiencies deriving from such agreements, although widely assumed, remain to be verified. Keeping a monopoly, like getting one, requires explanation of how higher costs are imposed on prospective entrants than upon oneself. This same question is, of course, as applicable to an assessment of the propriety of mergers as it is to contracts.

4. Reproduced from Bork and Bowman, "Goals of Antitrust."

scale—whether due to engineering and production developments or to new control and management techniques—which make larger size more efficient. This increased efficiency is valuable to society at large, for it means that fewer of our available resources are being used to accomplish the same amount of production and distribution. By inducing courts to strike at such trends in their very earliest stages, the concept of incipiency prevents the realization of those very efficiencies that competition is supposed to encourage. But it is when the incipiency concept works in tandem with the unsophisticated, but currently ascendant, theory of exclusionary practices that its results are most anticompetitive. Where a court or Federal Trade Commission lacks the means to distinguish between tactics that impose greater costs on rivals and those that are normal means of competing, what evidence can it look to in its effort to discern an incipient lessening of competition? The obvious resort is to evidence that a competitor has been injured, for it is through the infliction of injury upon competitors that the exclusionary devices are thought ultimately to injure the competitive process itself. There seems no way to tell that a competitor has been "injured," however, except that he has lost business. And this is precisely the meaning that the statutory test of incipient lessening of competition or tendency toward monopoly is coming to have. In case after case the FTC, for example, nails down its finding that competition is injured with the testimony of competitors of the defendant that his activities and aggressiveness may cost or have cost them sales. The conduct that threatens such "injury" is then prohibited. That this result is profoundly anticompetitive seems never to occur to the Commission or most courts.

Efficiency from Use-Restrictive Licensing

Economic appraisal is required for a systematic analysis of the problems of patent exploitation. Correct predictive analysis is an essential precondition for normative recommendations. The following two chapters detail the nature of monopoly maximization and relate it to patent exploitation. The analysis attempts to show that, given the patent monopoly, proscribing the means by which patentees may exploit the competitive superiority of their patents is plausibly explained without resort to the implausible monopoly-extending hypothesis. These restrictions can lead to resource allocation in which both the patentee and the community can be expected to be richer, not poorer, than if these practices were proscribed. Imposing conditions on licensees, in the absence of collusion with competitors, predictably leads to results which compel a conclusion that the public interest would *not* be fostered by repressing rather than supporting a patentee's freedom to exploit by noncollusive means, in his self-interest. Use restrictions, so imposed, include the right to exclude others from making, using, and selling. They also apply to processes, machines, manufacture, or composition of matter.

The demand for a patent, it will be demonstrated, is often a joint demand depending upon the availability and the prices of other products or services with which it is used. So it is with most unpatented goods. This is most obvious for intermediate products or services (inputs) which are used with other materials and services to produce final products. But it is often, if not generally, characteristic of final products as well. Thus the demand for automobiles is affected by the quality and price of gasoline, tires, batteries, and efficient repair service, just as the demand for a mimeograph machine depends upon the quality and price of stencils, ink, and paper. And so it is with patented items, whether they involve processes or products. A property right in an idea—a patent—is often thus usefully considered as a complementary good. Its usefulness is impaired if those goods with which it is used are provided inefficiently. This will lower both the reward to the patentee and its usefulness to society. Restriction on the efficient supply of complementary products or services, whether arising from inept utilization of productive, distributive, or sales-promotion techniques or from monopolization or cartelization of suppliers of these services, makes for less reward to the patentee. A patentee's "maximizing" interest, like the interest of consumers and of the community in general, is in eliminating all forms of output restriction by others in the supply of all complementary products and services. This does not preclude the desirability of control *by the patentee* of complements having unique cross-demand relationship to the patent.

The interest of the patentee, to reemphasize a central proposition, is precisely the opposite with respect to items competing with the patent. Restricting the supply of substitutes for a patent would benefit a profit-maximizing patentee, but the effect on consumers would be adverse, just as if a cartel of competitors were formed. Thus if two competing patents were pooled or if agreements were made between the patentee and the producers of any competing products or processes to eliminate competition with substitutes, this would clearly signal the existence of what has here been termed "patent extension." The reward no longer measures competitive superiority over all substitutes, but rather monopolization of that trade which is not measured by the competitive superiority afforded by the patent. Here the result is the same as if competing producers without patents, or with invalid patents, combined to restrain trade by restricting output. This collusive output restriction is not unrelated to the reward accruing to the patentee, but it is unrelated to the reward attributable to the patent. Allowing patentees to make agreements with competitors would without doubt increase the incentive for patentable innovation. But any subsidization scheme for the production of any economic good will have such an effect. The patent has been justified not as a subsidy because inventive activity is more desirable than other activity but because the advantage it affords to users would not be forthcoming were no protection afforded to that which consumers wanted produced. Good short-run allocation, reduced by the temporary monopoly which any good patent involves, is sacrificed for the assumed greater benefit to be derived from better long-run allocation resulting from new and better products or production methods. Monopolization of the nonpatented, the combination of competing patents, or agreements between a patentee and the makers of unpatented substitute products would not meet this test. Cases involving arrangements of this latter type, subsequently discussed in chapters 10 and 11, involve trade restraint not ancillary to the achievement of an overriding benefit.

An economic analysis of the means monopolists find useful in maximizing profit, and the predictable effects of the application of these means, is the subject of the next two chapters. On this analysis rests the case evaluation that composes the remainder of the book.

5

More Efficient Use of Patent
Monopoly through Use Restriction

If the conclusion is accepted that patentees cannot use the monopoly
the law grants them to achieve additional monopoly not ascribable
to the competitive superiority which the patent affords, the propriety
of allowing patentees to extract the full differential value of the patent is still, for some critics if not for the courts, a problem deserving
more careful attention. In this chapter and in the following chapter
various forms of restriction on use—profit-maximizing devices—which
patentees make with licensees will be analyzed in terms of their effect
upon resource allocation. Many, if not most, will be shown to be
efficient—not only efficient privately in terms of increasing patent
revenue, but efficient socially, in terms of consumer interest when
compared with the monopoly alternative where use restriction is outlawed and where a single uniform royalty rate is insisted upon for all
prospective licensees. Chapter 6 continues this efficiency analysis, but
there attention will be focused on price-restrictive licensing, with
special emphasis on resale price maintenance. Here monopoly maximization will be analyzed in broader terms not limited to special forms
of price restriction. Successively more complicated situations will be
discussed, beginning with a simple end-product patent monopoly.

Exploiting the full value a patent provides over substitutes involves
a profit-maximizing process entailing (1) differentiating more urgent
from less urgent uses, (2) having the patent utilized most efficiently
(lowest cost production of the end products in which the patent is
utilized), and (3) provision for the pricing of essential commodities
or services jointly required for use with the patent.

For those familiar with the rudiments of traditional monopoly price
theory, these conditions will be recognized as involving (1) price discrimination, including both market segregation of customers with

different demand elasticities and control over quantities available to individual customers when decreasing demand elasticity for successive units used by each can be exploited (the all-or-none offer case);[1] (2) the uniform interest of both competitors and monopolists in reducing costs (the most economical provision of the product and its essential complements);[2] and (3) the advantages of setting more than a single price when two products must be used together and the price of one affects the sales of the other (cross-elasticity of demand).[3]

1. Market segregation by a patentee might involve a patented product, say a plastic with two uses. Suppose in one use close substitutes are available, for example, in containers where relatively inexpensive glass and metal are available, but that in the other use, say dentures, the alternative material is very expensive. In such a case charging denture users higher royalties than container users, if cross-selling by users could be avoided, would increase net returns to the patentee.

Similarly, even if there were only a single use for a patented product, even by a single user, if this user valued successive increments of the product differently, a patentee would like to be able to exploit this demand pattern. Suppose, for example, the customer would pay 25¢ for the first unit, but only 20¢ for the second after he had the first, and 10¢ for the third after he had the second, but would pay nothing for a fourth after he had the third. Under these circumstances this customer, rather than do without the product, would buy three, paying 25¢, plus 20¢ plus 10¢ (55¢). Charging 55¢ for three units (thus the designation "all-or-none") would give the patentee more revenue than setting a single price and allowing the customer to take as much as he might then choose.

2. If, for example, a patented product could not be marketed except through retailers who by means of resale price maintenance agreements insisted upon markups substantially greater than those prevailing under competitive retailing, it would clearly be in the interest of the patentee to lower the cost of the retailing "complement" so that his patented product would have greater sales. And for similar reasons, if his patented product were manufactured either by the patentee or by licensees, the patent reward would be greater the more efficiently (less costly) this manufacturing could be done.

3. This kind of relationship might be exemplified by a "bacon and egg" example. These two products can be either substitutes (higher egg prices making for more consumption of bacon) or complements (higher egg prices making for less bacon consumed). In either case, depending upon the relative prices of bacon and eggs, they can be expected to be used in variable proportions. It is also conceivable that the cross-effect of the price of eggs on bacon demand is not the same as the cross-effect of the price of bacon on eggs demand. Suppose, therefore, that bacon is a patented product which is salable only for use in conjunction with eggs, an unpatented product sold competitively. If the owner of the bacon patent were to discover that raising the price of bacon (eggs remaining at the competitive price) had the effect of greatly reducing the proportions of bacon to eggs, whereas raising the price of eggs (while bacon prices were maintained or lowered to cost) had a much smaller cross-effect on the demand for bacon, then, it would follow that the patentee could gain revenue from "bacon and egg" customers by tying their purchases of bacon to

Understanding how and why these various monopoly pricing principles apply to patent examples is essential in determining whether specific practices should be permissible under patent or antitrust law.

Beginning, then, with the single-market end-product monopoly case, for the purpose of setting the stage for the more complicated cases which derive from it, various kinds of patent-licensing contracts will be examined, including, specifically, patents on input factors used in fixed and variable proportions, joint demands for complements and substitutes, and various aspects of price discrimination. These will successively be reviewed as examples of how and why patentees employ these methods efficiently to extract the maximum return from their patents.

Single-Market End-Product Monopoly

The basis for understanding any monopoly is, of course, the fact that monopolists take conscious account of the influence of output on price. The ability to affect price by varying output defines monopoly power. A valuable end-product patent monopoly is a monopoly prototype. It exemplifies the textbook model in which the monopolist, facing by definition a declining demand curve, increases his output only by lowering price; and effects of the lower price, being borne by him and not, as under competition, largely by rivals, makes marginal revenue (the additional revenue from selling one more unit) less than the price.[4]

The monopoly seller can therefore be described as a price searcher. Given the incomes, the tastes, and the prices of complementary and substitute products available to potential buyers of his product, and given the costs of producing and distributing the varying amounts of his product that these customers require, the monopolist searches for that price, or that amount of output, which will maximize the differ-

---

sale of eggs from the patentee. The patentee would then raise the price of these eggs above the formerly competitive price and lower the price of bacon below that which he would charge if eggs were priced competitively, while at that same time substantially increasing his revenue.

Moreover, it is notable that this form of patent "exploitation" does *not* provide an equivalent of an additional egg monopoly. It is useful to the patentee only with those customers who demand bacon with their eggs, and but for the "bacon invention" there would be no such customers.

4. See, for example, Stigler, *The Theory of Price,* 3d ed. (New York: Macmillan Co., 1966), p. 195.

ence between his total cost and his total revenue. Achieving this result when all output is sold at the same price is the equivalent of selling that amount of product at which the marginal revenue (MR) from additional sales is equated with the marginal cost (MC) of these sales.[5]

Maximum profits are obtained when an increment of output adds as much to revenue as to cost. (Nobody is presumed to purposely spend an additional dollar to get an additional ninety cents.) This incremental method of analyzing the wealth-maximizing position of a monopolist can be shown graphically by plotting prices or costs on a vertical axis and output or sales on the horizontal axis (each for the same relevant period). The demand curve, sloping downward to the right, reflecting the inverse relationship between the selling price and the amount of sales which can be made, can also be read as an average revenue curve (AR). It shows, for any amount of output or sales (on the horizontal axis), what revenue can be obtained per unit of sales (AR). This is the price (P) for that amount. Once this demand curve, or average revenue curve, is established for various prices, or equivalent amounts of sales or output, there is derivable from it a curve which shows for each of these amounts the additional revenue obtainable from one additional unit of output. This is the marginal revenue (MR). It must be below and to the left of a downward-sloping average revenue curve.

Marginal cost (MC) bears the same kind of relationship to average cost (AC) as marginal revenue does to average revenue. If average costs increase with output, marginal cost is above and to the left of average cost for any output. If average costs are declining, marginal cost is below and to the left of average cost. And if, as is usually the case, costs first decline and then rise with increasing outputs, the marginal cost curve will intersect the average cost curve at the latter's lowest point.[6]

---

5. This formulation is general. It is as true for a competitive producer (a price-taker) as it is for a monopolist (a price-searcher). In the former case, however, the output of the single firm is presumed to be so insignificant as to have no effect upon the market price. That price represents the competitor's marginal revenue (MR) for any of his outputs, and he produces to the point where his marginal cost equals the price (P=MR).

6. This point of intersection between marginal cost and average cost at the latter's lowest point is equally relevant for average total cost and for average variable cost (fixed cost excluded). A decision about whether to produce, and how much to produce, involves only variable costs. In the long run all costs

An example of these relationships is depicted in figure 1.

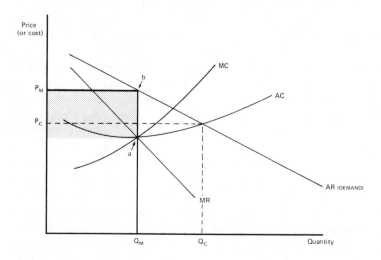

Fig. 1. Monopoly pricing of an end product in a single market.

Given the demand curve (the average revenue curve) in figure 1, and given the costs shown (the lowest available to the patentee whether he made the product himself or had it made by others), there is one price (P_M) and one quantity (Q_M) which will provide more net revenue to the patentee than any other single price or quantity. The "maximizing" quantity (Q_M) is shown by the intersection of the marginal cost curve (MC) and the marginal revenue curve (MR). With quantity Q_M customers will pay up to price P_M. The extracompetitive return available to the patentee, the difference between total revenue and total cost, is shown by the shaded area in figure 1.

Were the product, the demand curve for which is shown by AR in figure 1, unpatented, and were the supply curve shown by MC in the figure the same as for the monopoly seller, the competitive price and quantity sold would then be indicated by the intersection of the marginal cost curve, MC, and the demand curve, AR. The dotted lines

are variable (AC in fig. 1). In successively shorter runs relatively more costs are "fixed" and therefore irrelevant for current output decisions. And because variable costs are avoidable, unless they can be recovered no output at all is predictable. Thus, in figure 1 the applicability of AC to output decisions requires AC to be read as average *variable* cost.

on the diagram indicate the lower price, P_C, and the larger quantity, Q_C. Given these competitive supply and demand conditions we can see from the diagram that if the product patent were awarded to a nonproducing patentee, he could achieve the precise equivalent of setting monopoly-product price at P_M by charging a flat nondiscriminatory, nonexclusive royalty per unit of the patented product produced. This royalty equivalent to setting the price at P_M would be a royalty rate identified in figure 1 by the vertical distance between point a (the intersection of MC and MR) and point b (the corresponding output on the AR curve).

This equivalence, a uniform royalty rate in lieu of fixing the price of the product, however, rests upon "other things equal" assumptions which diagraming (as in fig. 1) has assumed in a rather heroic manner. Patentee price-searchers, or any other price-searchers, do not have the precise demand schedules economists draw for illustration. They must estimate or guess, on the basis of experience, about demand conditions. Knowledge about demand is not costless, therefore, and these costs may vary under differing licensing arrangements.

It is also most unlikely that the costs incurred in a "do-it-yourself" production scheme will be identical to those incurred when production is under license by others. The differences in the size or in the manner of operations are bound to introduce either economies or diseconomies. Moreover, the costs to a firm, especially one whose output affects price, are significantly related to the firm's estimation of demand and its variability as well as to estimation of the alternative costs of licensing others to produce. Achieving minimum costs in the production of any product, being related to rates of output in turn dependent upon estimation of demand, thus becomes more uncertain with longer forecast periods. Long-run costs of the type depicted in figure 1, in which the maximizing output occurs at minimum cost, represent an equilibrium monopoly adjustment akin to perfect forecasting—that is, both demand and costs have been drawn in such manner that the maximizing output (Q_M) is achieved at that precise point where average cost is at a minimum. Forecasting is not precise. Only if demand and cost were precisely predictable would the optimum profits depicted in figure 1 be possible.[7]

7. Similarly, were the monopoly to be eliminated and the production subject to competition it is clear that costs are not minimized for this larger output. As the dotted lines in figure 1 indicate, the marginal costs are substantially higher than average minimum cost and consequently a rearrangement of production is signaled.

The decision whether to manufacture or sell oneself or to license others to manufacture or sell a patented end product will, of course, depend upon whether the cost of producing and distributing the product through the patentee's firm is higher than the cost of having these tasks performed by others. It is in the patentee's interest to have these tasks performed as efficiently and cheaply as possible. Higher manufacturing or distribution costs lower the net value to the patentee. A patent is more valuable the less expensive its complements are. A patentee's potential reward depends upon how efficiently (and therefore inexpensively) the products and services with which it must be used are provided. A patentee, to achieve efficient manufacture or distribution, may, in addition to licensing others, improve efficiency by imposing conditions of use upon licensees.

Derived Demand for a Patented Input: Used in Fixed Proportions

Figure 1, a textbook model of monopoly pricing, exemplifies how the owner of patented end product could be expected to price his patented product, given knowledge about demand and cost conditions and further assuming (1) that only a single price could be set (the final market would not profitably be subdivided); (2) that the demand could not be affected either by further promotional activity or by manipulation of the price of substitutes for or complements to the monopolized end product; and (3) that the costs of having others produce or sell the product were not lower than when the monopolist is the sole producer.

Maximizing the monopoly profit by setting the appropriate single price for an intermediate product or a process is accomplished in precisely the same manner as for an end product. The demand curve and the cost curves would merely be for different commodities, reflecting a different set of alternatives with respect to use on the demand side (conceivably either more or less responsive to price change) and also a different set of alternatives with respect to inputs on the cost side (also conceivably more or less elastic with respect to cost change).

When producers sell directly to consumers the value of the goods produced is judged directly. A consumer demand curve reflects the relative importance users attach to a particular product. The demand for final goods thus reflects their "utility." The demand for intermediate goods (factors of production) reflects this "utility" indirectly, their demand being derived from the demand for end products. The name economists give to the analysis of those things affecting the demand for a factor of production is the theory of marginal productivity. This involves proportioning the various inputs, the economical joint use of which makes up a composite cost curve. (An example of such a composite curve was represented in figure 1.)

Productive factors (inputs) necessary for the production of end products are seldom constricted to rigidly fixed proportions. Thus, for example, the amount of land and labor used to produce a given crop, or the amount of wood and glass used to produce a house vary as the relative prices of these input factors change. And, usually, the longer the adjustment period (the longer-run demand) the greater the variability. A fixed-proportion case, however, provides a useful if simplified example of the profit potential of a patent on an input as contrasted to a patent on an end product (as was diagramed in figure 1). Let it be assumed, therefore, that there is an unpatented final product X, for example, a one-bladed knife consisting of two parts: A, a patented blade, and B, an unpatented handle. The fixed-proportion assumption is that there is only a single production function. Thus 1A (a blade) + 1B (a handle) equals 1X (a knife). This means that no knives (X) can be produced unless the owner of the blade (A) patent provides the patented blades; and, given one-to-one fixed proportions, the demand for knives, D_X, calls for the same derived demand for patented blades (D_A), and also, of course, for unpatented handles (D_B).

How, in this kind of situation, should the owner of the blade patent (A) maximize the return on his patent? Several possibilities exist. First, he can manufacture all the knives himself. He would then set the end-product knife price (P_X), just as if he had a patent on the whole knife rather than just a patent on the blade. Also, he would either purchase unpatented handles (input B) or make them himself, depending upon which was more economical. A second option would be to manufacture only the patented blades, selling them to knife manufacturers at the maximum price (P_{A_M}). This price would depend upon the cost of producing the blades in relation to derived demand for them.

If the knives (X) and the handles (B) were each competitively produced and provided at the same cost that the patentee incurred when he made them himself, then the profit under this second option would be exactly the same as under the first. Here, as in the end-product example, cost reduction in the supply of complements is decisive to profit maximization.

A third option (and again the same kind of cost considerations would be relevant) involves no manufacture at all by the patentee. The patent would be licensed to blade makers. They would be charged a royalty on either the number of blades, or what is the same thing in this example, the number of knives produced. Once again, if the licensees are competitive and outsiders' costs are the same as the patentee's for manufacture and sale, the optimal rate would give the patentees an equivalent profit to that provided by the other alternatives just described.

From the foregoing fixed-proportion example it might appear that a patentee holding a patent on a complementary input factor such as a knife blade (A) could maximize his profit by imposing no conditions on the supply of handles (B) or knives (X). The example suggests that the patentee has no need to impose conditions upon licensees in order to maximize his profit. Setting an appropriate single royalty rate on blades seems sufficient for maximizing the revenue from a patent on input factor A, the blade. This conclusion is illusory. Setting the price on a productive factor, A, usable in a fixed proportion with factor B, or final product X, for which it is essential, is the equivalent of setting the price of the final product only *if* all other factors are provided competitively. The maximizing price for factor A (blades) depends upon the costs and prices of other factors. For example, were separate patent monopolies to exist on product A (blades) and on product B (handles), each of these patentees would, of course, prefer to have the other set the lowest possible price (the competitive price). Without agreement between the two patentees the possibility exists that each in attempting to maximize his profit by independently setting his own price would so contract output that the resulting price to users will be too high to maximize their joint profits. Also, consumers would pay a higher price for less of the final product, and the entire community would be poorer. Any agreement concerning use of an input factor which makes for more efficient production of the final product will, as the following diagrams indicate, make for lower prices to consumers as well as for more profit to the patentee.

The fixed-proportion case, in which the productive factor A is combined with productive factor B in such manner that 1 A plus 1 B equals 1 final product X, is diagramed in figures 2, 3, and 4. For purposes of simplifying the exposition it is assumed that the costs of producing A and B are identical and do not vary with output.[8]

Figure 2 shows the single maximizing output and price of a patented product X when its demand is AR_X and its cost of production is MC_X, the summation of the cost of A (MC_A) and the cost of B (MC_B). Just as in figure 1, the intersection of the marginal cost and the marginal revenue curves indicates output (Q_{X_M}) and price (P_{X_M}) leading to maximum profits shown by the shaded area in figure 2.

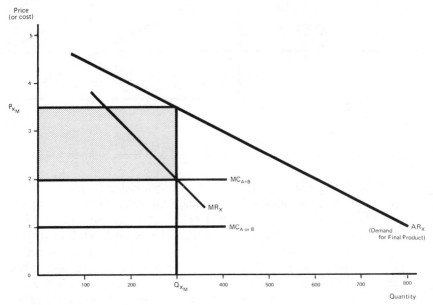

Fig. 2. Monopoly pricing of an end product with two fixed factors.

Figure 3 shows how this identical result in terms of output, final product price, and profit arises from a patent on an input in a fixed-proportion case. Hence the patent monopoly on input factor A, rather

8. Assuming equal and constant costs merely makes diagraming simple and facilitates comparison among figures 2, 3, and 4. The same kind of result could be derived were the costs assumed to be the same as those previously shown in figure 1.

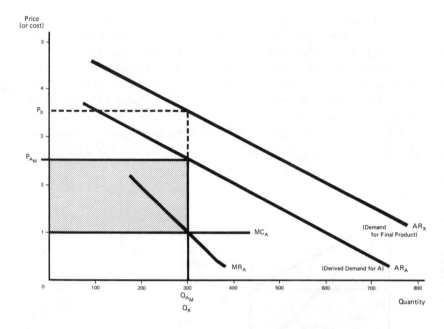

Fig. 3. Monopoly pricing of factor A when factor B is competitively priced.

than on final product X, is shown to be identical only when *input B* is competitively supplied—that is, when the price of B (P_B) equals its cost (MC_B). Because one unit of B had to be paid for in order to sell one unit of A, the derived demand for A (AR_A or D_A) for any price of A (P_A) is the demand for X less the cost of getting the requisite amount of B. This demand curve for A is lower than and to the left of the demand curve for X. (Here it is also parallel to X because of assumed constant cost of production for B.) Marginal revenue for sale of A (MR_A) derivable from AR_A intersects MC_A at output Q_{A_M}, the monopoly output for factor A. Given the competitive price of B ($MC_B = P_B$), it can be seen that the price and output of the final product X is precisely the same in figure 3 as it is in figure 2. And the shaded area in figure 3 representing monopoly return to the holder of a patent on A is precisely the same as was the profit to the holder of the end-product patent represented in figure 2.

It is very important to understand that the equivalent results shown in figures 2 and 3 depend upon the fact that factor B is competitively priced. Were the price of B higher the derived demand for A would of course be lower. In that event, there would be less output of A, and correspondingly less output also of B and of X. This in turn, although making for less profit to the monopoly seller of A, would also raise the price of the final product (P_X) to a *higher* level than were there a monopoly of X (higher than P_{X_M} shown in figure 2).

The overly restrictive possibility of a double monopoly is shown in figure 4. The demand curve for the final product X (AR_X) is again the same as in figures 2 and 3. The cost of producing factor A and factor B is also as before. In figure 4, however, it is assumed that factor A is priced by one holding a patent on A at the level represented by P_{A_M}) in figure 3. Given that price of A, figure 4 shows the best result obtainable by the holder of a patent on factor B. The demand for B (AR_B) is derived in exactly the same manner as was the demand for A in figure 3. So is the maximizing output and price for sale of B given this price for A. Output is lower, the price of the final product is higher, consumers are worse off, and the joint profits of the producers of A and B, shown by the shaded area in figure 4, are lower than those shown in figures 2 and 3. The solution

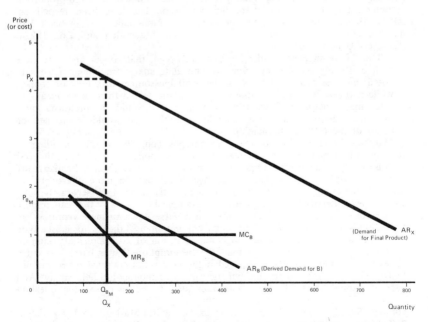

Fig. 4. Monopoly pricing of factor B when factor A is priced as in figure 3.

in figure 4 is both indeterminate and inefficient. It is indeterminate because after the producer of B sets the price as shown as P_{B_M} , at that price of B, P_{A_M} (the monopoly price for A shown in figure 3) is no longer appropriate for A. Since the price of B is now higher, there is a lower derived demand curve for A, calling for a lower output which in turn further raises the price of final product X. This in turn calls for further adjustment by B. The result, interestingly enough, seems to become progressively more inefficient. In circumstances of this kind, keeping the parties at arm's length—forcing each to set a separate price or royalty rate and proscribing further agreement—would benefit neither patentees, patent users, nor the community at large. All would be the worse for it.[9]

Derived Demand for a Patented Input: Variable Proportions

The foregoing fixed-proportion example (one blade and one handle

9. This conclusion, the inadvisability of preventing merger or agreement between two noncompeting monopolists, is not limited to fixed-proportion complementary monopolies. Also, the conclusion has long been recognized. Alfred Marshall discusses the two noncompeting monopolies case in book 5 of his *Principles of Economics*, 8th ed. (London: Macmillan and Co., 1927). At page 493 he writes:

Thus if we supposed, following Cournot's lead, that copper and zinc were each of them useless except when combined to make brass: and if we supposed that one man, A, owned all the available sources of supply of copper; while another, B, owned all those on zinc; there would then be no means of determining beforehand what amount of brass would be produced, nor, therefore, the price at which it could be sold. Each would try to get the better of the other in bargaining.

Marshall, however, in subsequent paragraphs (pp. 494–95) is unwilling to recommend merger of two complementary monopolies in the public interest because of "perhaps greater importance on the other side." Marshall, like many later economists, suggests that competitive entry may be more effectively retarded if the complementary monopolies are jointly rather than separately held. But he never details by either theory or example how or why this can impose higher costs on outsiders so as to have an adverse effect on new ventures. He thus discloses no "foreclosure" or "incipient monopoly" theory to substantiate his conjecture. His unwillingness to condone fusion of complementary monopolies seems to rest on no more than the presumption that a barrier to entry arises because more capital is required if the new venturers must overcome not two monopolies rather than one, but the same two monopolies held singly. And even if capital costs of entry were presumed to be increased the question remains, as I attempted to explain in chapter 4, Why is not the capital forthcoming? See also Stigler, "Imperfections in the Capital Market," 75 *J. Pol. Econ.* 287 (June 1967), reprinted as chapter 10 in *The Organization of Industry* (Homewood, Ill.: Richard D. Irwin Inc., 1968).

for a single knife), as was previously stressed, is a rather special case of joint demand. A more general relationship involves variability in the proportions of inputs to produce a given amount of final product (or a product equivalent providing the same customer service). The ability to vary the proportions of general factors, such as labor and capital, is widely recognized as typical for the production of innumerable manufactured products; and the longer the adjustment time the greater the possible variability. Thus, to take a popular example, as the wages of elevator operators are increased relative to the cost of automation there is incentive for building managers to provide elevator service with proportionately more capital and proportionately less labor. This kind of phenomenon is equally applicable to more specific factors. When the proportion of any input factor in a productive process is variable, how much or how little of a particular factor will be utilized will depend not only upon its price but also upon the prices of the other factors with which it is jointly used as well as upon how varying the proportions affects output. The cost and price relationships between these joint factors are therefore crucial to achieving any output most efficiently.

A patented product or process often is subject to the kind of variability just described. The limits of this variability—the ability of a patentee to raise the price of a patented input without having it substantially or even totally displaced—will depend upon what is described in economic terminology as the law of diminishing marginal returns. This law states: "As any input is increased by unit amounts, the marginal products (although possibly increasing at first to a maximum, called the point of diminishing marginal returns) will thereafter decrease."[10] The amounts and the proportions of use of these joint factors will thus vary as the relative prices of the factors vary. Consequently, for any given output, alternative combinations of inputs (production possibilities) exist, and choice among them turns upon the relative prices of the variable input factors.

The profit-maximizing task for a patentee holding a patent on an input factor is complicated by the variability of input proportions. As he raises the price (or royalty) on his patented input, he encourages partial displacement of the patented input in such manner as to cause inefficient[11] proportioning of inputs by his customers. Suppose, as an example of variable proportioning of a patented input, that there is a patented machine for dispensing salt into cans and that the use of this patented machine substantially lowers the cost of canning as contrasted to the manual method formerly in use. Now, to illustrate variability, assume that as the patentee raises the price of (or the rental for the use of) the machine to licensees (the price of competitively produced salt remaining the same) the machine is used less and less and more and more salt is used or wasted by alternative inefficient dispensing methods, with the further result that the real cost of any output is increased. Under these conditions, setting a profit-maximizing price on the machine to licensees without restrictions upon use can be shown to force inefficient proportioning of machine use to salt use.

In the previous example, where proportions of input (a blade and a handle to make a knife) were not variable, whether the blade was priced at $2.00 and the handle at $1.00 or whether each was priced at $1.50 did not determine whether production was efficient. There was no alternative production function other than one to one for blades and handles in the production of the knife. And this was so, of course, whether the licensee manufactured the knife himself or licensed others to do so. In the variable-proportions example, however, what the patentee would do (or could do in the absence of use-restrictive licensing) is the key to understanding not only how a patentee may maximize his patent return,[12] but also how the community may get more of what it wants at less cost through more efficient production. To illustrate how this might work in the salt-dispensing example, let it be assumed (solely for simplicity of exposition and as equally applicable to more complicated cases) that there are, as in the previous fixed-proportions example, only two input factors, A (the

11. "Inefficient" here is "socially inefficient" with respect to the allocation of resources relative to their real costs. This is not privately inefficient to the customer, because he correctly apportions use in terms of the relative prices he is charged, which are his costs.

12. Thus, if a patentee in pricing factor A should, for example, set a price of $4.00 whereas the price of another partially substitutable factor B was priced at $1.00, the maker of the final product can be expected to substitute B for A to the point where their marginal contributions are just equal. In economic terms this proposition is expressed as:

$$\frac{\text{MPP}_A \text{ (marginal physical product of A)}}{\text{MC}_A \text{ (marginal cost of A)}} = \frac{\text{MPP}_B \text{ (marginal physical product of B)}}{\text{MC}_B \text{ (marginal cost of B)}}$$

patented machine) and B (competitively supplied salt). And here, as in the previous example, it will be assumed that each of the factors (machine use and salt) is supplied at equal per-unit cost (to the patentee) irrespective of how much is produced. Let this constant unit cost for A (machine use) or B (price or cost of salt) be $1.00 per unit. Given these costs, if the machine patent owner were to carry on the canning operation himself rather than licensing others to do so, given variable proportion possibilities, he must decide what proportions of machine (A) and salt (B) to use in producing his final product (X). This will depend upon how varying the proportions of A and B will affect final output (X). To make this assessment one needs to know about what has been described as "marginal productivity." This involves describing a production function. In the salt-dispensing case we must ask what can be expected to happen to output (X) when, for example, machine use (factor A) is held constant and increasing amounts of salt (factor B) are used (or wasted). Table 1 illustrates a variable-proportion production function, showing how marginal product declines as increasing units of one factor are added while the other (or others) are held constant.[13] This is thus an example of the previously mentioned law of diminishing returns.

TABLE 1
Units of Factors A and B Required for the Production of Product X

Factor A	Factor B	Units of Product X	Marginal Product of B (MPP_B)
1	1	1.0	1.0
1	2	1.4	.4
1	3	1.7	.3
1	4	1.9	.2
1	5	2.0	.1
1	6	2.0	0

It should be apparent, given the production possibilities in table 1 and the previous assumption about the relative cost for factors A and

13. To simplify the exposition it is assumed that the ratios of factor A to factor B for the production of final product X are the same over all the ranges of output of X. Thus, if 1A + 1B provide 1X, then 2A + 2B provide 2X, and if 1A + 2B provide 1.4X, then 2A + 4B provide 2.8X, etc.

B ($1.00 each), that if the patentee were to produce the final product
(X) himself his lowest cost for any given amount of final product
would be achieved only by using factors A and B in the proportion
of one to one. And it would be equally true if he were to license others
who had these same production possibilities, and factor B (salt) was
available at a competitive price of $1.00 per unit, that they too would
be producing efficiently only were they to use the factors in this same
proportion.

Use-restrictive licensing, either by tying the sale of salt to the use
of the machine or by alternative means of imposing restriction upon
use of a patented product, will now be shown to be a plausible means
of achieving this kind of efficiency.[14] This demonstration involves
deriving the demand for a patented input (A), given final demand
for the end product (X). Two alternative demand schedules are
shown for final product X. The first, diagramed in figures 5 and 6,
is as follows:

Price of X (P_X)	Demand for X (D_X)
$10.00	0
9.00	50
8.00	100
7.00	150
6.00	200
5.00	250
4.00	300
3.00	350
2.00	400

14. There is an alternative and equally if not more plausible explanation of
why the sale of salt may be tied to the sale or lease of a salt-vending machine.
It involves the use of salt sales to the machine user as a metering device to
measure intensity of machine use. This is a form of price discrimination and
is explained in a subsequent section of this chapter.

It should be noted that the variable-proportions example in this section relates to apportioning factor inputs for the efficient production of a final product.
A similar analysis can be applied to end-product substitutes when their demand
is joint. If, for example, there were a patented consumer product useful only
with another unpatented product, and consumers within limits could substitute
one for the other, this same kind of analysis would be applicable.

An alternative demand for X, shown in figures 7 and 8, is:

Price of X (P_X)	Demand for X (D_X)
$ 5.00	0
4.50	100
4.00	200
3.50	300
3.00	400
2.50	500
2.00	600
1.50	700
1.00	800

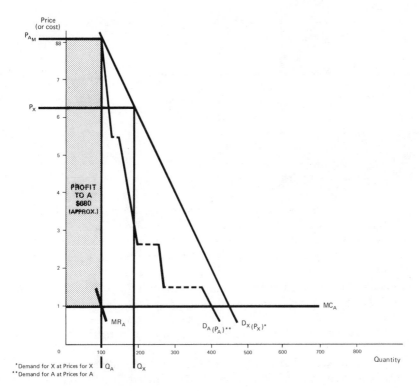

Fig. 5. Monopoly pricing of variable factor A without use restriction.

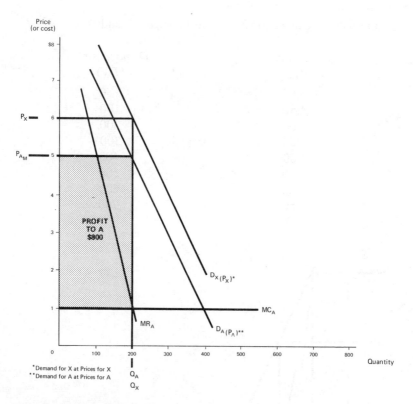

Fig. 6. Monopoly pricing of variable factor A with use restriction.

Now, given the demand for product X ($D_{X_{P_X}}$) in figures 5 and 7,
given the cost of supplying patented input factor A (MC_A in figures
5 and 7), and given the effects on the production of X when factor B
is substituted for factor A (as in the production function table), a
demand for patented input A may be derived for various prices of
A. Two such derived demands are shown as $D_{A_{P_A}}$ in figures 5 and 7.

The derivation of the demand for A ($D_{A_{P_A}}$) in figures 5 and 7 is
shown in tables 2 and 3. For ease of calculation a discontinuous case
has been assumed. In other words, it is assumed that the proportions
of factors A and B to produce X, shown in the following tables, are
the *only* proportions. This, of course, converts the variable proportion

example into a series of fixed proportions. The most advantageous of these for the maker of X are shown by italics in each of these tables; and in a final column profits (PR_A) are shown for various prices of a (P_A).

The derivation of the demand for a patented input (A) shown graphically in the foregoing figures shows the results of use-restrictive licensing as contrasted to the results when use restriction is *not* applied under two alternative demand schedules for the final product. In the first example, as is shown in figure 5, nonrestrictive licensing results in 97 units of A being sold at slightly over $8.00. But at this price, since only 1 unit of A and 4 units of B are used in producing 1.9 units of product X, 184 units of X are produced, which, given the demand for X, will bring $6.32 for each unit of X sold.

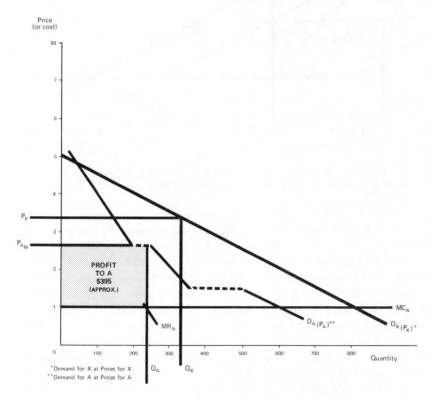

Fig. 7. Monopoly pricing of variable factor A without use restriction (alternate to figure 5 given more elastic demand for end product).

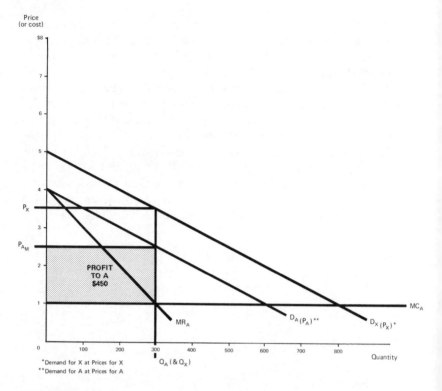

Fig. 8. Monopoly pricing of variable factor A with use restriction (alternate to figure 6 given more elastic demand for end product).

Figure 5 indicates how a patentee, attempting to exploit a patent on an input factor, usable in variable proportions, forces inefficient resource use by setting the price of the patented factor while allowing buyers to purchase as much or as little as they wish without restriction on use. Given the conditions posited in this example, too little of the patented product A is produced at too high a price. Figure 6 indicates how both the consumers of product X and the owner of the patent on input factor A would be benefited were the sales of A conditioned on use in making product X in the most efficient manner—in the ratio of 1A to 1X. Various means might be used to achieve this result. One of the simplest would be to condition the amount of sales of input A to a licensee's output of product X on a one-to-one basis. This would force the licensee-manufacturers of X to efficient resource use, and would increase the sales and lower the price of patented input A, while

TABLE 2
Arithmetical Derivation of Demand for A and Maximum Profits Shown in Figure 5

Price		Cost to Maker of X with Variable Proportions					Demand X	Demand A	Profit
(P_A)	(P_B)	1A to 1X (1B)	1A to 1.4X (2B)	1A to 1.7X (3B)	1A to 1.9X (4B)	1A to 2X (5B)	(D_X)	(D_A)	(PR_A)
$10.00	$1.00	$11.00	$8.57	$7.65	$7.37	$7.50	131.5	69	$621.00
9.00	1.00			7.06	6.84	7.00	158.0	83	664.00
8.50	1.00			6.76	6.58	6.75	171.0	90	675.00
8.00	1.00			6.47	6.32	6.50	184.0	97	679.00
7.50	1.00			6.18	6.05	6.25	197.5	104	676.00
5.50	1.00		5.36	5.00	5.00	5.25	250.0	{ 131 / 147	{ 590.00 / 662.00
2.65	1.00	3.65	3.32	3.32					
1.50	1.00	2.50	2.50	3.21					

TABLE 3
Arithmetical Derivation of Demand for A and Maximum Profits Shown in Figure 7

Price		Cost to Maker of X with Variable Proportions					Demand X	Demand A	Profit
(P_A)	(P_B)	1A to 1X (1B)	1A to 1.4X (2B)	1A to 1.7X (3B)	1A to 1.9X (4B)	1A to 2X (5B)	(D_X)	(D_A)	(PR_A)
$5.00	$1.00	$6.00	$5.00	$4.71	$4.74	$5.00	58	34	$ 36.00
4.00	1.00		4.61	4.41	4.47		118	69	
3.30	1.00		3.78	3.71	3.84		270	159	366.00
3.00	1.00		3.57	3.53	3.68		294	172	
2.67	1.00		3.33	3.33	3.51		333	⎰195	395.00
2.50	1.00	3.50	3.21	3.24	3.42		358	⎱238	384.00
1.50	1.00	2.50	2.50	2.65				256	

at the same time increasing the patentee's profits and lowering the price of X to consumers. This result, forcing the most efficient proportions of A and B, is shown in figure 6. Forcing licensees to use patented input A with unpatented input B in the ratio of one to one (as in figure 6, where the cost of providing each was assumed to be equal) was a means of lowering the costs of producing X by licensees below the costs these licensees would incur were the patentee merely to set the price of patented input A with no conditions imposed by the patentee (as in figure 5). Allowing the patentee to lower the maximizing price of patented input A below that depicted in figure 5 and to raise the price of unpatented input B above the competitive level made it possible for the patentee to set the prices of the two inputs in proportion to their real costs and thus to compel a use which was more profitable to the patentee, and in this particular case, also less costly for licensees, and therefore less costly to consumers.

In the foregoing example, the efficient apportioning of scarce resources among alternative uses in the interest of both the patentee and the community as a whole was achieved by imposing "conditions of use" on licensees making end products. The example at the very least indicates the shortsightedness of any general rule automatically proscribing restrictions upon use. The example involved substitutable inputs. It involved cross-elasticity of demand between factors A and B. In other words, as the price of input A was increased, the price of B remaining constant, it showed how the demand for B increased. And, of course, in searching for that price, and those terms of sale which would maximize the return from his patent, the owner of the patent on input factor A in the example took this cross-elasticity into account. In doing so he could be said to have "tied" the sales of input A to the output of final product X. And although in this particular tie-in example, if it may be so characterized, producers of product B were prevented from making sales otherwise available, it achieved not only greater reward for the patentee but also lower prices for consumers.

Lower prices to consumers, however, do not necessarily follow because variable input proportions exist. Given different demands, different costs, or a different production function, output of the final product X could be restricted rather than expanded, even though the patentee's profits would be increased. In such a case, depicted in figures 7 and 8, the output expansion effect of forcing the maker of X into more efficient production is swamped by the greater effect occasioned by the more elastic demand.[15] In either case, however, inefficient proportions of resources are used in producing any given quantity of the final product. Moreover, whether or not consumers of the final product pay more for and get less of the product than they would were no use restriction imposed, no payment can be extracted by the patentee which is not ascribable to the competitive superiority afforded by the patented resources without which the consumers would be even worse off.

The maximum reward achievable by a patentee in either of the foregoing examples (as indicated in figures 6 and 8) could be achieved by an alternative means involving a more conventional tie-in arrangement. The owner of the patent on input A might require that no amount of patented input A could be purchased by makers of product X unless they also purchased all their requirements of input B from the patentee. In such case, rather than charging a maximizing price for A and forcing the sale of one unit of A for each unit of X produced (allowing B to be purchased competitively at $1.00), the patentee could achieve the same result by equalizing the prices of A and B (total cost to X remaining the same). This too would eliminate X's inducement to shift to inefficient proportions of A and B. This alternative would be workable, of course, only if the makers of product X could be effectively prevented from access to the competitive market in which B is sold for $1.00. But this kind of problem is typical of most tying sales.

End-Product Pricing: A Parallel Derived-Demand Example

Patented inputs, like other inputs, the demand for which is derived from the services they provide, will lead to greater return as the end products in which they are essential are more valuable, and as alternative inputs (a substitute patent, for example) are not readily available. The means by which a patented input can be used in combination with other resources is not different conceptually from the various ways a final product can be combined with other products or services. In each case, as the price is raised or lowered the amounts demanded fall or rise. Final goods are combined in different proportions in consumer budgets as prices change. And similarly, inputs generally used in

---

15. This, of course, is most efficient given the production function in the example and given the equal cost of the substitutable factors A and B.

variable proportions vary as their relative prices change. A true fixed-proportion case, given significant adjustment time, is practically unknown. There are few if any equivalents of rigid proportions of patented inputs in the same sense as they exist in chemistry—for example, of oxygen and hydrogen in water.

Pricing anything high enough will always cause some substitution for it. This is true of end-product patents, intermediate-product patents, or process patents. Suppose, for example, a patent were issued on a synthetic fiber, nylon, one of whose claims was its use in the manufacture of ladies' hosiery, so that no hosiery manufacturer could make or sell hosiery containing nylon without the explicit consent of the patentee. To simplify the example let it be assumed that nylon (as is of course not true of this many-use product) has no use except in ladies' hosiery. Now let it further be assumed that in making hosiery it is possible to use nylon in combination with other materials, including varying proportions of cotton, rayon, or silk with corresponding effect upon relative durability, sheerness, and style. In other words, the assumption is that patented nylon makes up only a part of the cost of the final product nylon hosiery.

This kind of question has been posed by Professor William Baxter with respect to adverse effects of allowing the patentee to set the price of a final product, for example, stockings containing "patented nylon" rather than setting *only* the price of the input, that is, the nylon price.[16] Baxter's conclusion is that such "end-product" pricing makes it possible for the patentee to raise the price of stockings to a level higher than would be the case if this right were denied him. This nutshell conclusion, Baxter has written, is derived because "the elasticity of demand for a factor input [nylon fiber in our example] is always greater than the responsiveness of the end-product [nylon stockings in our example] to a price change in the same factor input."[17]

This is an explanation, however, that is neither useful nor relevant to the problem. Of course, if nylon made up 10 percent of the cost of stockings and its price were cut in half, the cost of stockings would

16. William Baxter, "Legal Restrictions and Exploitations of Patent Monopoly: An Economic Analysis, 76 *Yale L. J.* 267 (Dec. 1966), at p. 303: "Under an endproduct royalty structure, a licensee pays nothing for incremental use of the invention in the production of any given product. And through royalties the patentee may drain off the full monopoly potential inherent not in the invention but in the unpatented endproduct."
17. Ibid., p. 300.

only be cut 5 percent if the amount of nylon in stockings did not increase. And even if this nylon price cut increased the use of nylon in stockings tenfold (variable proportions), it would still be a truism that the cost of nylon would be less than the cost of the stockings. In other words, a cut in the price of nylon would lead to a less than proportionate cut in the cost of stockings. But this does not mean that the owner of a patent on nylon fiber will sell more nylon at the same or a higher price by setting stocking prices than by setting nylon prices.

In the foregoing example, the variability in the use of the patented input factor, nylon, in the production of nylon stockings will not allow a patentee to restrict the nylon in stockings and thereby increase return to the nylon patent. This also holds for the more extreme case, the nylon-processing patent. Suppose there is a nylon-processing patent but that nylon is unpatented. Suppose further that alternative processes for producing nylon usable only in nylon stockings are very close, but that nylon stocking demand is extremely inelastic for competitively priced stockings. This is to say that rayon, silk, and leg makeup are very imperfect substitutes for nylon. How, it must be asked, can end-product pricing of the nylon-process patent overcome or eliminate the substitution effect of alternative processes[18] with the result that greater output restriction of the end-product, nylon stockings, is more achievable than that achievable by the direct pricing of the process?[19] A moment's reflection shows that the key question is what end-product producers would be willing to, or would have to, pay for nylon where nylon is produced cheaply without patent infringement.

Take, for example, a most extreme and economically implausible case, one in which all nylon-stocking customers would pay $3.00 a pair and would buy none if the price were higher and no fewer at any price competitive sellers would be willing to offer them—a vertical demand curve with an upper limit of $3.00 a pair. This would be the price extracted from consumers if there were a patent on nylon stockings. Assume alternatively that there existed a patent on a process

18. This example concedes that by no means typical condition that the demand for the process is more elastic than the demand for the final product of which it is a part. See Stigler, *Theory of Price*, pp. 242–44, and his Appendix B, n. 14.
19. This example purposely excludes the possibility of price discrimination in different end-product markets. That is a different case subsequently discussed. A single end-product market is assumed in order to focus exclusively upon the "variable proportions" case suggested by Baxter.

for producing nylon stockings which saved 10¢ a pair in production cost over alternative nonpatented methods of producing unpatented nylon usable only in stockings. Assume further that the nonnylon cost of producing and selling stockings is 50¢ a pair and the cost of nylon produced without the process patent is also 50¢ a pair, irrespective of how many stockings are produced. If there were no nylon-processing patent, the cost of, and the competitive price of, a pair of nylon stockings would then be $1.00.

Under the conditions just assumed, a patent on nylon stockings would be worth $2.00 ($3.00 less $1.00 cost) times the number of pairs demanded.[20] Suppose this inelastic demand is 10,000 pair for a given time period. A nylon stocking patent would then be worth $20,000 for this period—10,000 times $2.00.

But assuming a patent on the process for producing a generic unpatented product, nylon, which saves 10¢ a pair over alternative methods of producing nylon, the Baxter analysis, stripped to its essential logic, suggests that the owner of the process patent, by end-product pricing, can in some unrevealed manner convert a 10¢ a pair advantage into something like the equivalent of the $2.00 a pair advantage if a monopoly on nylon stockings existed.

The answer should be obvious. No rational nylon stocking manufacturer would use any patented-process nylon priced any higher than nonpatented processed nylon. This is to say that Baxter has not revealed the trick (end-product pricing, tie-in sales, or whatever) by which the owner of the nylon-processing patent could extract more than 10¢ a pair for his process. In fact, charging 10.1¢ would dry up his market completely. And relaxing the implausible assumption that the demand for nylon stockings is not completely inelastic but, as Baxter suggests, only less elastic than the demand for the process patent, of course, leaves the essence of the conclusion unchanged—nobody will pay more for a process patent than the differential advantage it affords. End-product pricing is not an obvious means by which patentees with process patents, or with patents on intermediate products, may control end-product prices.

If, unlike the foregoing example, however, some amount of an essential (patented) input is required to produce the end product, then a patentee's net revenue may be increased by limiting input sub-

20. Assuming in this simplified example that licensing and using the nylon-processing patent did not change costs.

stitution. Insofar as a patented input is not completely replaceable, that is, *some* input A is required to produce end product X, then, of course, no end product would be possible but for the patent. Moreover, given variable proportions, as the owner of patented input A raises the price of A there will be, as figures 5 and 6 have indicated, a double substitution effect. First, the cost of final product X will be increased, thus increasing its price and lowering the amount of final product demanded. Second, as the price of input A is increased, relatively less of A and more of substitutable inputs will be used, further decreasing the derived demand for the patented input even though some use of A is essential.

As was shown in figures 5–8, output restriction is not uniquely predictable. End-product pricing (or an equivalent pricing method) can be output expanding. But imposing conditions of use, including end-product pricing, can be used to achieve more efficient production or distribution and thus to lower rather than raise the price of the products in which the patent is essential. The variability of proportions of use of a patented input factor can give rise to the kind of situation described in figures 5 and 6. And, output effect notwithstanding, setting the input price of a variable input factor and leaving the patent user free to buy as much or as little as he wishes makes for inefficient production of the output. Too little of the more efficient input is utilized, and production of that amount of end product produced is wasteful.

The case that patented inputs are misallocated or underallocated when a patentee having exclusive rights to such inputs is allowed to price or condition the sale of end products, rather than to price the input directly, cannot be grounded on the existence of variable proportioning of input factors. The conclusion that "free market assessment is thwarted if the patentee is permitted to sell not the bare right to use the invention but the right to monopolize generic end products in which it is useful"[21] suggests leveraging to additional monopoly. But even without leveraging consumers may be benefited.

The conditions of sale or lease in disposing of or licensing a process or an intermediate-product patent are plausible means of achieving

21. Baxter, "Legal Restrictions," p. 353. An end-product monopoly may, of course, be more valuable than a monopoly over one of its inputs. The *right* of a patentee with a patent on an important factor to "monopolize" a general end product would indeed be improper if this right could be exercised by some form of leveraging.

efficiency just as was the exclusive dealing device described in the previous chapter. And it should be stressed again that even if particular competitors may be unable to participate in particular markets because end-product use or use with other products is specified, this "competitor" effect should not be confused with effect on competition.

Cross-Elasticities in General: Substitutes and Complements

The market demand for a particular input is a function of the quantity and price of other jointly used inputs, as well as a negative function of the price of that particular input. The same is true of all goods, however, including consumer goods. If a larger number of eggs causes a *higher* demand for bacon (see n. 3 supra), the two goods are complementary. If, on the other hand, a larger number of eggs causes a *lower* demand for bacon the two products are substitutes. In the previous example of patented input A and competitive input B usable in variable proportions in the production of product X, the two inputs were substitutes, since it was possible to produce a specified rate of output X with less of one input and more of the other. The example also exposed another meaning of substitution. More of one input (B) caused a *lower* marginal product for the existing amount of the *other* resource (patented A). There was a negative "crossover" effect upon the marginal product, and therefore upon the demand for the other resource. The interaction between two joint inputs need not bear this negative relationship; it might well be positive. Similarly, this is also true of joint demands for final products. Neither need these "cross-effects" be symmetrical. The "cross-effect" of a change in the price (or quantity) of joint product A on the demand for joint product B, whether positive (complement) or negative (substitute) need not be the same as a change in the price (or quantity) of product B upon the demand for product A.

When these asymmetrical cross-elasticities exist there is strong incentive for a patentee with a monopoly over one of them to take them into account. If, for example, a tie-in is to maximize the patented reward by taking advantage of cross-elasticity of demand, this is done by lowering the price of the tying product and raising the price of the tied product as compared with the prices which would exist were no tie-in allowed. This use of a tie-in works to maximize profits when the asymmetrical cross-demand effect from a given increase in the price of the tied product causes less decrease in demand for the final product than would a similar increase in the price of the tying product.

When cross-elasticities of demand between two joint products, one of which is patented, are such that raising the price of the unpatented product above the competitive level lowers the price of the patented product below what would otherwise be the monopoly price, then a profit-maximizing patentee has incentive to set both prices.[22] A tying contract is a means of achieving this result.

Cross-demand relationships between joint products complicate profit maximization for a patentee. The nature of the problem is exemplified in figures 9–12. In these examples the demand for patented product A changes as the price of complement B changes. In figure 9 the demand for A shown is applicable only when product B is priced competitively at $1.00 per unit. The cost of producing product A is presumed to

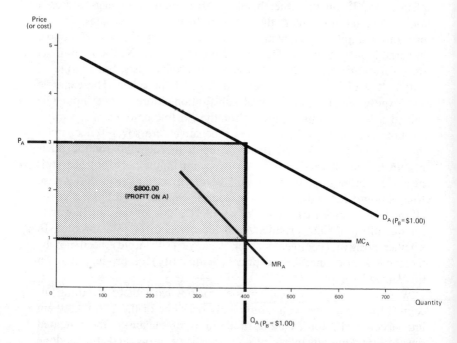

Fig. 9. Monopoly price and output of product A when complementary product B is competitively priced.

22. Were the profit-maximizing price for the tied product below the competitive price, of course no tie-in would be required. The patentee could merely purchase the product in the competitive market and sell the "required" quantities at the lower price.

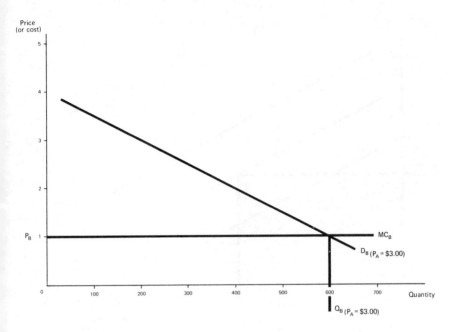

Fig. 10. Competitive price and output of product B when complementary product A is priced as in figure 9.

be $1.00 (MC = $1.00) for all levels of output in this example. In figure 9, therefore, given the demand for A (D_{A, P_B} = $1.00), and given $1.00 per unit production cost for producing A (MC$_A$ = $1.00), pricing at $3.00 and selling 400 units maximizes the patentee's profit. This profit, shown by the shaded area in figure 9, is $800.

At the $3.00 maximizing price for A, the demand for competitively produced product B, *for use with product A* (other uses can be assumed to be beyond the control of the holder of the patent on A), is shown in figure 10. The cost of producing B is assumed to be $1.00 per unit (MC$_B$ = $1.00) for all levels of output. Thus, as is indicated in figure 10, when A sells for $3.00, 600 units of B will be sold for use with A at the competitive price of $1.00 for B.

Now, given these demands and costs for the production of products A and B, it will be assumed that for every 25¢ increase in the price of B there will be a decrease of 50 units in the demand for A (and conversely for decreases in the price of B). For each decrease of 25¢ in the price of A (and conversely with an increase), assume that the demand for B is increased by 25 units.

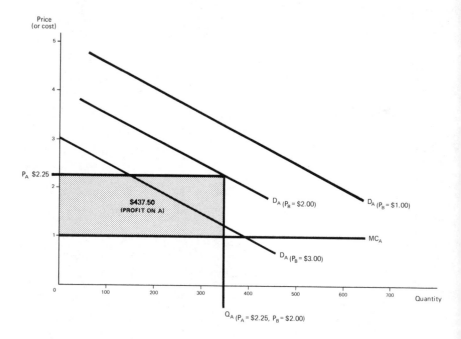

Fig. 11. Price and output of product A with joint maximization of complements A and B.

Given this joint relationship[23] (and assuming for brevity of arithmetic exposition price increments of 25¢), table 4 indicates the effect on profits of varying the prices of A and B. The effect on profits of lowering the price of A from $3.00 to $2.25, and raising the price of B from $1.00 to $2.00, is shown in figures 11 and 12.

By taking account of the cross-demands between joint products A and B, the owner of patent A, in the example provided, is able to restrict the sales of both A and B to below the amounts which would have been available to customers had this method of pricing been foreclosed. This particular outcome was a result of the demands and costs posited. Other examples of cross-demand, involving either complementary or substitute products, could be provided in which the

23. This same method of dual pricing would be applicable to a situation in which the cross-effect was in the opposite direction—a higher price of one product leading to *higher* rather than lower demand for the other. This substitution effect, as with complements, would also provide a feasible rationale for tying only for uses of the tied product requiring use with the tying product.

output of either product is expanded while the other is contracted, or in which both outputs are expanded.[24] The output restriction effect of setting two prices instead of just one was against the interest of consumers, as is shown in figures 11 and 12, and resulted from the particular demand and the cost conditions used (see table 4). But even when output restriction results from dual pricing (as it need not), this is not the result of the creation of a second monopoly due to setting the price of the second product. Whether this cross-demand reflects complementary or substitution effects or the ability of a patentee to raise the price of either the patented or the unpatented product, the

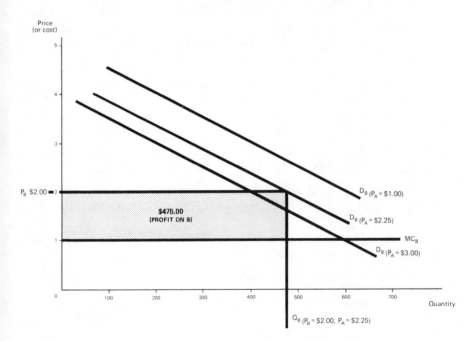

Fig. 12. Price and output of product B with joint maximization of complements A and B.

24. See Harold Hotelling, "Edgeworth's Taxation Paradox and the Nature of Demand and Supply Functions," 40 *J. Pol. Econ.* 577 (Oct. 1932), at p. 578. "For some pairs of related demand functions a tax on one commodity will cause both to increase in price, for others, one commodity will increase and the other will decrease in price. [But there is a third class] for which both commodities will decrease in price, when the seller pays the tax."

The charge a patentee might impose on his licensees can be viewed as a "tax" in applying the Hotelling analysis in the patent licensing context.

TABLE 4
Demand for Joint Products

Prices		Demand			Profiit A	
P_A	P_B	D_A	D_B	TR_A	$- TC_A$	$= PR_A$
$3.00	$1.00	400	600	$1,200.00	— $400.00	= $800.00
	1.25	350	550	1,050.00	— 350.00	= 700.00
	1.50	300	500	900.00	— 300.00	= 600.00
	1.75	250	450	750.00	— 250.00	= 500.00
	2.00	200	400	600.00	— 200.00	= 400.00
2.75	1.25	400	575	1,100.00	— 400.00	= 700.00
	1.50	350	525	962.50	— 350.00	= 612.50
	1.75	300	475	825.00	— 300.00	= 525.00
2.50	1.50	400	550	1,000.00	— 400.00	= 600.00
	1.75	350	500	875.00	— 350.00	= 525.00
	2.00	300	450	750.00	— 300.00	= 450.00
	2.25	250	400	575.00	— 250.00	= 325.00
2.25	1.75	400	525	900.00	— 400.00	= 500.00
	2.00	350	475	787.50	— 350.00	= 437.50
	2.25	300	425	675.00	— 300.00	= 375.00
2.00	2.00	400	500	800.00	— 400.00	= 400.00
	2.25	350	450	700.00	— 350.00	= 350.00
	2.50	300	400	600.00	— 300.00	= 300.00
1.75	2.25	400	475	700.00	— 400.00	= 300.00
	2.50	350	425	612.50	— 350.00	= 262.50

NOTE: For a more precise geometric solution for this kind of case see Bailey, "Price and Output Determination for a Firm Selling Related Products," 44 *Am. Econ. Rev.* 82 (1954).

aShown as shaded area in figures 9 and 10.

bShown as shaded area in figures 11 and 12.

	Profit B		
TR_B	$- TC_B$	$= PR_B$	PR_{A+B}
$600.00	— $600.00	= $000.00	$800.00[a]
687.50	— 550.00	= 127.50	827.50
750.00	— 500.00	= 250.00	850.00
787.50	— 450.00	= 337.50	837.50
800.00	— 400.00	= 400.00	800.00
718.75	— 575.00	= 143.75	843.75
789.50	— 525.00	= 264.50	887.00
831.25	— 475.00	= 356.25	881.25
825.00	— 550.00	= 275.00	875.00
875.00	— 500.00	= 375.00	900.00
900.00	— 450.00	= 450.00	900.00
900.00	— 400.00	= 500.00	825.00
918.75	— 525.00	= 393.75	893.75
950.00	— 475.00	= 475.00	*912.50*[b]
956.25	— 425.00	= 531.25	906.75
1,000.00	— 500.00	= 500.00	900.00
1,012.50	— 450.00	= 562.50	*912.50*
1,000.00	— 400.00	= 600.00	900.00
1,067.75	— 475.00	= 592.75	892.75
1,062.50	— 425.00	= 637.50	900.00

power to raise prices is limited to those uses of the tied product that but for the existence of the patented product would not exist.

Any firm seeking to maximize joint profits from related products will not consider each market in isolation. When making price and output decisions, a patentee's ability to raise the price of a related unpatented product depends upon, and is limited to, those joint uses in which the patent is essential. Otherwise, of course, attempting to raise the price of the unpatented complement would merely divert buyers to alternative suppliers. If, for example, a shoe machinery company had a patent on a stitching machine but no patent on a soling machine, competitively supplied to shoe manufacturers who required both of these complementarily related machines to produce shoes, the patent on the stitching machine could be used to raise the price of unpatented soling machines only to those shoe manufacturing customers who could not do without the patentee's stitching machine. The existence of a valuable patent on a stitching machine by no means guarantees its indispensability. And, as in the previous nylon example, if the patented stitching machine had substitutes that shoe manufacturers could use, but whose cost was higher than the cost of the patented stitching machine, there would be no means (in the absence of agreement with makers of competing stitching machines) by which a cost could be imposed upon shoe manufacturers greater than the comparative advantage provided by the patented stitching machine. And this conclusion is as true of dual pricing of complements as it is of single pricing of the patented machine. Leveraging to new monopoly is not involved. What is involved is an exercise by the patentee of his interest in exploiting the full advantage his patent affords users by imposing particular conditions of use.

Price Discrimination

The first example (fig. 1) demonstrated how the owner of an end-product patent maximizes the net returns achievable from his patent monopoly. One of the assumptions necessary to the conclusion reached was that all sales were made in a single market at a single price. The demand curve in that example revealed the revenue obtainable for differing amounts of *total* sales; the possibility of charging different prices to different customers was assumed not to exist. A demand schedule showing amounts salable at various prices is typically the summation of the demands of a number of different potential buyers, some of whom, or some groups of whom, may be willing to pay considerably more or less for the product than others. Differing tastes, differing incomes, or differing access to close substitutes for, or complements to, the monopolized product may bring this about. Sometimes these differences can be exploited by a patentee and sometimes they cannot.

"The essence of discrimination is to separate buyers into two or more classes whose elasticities of demand differ appreciably, and this usually requires that the product sold to the various classes differ in time, place, or appearance to keep buyers from shifting."[25] Neither the creation nor the maintenance of separate markets is a costless operation. For discrimination to be practicable it must be achievable at costs which are reasonable in light of the potential profits. The most likely product candidates for discrimination, therefore, are those which do not lend themselves readily to resale from low-price buyers to high-price buyers. The existence of a patent provides no automatic means of overcoming these difficulties; but certain kinds of licensing arrangements in particular circumstances do provide means which make price discrimination economically feasible. Thus, when demand conditions vary in different territories, varying license rates by territory may be feasible; similarly, if a patented product has several end-product uses in which the economic proximity of close substitutes differs substantially, licensing the different uses at differing rates may be practicable. Similarly, if a patented machine were useful to both intensive and extensive users but worth more to the former than to the latter, leasing the machine at rates related to machine output might be a means of increasing patent revenue by discriminatory charges.

All of these price discrimination examples describe means by which a patentee maximizes the return ascribable to the differential advantage the patent affords. Leveraging to new monopoly is not involved. The only difference between the price discrimination case and the single market–one price monopoly case is divisibility of use on the basis of different degrees of unique usefulness (elasticity of demand). And for this condition to apply (differing demand elasticities), these markets are often noncompeting. But it is differing demand elasticity that is crucial; otherwise a single price would be profit maximizing. A discriminatory patent license contract, in the absence of provision

25. Stigler, *Theory of Price*, p. 209.

or understanding for the elimination of competition with patent substitutes, is an economically explicable means of exploiting this absence
of competition between markets, but not of creating it.

The following diagram, figure 13, indicates how, with two separate
markets, price discrimination can increase net return to a patentee.[26]

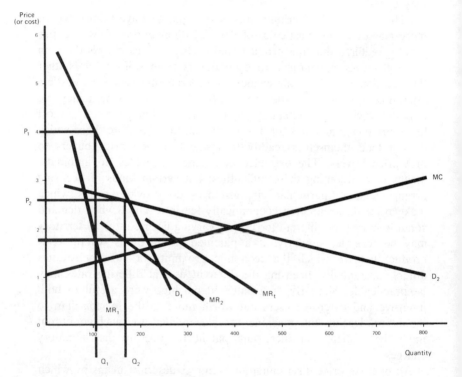

Fig. 13. Discriminatory pricing in two markets.

The general rule about price discrimination illustrated in this diagram is that a monopolist will maximize his profit only when he
equates the marginal cost for his total output with the marginal revenue in each market.[27] This is indicated in figure 13 by the horizontal

---

26. For simplicity of exposition, not affecting the nature of the outcome, we
will assume that the markets are not interdependent.
27. Again, correction for possible interrelation of demand between the two
markets is ignored.

summing of the marginal revenue curves (MR_1 and MR_2), noting the intersection of this summed curve (MR_t) and apportioning the output to be produced for the two markets by the intersection respectively of MR_1 and MR_2 with a line horizontal to the intersection of MR_t and MC. (This is necessary to allow for the fact that output in both markets is required to arrive at the appropriate cost level when incremental costs are not constant at various output levels.)

Once the appropriate output division is made in the manner indicated, the separate prices are determined in each market exactly as they were in the single-market case depicted in figure 1. The two profit areas are then, of course, summed.

The two separate demand curves appropriately describe (as did figure 1 for the single-product case) market-use subdivision of end-product patents, intermediate-product patents, or process patents. In any of these markets it is differing demand elasticity which makes the price discrimination process profitable. Means of accomplishing discrimination vary under different circumstances. Patent-tying contracts, for example, which the courts condemn almost automatically, may be used to separate users whose demands differ as in D_1 and D_2 in figure 13.

An early (1895) case provides an apt example.[28] A machine was invented for stapling buttons to high-button shoes, an operation formerly done by hand at higher cost. The patentee had a number of prospective customers for his machine, some of whom made a great many shoes, others only a few. The invention saved each user a fixed amount on each button attached. Thus the machine was worth more to the more intensive users. An attempt to charge different prices to the different users, however, would have encountered two problems. First, advance knowledge of how intensively each buyer would use the machine would be difficult to come by. Second, preventing those who paid a low price from reselling to those who paid a high price might have proved impossible. A tie-in would resolve the difficulties. The machine might be sold at cost, on condition that the unpatented staples used in the machine be bought from the patentee. Through staple sales, the patentee could measure the intensity with which his customers used the machines. Hence by charging a higher than com-

---

28. The case is Heaton-Peninsular Button-Fastener Co. v. Eureka Specialty Co., 65 Fed. 619 (C.C.W.D. Mich. 1895). The example is from Bowman, "Tying Arrangements and the Leverage Problem," 67 *Yale L. Rev.* 19 (Nov. 1957).

petitive price for the staples the patentee could receive the equivalent of a royalty from his patented machines.[29]

A tying sale may thus be used as a "counting device" for setting discriminatory prices on the tying product, and as such creates no new and additional monopoly over the tied product. Exactly the same result might be achieved by attaching a meter to the button-stapling machine to measure the intensity of use, then leasing the machine and charging a meter rate.[30] Such other devices, however, might well be more costly. Tying here is used simply as an efficient means of insuring the full monopoly return on the tying product where a monopoly already existed. No leverage can be found; and the output of the tied product, staples, is exactly the same when machine payment is charged directly and staples are sold competitively as when the staples are tied to the machine. So far as staples used for shoes are concerned, the outputs under the two equivalent methods of discrimination are identical.

Although the use of a tie-in sale as a counting device is consistent with the facts of a large number of tying cases—for example, the tying of ink to mimeographs, punch cards to computors, or rivets to riveting guns—it does not provide the only rational explanation of tying practice when variable proportions are involved. The example suggests a means by which a monopolist can separate markets to achieve the maximum return from each of the various markets in which the single product can be sold. In this instance, the higher price charged for the tied product is in lieu of the proper pricing of the tying product

---

29. The same "discrimination" result could conceivably have been achieved by giving the machine away and charging a still higher price for staples, except that the machine might be provided to infrequent users. Under these circumstances the patentee might not even secure a return which would cover the cost of supplying the machine.

30. Although each user of a patented button-fastening machine pays the same rate per pair of shoes manufactured, use of the tying device or of a meter has the effect of a different sales price for the machine according to intensity of use. This is discrimination if the large user pays a higher price relative to cost than small users. Whether the machine manufacturer's royalty comes from the sale or lease of the machine or from the sale of the staples or the buttons, the maximum that can be charged is fixed by the amount the machine saves the users. If those to whom the machine is "worth" more can be charged more for the machine, either in the form of a machine charge or indirectly by compulsory purchase of a tied product, the patentee is being rewarded for his machine patent. Interestingly enough, Judge Lurton used almost precisely this reasoning in deciding both Heaton-Peninsular Button-Fastener Co. v. Eureka Specialty Co., 77 Fed. 288 (6th Cir. 1896), and Henry v. A. B. Dick Co., 224 U.S. 1 (1912).

without the tie-ins. We must remember that profit maximization on only a single product is involved. The example takes no account of the possible effect that the price or the quantity sold of the tying product may have on the sales of the tied product, or of the effect that the price or the quantity sold of the tied product may have on the sales of the tying product when the demands for the two are related. That case was discussed in the previous section.

Separation of Markets

The ability of a patentee (or any monopolist) to maximize profits by charging different prices in different markets has been explained as depending upon the existence of differing demand elasticities. These differences typically reflect the existence of classes of customers who value a product or service differently because of the relative closeness or remoteness of substitutes. The previously cited example of a plastic for use in containers or in dentures represented this situation in an end-product market. So did the button-fastener example. In sales to competing intermediaries—to manufacturers, distributors, or retailers —charging different prices would maximize profit for a patentee only if each intermediary had different elasticity of demand (as, for example, that based on intensity of use measured by counting under a machine patent). Often, discriminatory pricing is profitable only if final uses can be separated and traced. Otherwise diversion of sales by an intermediary would prevent the patentee from deriving the benefit of the differing demand elasticities of final customers. A patentee does not maximize his profits on a patented product by charging different prices to inefficient than to efficient competing intermediaries all selling or reselling to a given class of customers. Subsidizing inefficient distribution is not in the interest of a patentee.

If, for example, a patentee were to classify competing licensees selling in the same market on the basis of their relative efficiencies, charging the more efficient at a higher rate than the less efficient, this would amount to subsidizing inefficient distribution, resulting in higher cost to consumers and less derived demand diminishing the profit to the patentee. Effective price discrimination is not achieved simply by eliminating competition among licensees.

A recent case[31] involving a restrictive licensing arrangement which discriminated between two groups of users of a patented shrimp-

31. Lapeyre v. F.T.C., 366 F. 2d 117 (U.S.C.A. 5th Cir., 1966).

peeling machine epitomizes how the Federal Trade Commission and the courts come to naive evaluative conclusions about discriminatory pricing by not understanding, or ignoring, this central prerequisite to effective price discrimination.

The Lapeyre family, through the Grand Caillou Packing Company, was engaged in the shrimp canning business on the Gulf Coast. The same family, through another company, Peelers Corporation, owned a patent on a shrimp-processing machine which it manufactured and distributed to shrimp-canning licensees. The family's shrimp-canning company, Grand Caillou Packing, accounted for only 7.4 percent of the country's shrimp-canning business. Before the availability of the patented shrimp-peeling machinery in 1949 almost all of the shrimp canning in the United States was done in the Gulf area, and all shrimp for this canning was peeled by hand. The peeling machine substantially lowered the cost of peeling by replacing expensive hand labor. A study by the patent owner of these savings to Gulf canners was the basis for a decision to lease the machine and charge for it in terms of the savings it afforded. The charge was 55¢ for each 100 cycles of the machine's roller. Apparently all Gulf canners paid this same rate. The advantage to Gulf canners was decisive at this rate, and hand peeling disappeared.

Smaller shrimp thrive in Pacific Northwest waters. On the average these run at least twice as many to a pound of raw heads-on shrimp as in the Gulf. Because it was found to take the same amount of hand labor to peel a shrimp irrespective of size, the relative advantage of the shrimp-peeling machine, which with slight modifications was usable for peeling Northwest shrimp, was greater for Northwest than for Gulf shrimp. Making a separate calculation for machine rentals for Northwest licensees, the patentee set a rate of $1.10 per 100 cycles of the machine roller. This was exactly twice the rate to Gulf licensees, and bore the same proportionate ratio to savings of hand-peeling as applied to Gulf licensees. The patentee thus charged Northwest canners twice as much as Gulf canners for identical machine revolutions on substantially identical machines.

FTC found this price discrimination to be illegal under section 5 of the Federal Trade Commission Act. The majority of the commission found that the purpose of the discrimination was to protect the Grand Caillou canning business (only 7.4 percent of the United States market) from Pacific Northwest competition. The effect, according to the FTC and confirmed by the court of appeals, was that the Lapeyres, who controlled both the machine peeling patent and the Grand Caillou Packing Company, used the patent to foreclose competition with its Gulf shrimp-canning business. This is indeed an odd explanation of the different licensing rates, since this competition could not have existed at all had the Lapeyres simply refused to license Pacific Northwest shrimp canners at all, as was their uncontested right.

Price Discrimination in Shrimp Peeling as a Means of "Foreclosing" Competitors

Conceptually, according to the appeals court, the problem of this shrimp-peeling case "is not one of the Robinson-Patman type discrimination, but of the duty of a lawful monopolist to conduct its business in such a way as to avoid inflicting competitive injury on a class of customers.[32] The commission, however, had found the price differential to be discriminatory and to have an adverse effect on commerce. The motive, according to the majority of the commission, was to protect Grand Caillou's interest from Northwest competition, and not, as Commissioner Elman believed, merely a means of maximizing the profit from a valid patent. The court of appeals, however, did not find it necessary to resolve this interesting economic question because: "Both the majority and Commissioner Elman found that the central characteristic was the same—the utilization of monopoly power in one market resulting in discrimination and curtailment of competition in another."[33] The commission was affirmed. The discriminatory licensing was illegal because "refusal to treat the Northwest and Gulf Coast shrimp canners on equal terms has substantially and unjustifiably injured competition in the shrimp canning industry."[34] This, the Court of Appeals statement notwithstanding, is a Robinson-Patman type problem.

The Federal Trade Commission's theory, affirmed on appeal, was a leverage theory—the use of monopoly power in one market (the patent market)—and so found to curtail competition in another market (inhibiting economical shrimp canning in the Northwest to protect shrimp canning on the Gulf Coast through price discrimination).

This case, it must be acknowledged, presents an anomaly for rational economic analysis, at least if the factual circumstances concern-

32. Ibid., p. 120.
33. Ibid., p. 121.
34. Ibid.

ing the competitive relationship between Gulf Coast and Northwest
shrimp canners portrayed in the FTC analysis can be accepted. In the
first place, if the analysis of profit maximization under price discrimination in the preceding section is correct, the discriminatory royalty
rates charged to competing Gulf Coast and Northwest shrimp canners,
if they sell in the same market are not a means of maximizing patent
reward. In the second place, if the fallacy of leveraging to additional
monopoly by foreclosing competitors analyzed in chapter 4 is correct,
there is no disclosed means by which a patentee can trade off lower
patent revenue from discriminatory pricing for a greater revenue from
the absence of competitors in the Pacific Northwest or anywhere else.
As I have indicated, had the Lapeyres wished to injure Northwest
competitors as a form of commercial sadism, rather than to maximize
profit, they could have done so far more effectively by refusing to
license them at all. And this alternative would have been far more
effective in eliminating troublesome outside competition than the discriminatory licensing system that was adopted. Equally puzzling, in
terms of the profit-maximizing interest of the Lapeyres, including their
Grand Caillou shrimp-canning interest, is the question of why, if
Northwest competitors were so undesirable, the Gulf Coast competitors were not equally undesirable. Grand Caillou produced less than
8 percent of the country's canned shrimp. It had several substantially
larger competitors in the Gulf Coast area. Why favor these competitors
any more than the Westerners? Short of such explanations as regional
philanthropy or a regional cartel, neither of which was even intimated
in the case, the commission's foreclosure theory would suggest no
licensing at all, not discriminatory licensing.

As to the Federal Trade Commission's theory (clearly implied if
not explicitly stated)—that taking less than maximum patent profits,
by using discrimination to prevent competing sales by efficient shrimp
canners, can be more than made up for by using the patent to reserve
this business for Grand Caillou, the patentee—it is merely the "leverage fallacy" revisited. Price discrimination, either by theory or by
convincing example, has not yet been shown to be a means of creating
monopoly by driving out or keeping out competitors. Either the competing canners, wherever they may be located, are able to supply the
same canned shrimp market more cheaply than Grand Caillou or
they are not able to do so. If more shrimp can be sold more cheaply
by allowing any other producers to compete with Grand Caillou, then
denying this right is for this patentee a decision to forego a patent

reward for a presumably greater reward from keeping a larger share of the market for itself. Neither the Federal Trade Commission nor the court of appeals made any attempt to explain how this could be done. Rather, they merely reverted to the timeworn, illogical presumption that an adverse effect on competitors—here Pacific Northwest shrimp canners—compels a finding of illegality because competitors were hurt, just as if there were an adverse effect upon competition.

There is some suggestion in the Federal Trade Commission opinion that the patentee had no economic rationale for the royalty rates it set in the different regions. According to record, the "double rate" for Northwest canners was directed by one Felix Lapeyre, a lawyer partner who "never worked in the shrimp industry and that his knowledge thereof was gathered by hearsay. . . . His reason for determining the rate . . . was . . . in order to adhere to our basic policy of charging a rate which was in proportion to the labor saved."[35] This suggests that the patentee was using price discrimination for sales in a single market (undifferentiated demand elasticity) in such a manner as not to maximize patent revenue. Were this the case, the Federal Trade Commission did both the country and the patentee a service by outlawing the discrimination—albeit unknowingly and by application of a fallacious rule. This ironic explanation, however appealing to an economist's sense of humor, is less plausible than another economically more rational explanation. Higher rates for canned shrimp sold in western markets would make economic sense if demand were less elastic there. This, of course, would be true irrespective of the source of supply. And even though the appropriate rate would depend upon the cost of supply, the patentee would have strong profit incentive not to disfavor low-cost suppliers.

Interestingly enough, "the record reveals that the principal market for canned shrimp in the United States consists of the eleven states which make up the western one-third of the continental country, excluding Alaska."[36] In 1956, 46.5 percent of canned shrimp consumption was in this area,[37] whose relative population is so small compared with the rest of the nation that its per capita consumption is obviously much higher than in the rest of the country, where Gulf producers would have a location advantage. Although per capita consumption

35. Grand Caillou Packing Co., Trade Reg. Rep. (1963–65 Transfer Binder) ¶ 16,927 (1964) at p. 21,973.
36. Ibid., p. 21,977.
37. Ibid., p. 21,978.

of a commodity is no irrefutable indicator of its demand elasticity, it seems most likely, in view of the very much higher canned-shrimp consumption in the west, that consumers there preferred canned shrimp over substitute foods much more than did consumers in other areas (i.e., demand was considerably less elastic).

If, under these conditions, there were no feasible way for the patentee to trace shipment destinations economically and charge particular licensees varying rates, the advent of production of canned shrimp in the Northwest by licensees, selling almost exclusively in the western market where demand was inelastic, would rationalize the economics of a discriminatory and higher royalty to western licensees. How the differential actually charged would be the same as the proportionate labor saved, the explanation given by Mr. Lapeyre, is neither suggested nor explained, either in the case or in this analysis. On the other hand, this traditional "counting" method of assessing royalty may well have been much closer to optimal (in profit-maximizing terms) than the single royalty rate insisted upon by the commission and affirmed by the court of appeals.

Baxter, in a critical analysis of discriminatory pricing of patents,[38] uses the Grand Caillou case as an example of how a patentee, by *profit maximization through royalty discrimination*, can misallocate resources against the interest of the public by forcing or keeping production away from the most efficient producers. He correctly concludes, given competing licensees, that charging them differently will make for a less socially efficient apportionment of production among them than that which would exist after the patent expired—the competitive allocation.[39] This, of course, is true of any charge for a patent,

38. Baxter, "Legal Restrictions." Professor Baxter would prevent patentees from charging discriminatory royalties. At p. 287 in the article referred to he writes, "One might argue . . . that any cost-related limitation on royalties was incompatible with the purposes of the patent laws, that the law calls for royalties commensurate with value to the licensee, and that 'value to the licensee' is a mere synonym for the licensee's elasticity of demand." He, however, finds this argument for discrimination unconvincing. He opposes profit maximization through royalty charges scaled to demand elasticity—"for it will diminish the patentee's ability to absorb potential cost advantage available to a segment of the industry." How? He is not convincing in his claim: "It thus will permit a partial shift of resources toward the more efficient segment, a shift in the direction of that allocation between segments that presumably will prevail after patent expiration" (p. 298).

39. Baxter's objection is not that a patent grant should exclude output restriction, but that discriminatory restriction is suspect. With discrimination, he believes, the restriction is inefficient for end-product users.

discriminatory or not. But, equally important, he slides over another relevant economic question: Is there less efficient apportioning of production with discriminatory royalties, not compared with competition after the patent has expired, but compared with single monopoly price while the patent is in force?

Price Discrimination and Product Output

The total output when markets are separated and different prices are charged will usually be different from the output of the product when a single price is charged.[40] Price discrimination has been criticized as an "inefficient" method of allocating a commodity among individuals, even though it does yield a larger revenue than a single-price system.[41] But possible ambiguity of the term "inefficiency" should be clarified before too easy conclusions are drawn about the desirability of outlawing price discrimination as a profit-maximizing device.

The "inefficient" resource allocation arising from price discrimination relates to how any *fixed stock* of goods is allocable among various users so as to maximize the satisfaction of users. Any trade among them that makes one of them better off without making others worse off, a precondition of honest trade, therefore makes the whole community richer. Because discrimination involves preventing this trade (arbitrage between separated buyers in the previous examples), it is in this sense socially inefficient. But it must be emphasized that this conclusion, relating as it does to a particular existing quantity of the product, ignores another aspect of efficiency associated with price discrimination—its effect upon the amount of the product produced. So even if no legal monopoly, such as a patent, were involved, price discrimination could result in greater output even in the short run. This is not, however, a precondition for justifying discrimination under a patent. Here short-run output restriction can in the long run lead to more of what consumers demand.

Numerous examples of output-increasing discrimination could be provided. A typical one involves exploitation of new territories.[42]

---

40. There is no simple rule that discrimination pricing leads to output restriction or output expansion. The relative convexity or concavity of the several demand curves makes for different results. See Joan Robinson, *The Economics of Imperfect Competition* (London: Macmillan and Co., 1933), pp. 188–95.
41. See, for example, Stigler, *Theory of Price*, p. 213.
42. New product markets would provide an equivalent example.

Suppose a patent is exploited by sales to only one area, and that very
high transportation cost is involved in reaching distant markets. In
these circumstances licensing new faraway producers at lower rates
than existing producers would increase production, increase range of
consumer choice in the new territory, and leave both producers and
consumers in the old territory in exactly the same position as before.
Here discrimination can be said to promote trade. Price discrimination
in this example clearly has a positive output effect. Evaluation of the
desirability of the result in this example, however, is not entirely in
terms of a positive output effect. The conclusion is facilitated because
the benefits to customers in the new territory are not at all at the
expense of consumers in the old territory. Were this not so, and if,
even with increased total output, slightly less output and a slightly
higher price were occasioned in the old territory, then approval of
the discrimination would call for a judgment that the larger amounts
of product available to customers in the new territory at the expense of
the smaller amounts taken from consumers in the old territory provided a net gain in economic welfare for the community as a whole.
Although an interpersonal comparison thus becomes a logical prerequisite to evaluating price discrimination in terms of output effect,
there is, on the other hand, no reason to suppose, in the absence of
evidence to the contrary, that the greater output is less likely rather
than more likely to benefit the community as a whole.

Examples could also be constructed indicating how, under particular demand and cost conditions, price discrimination could lead to
decreases in output. For the same kind of reasons calling for approval
of price discrimination which is output expanding, it has been suggested that price discrimination deserves proscription when it results
in output contraction. But evaluating this contention, especially in the
patent context, merely raises the question whether a patentee should
receive the "full reward" provided by the superiority of his patent in
some circumstances but not in others.

Why, it needs to be asked, if temporary monopoly (by nature restrictive) is what a patent monopoly necessarily involves, should it
be more reprehensible to achieve it from several demand curves than
from just one? And, for that matter, how can one be sure when return
is maximized by a single price that this is more or less "restrictive"
than in those other cases where markets can be segregated? The nature
of the patent grant is the right it affords the patentee to exclude others
from making, vending, or *using* without his permission. The permis-

sible divisibility of these rights, especially exclusion from use, discussed in chapter 7, has not turned upon an economic evaluation
of output restriction. Rather, leveraging to additional monopoly unrelated to the competitive superiority afforded by the patent has come
to be the criterion by which such practices as tie-in sales, discriminatory licensing, price-restrictive licensing, and other forms of limitations on use have been proscribed.

The Outer Limits of Discrimination

In the previous price-discrimination example (fig. 13) total demand
was subdivided into only two user classes, so that the profitability of
price discrimination could be illustrated simply. Whenever one price
is set in any market, whether in a single market as in figure 1 or in
one of the subdivided markets as in figure 13, the monopolist can be
expected to be making some sales to consumers who would be willing
to pay more and foregoing sales from other customers who would buy
if the price were lower. Figure 14 illustrates the outer limits of these
profit potentialities.

In figure 14, as was previously indicated in figure 1 for different
demand and cost conditions, the single profit-maximizing price (P_M)
and quantity (Q_M) is indicated by the intersection of the marginal
cost (MC) and marginal revenue (MR) curves. The difference between total revenue and total cost is shown for the single maximizing
price (P_M) by the shaded area (f b d e). When this price P_M (o f on
the vertical axis, and m b to the demand curve) is charged, those
consumers who would have paid more rather than do without the
monopoly product (those represented on the segment a to b on the
demand curve D) would have been willing to pay approximately[43]
the additional amount measured by triangle a b f (vertically lined in
figure 14) for the same total output (o m) as when single priced
($P_M =$ o f, or m b).

Exploiting the potential profits in this a b f area (sometimes referred
to as consumer surplus) involves further customer segregation of precisely the same sort, and with the same increased and costly impediments, as detailed in the description of the movement from the

43. Approximately, because no correction is made here for the lower real
income buyers would have if they spent more for the same quantity of output
previously purchased.

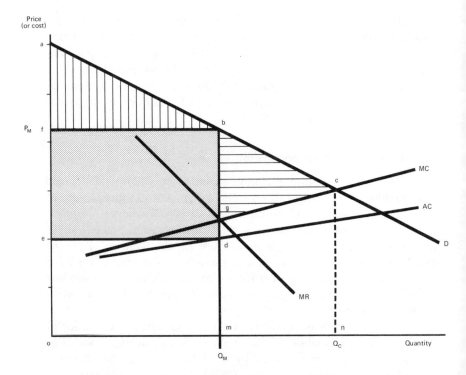

Fig. 14. The outer limits of discriminatory pricing.

one-price case (fig. 1) to the two-price case (fig. 13). At the extreme (sometimes referred to as "perfect discrimination," where the monopolist costlessly extracts all the a b f revenue and all the b c g revenue as well) it not only would be necessary to be able to price each individual customer separately, but it would pay a patentee to subdivide successive unit purchases of each individual customer when his successive purchases provided decreasing usefulness.[44] (This, however, involves all-or-none-offer equivalents subsequently discussed and not shown by the demand curve in fig. 14.)

44. A demand curve for a market typically (it need not) involves a combination of both factors—even for a single buyer there is downward-sloping demand curve. An individual consumer with a limited budget is not indifferent to his valuation of successive purchases of a single good—for example, that first cup of coffee after breakfast contrasted with the possible tenth before going to bed. (And although the road to this same conclusion for nonconsumer goods is more circuitous, the destination—conclusion—is still the same.)

The desirability of a patentee's receiving the value represented by a b f, or any part of it, as contrasted to leaving it with the buyers of the patented product (output of the patent product here is unaffected) is, I submit, a political problem of "just rewards," which, even disregarding incentive for invention effects, is, for reasons already indicated, an extremely skewed and most inappropriate function of antitrust or patent law.

If this last conclusion is accepted with respect to a patentee's exploitation of any of the profits in triangle a b f, the case is even stronger for allowing the patentee to attempt to exploit all or part of area b c g. A patentee's exploiting the profit potential of this area (indicated by horizontal lining in fig. 14), again involving discriminatory segregation of customers of the same sort as required for the exploitation of area a b f, has an output effect which benefits the patentee and those otherwise excluded consumers of the patented product without having any deleterious effect on those consumers still paying the higher price. In fact, the interesting effect of the extreme case, full and costless exploitation of this potential market by a monopolist, would be the same output of the patented product (o n or Q_C output in fig. 14) that would be achieved under competition. And this output effect is the very reason competition has been shown to deserve support. It follows, therefore, that a partial exploitation, which might be found practicable either by direct pricing or by other contractual means, would also be a means of promoting rather than restraining trade and not an appropriate target for proscription under either antitrust or patent law.[45]

The prerequisites for effective, profitable price discrimination which have been outlined included not only the cost of separating and keeping separate (avoiding arbitrage among customers), but also the cost of identifying the separable markets. It is rather simple to draw a demand line for illustrative purposes, as in the foregoing figures. It is quite another matter to have firm confidence in it for precise business decision-making purposes, especially in ranges varying substantially from going prices. The cost of discovering the aggregated consumer surpluses depicted in figure 14 can be expected to vary with number and diversity of the customers served. Still, especially when customers

45. This particular form of price discrimination, when identifiable, can be said, therefore, to belong in the "efficiency creating" category of patent practices. This relates to area b c g. Area a b f is neutral in this respect.

are few and consumption patterns are predictable, a monopolist may find it profitable to utilize devices designed to exploit an individual customer's downward-sloping demand curve for a patented product or process.

Multipart Pricing, All-or-None Offers, Lump-Sum Pricing, and Full-Line Forcing

Multipart pricing (charging successively lower prices as customers increase their purchases), all-or-none offers (withholding the right of customers to purchase at all unless specified quantities are taken), lump-sum pricing (charging customers a fixed sum for the right to purchase at a special price), and full-line forcing (the seller's requirement that buyers of a particular product may have it only on the condition that other products be bought exclusively from the same seller [the tie-in sale]) are alternative and rather widely used means which patent owners, or others with monopoly power, find useful in extracting the value of their product from its users. This larger reward, as in the foregoing examples, would not be available if a patentee were limited to setting a single price or a single royalty with no limitation on amounts taken or conditions of use. Lump-sum pricing, all-or-none offers, and full-line forcing are similarly explainable as means of maximizing the "competitive" advantage afforded by useful invention. They can be viewed as means by which a patentee attempts to keep for himself as much as possible of the net advantage the patent affords users.

As Professor Burstein[46] and, subsequently and in greater detail, Richard Markovits[47] have indicated in thoughtful articles on this subject, arrangements of this type, involving merely partial vertical integrations by contract, are not means of creating monopoly or extending monopoly into new markets. These are devices for profit maximization from a given degree of monopoly.

Burstein, however, contends that this is not to justify them. "It cannot be strongly enough emphasized," Burstein writes, "that the inadequacy of an hypothesis [monopoly extension] as an explanation of a

46. M. L. Burstein, "A Theory of Full-Line Forcing," 55 *Nw. U. L. Rev.*, 62 (Mar.–Apr. 1960).
47. R. S. Markovits, "Tie-Ins, Reciprocity and the Leverage Theory," 76 *Yale L. J.* 1397 (1967).

type of industrial behavior does not necessarily vitiate decision rules adopted by courts of law that have claimed to have founded their decisions on this hypothesis."[48] Although Burstein recognizes that "the legislative mandate can be improperly executed by the courts if the courts work with 'bad' economic theory" (monopoly extension or leveraging theory), and also that "if the legislature uses the same 'bad' theory it is apt to countenance results that are in fact at variance with its intent," he still thinks that "a balance of competing desiderata"[49] should be struck. The balancing factor in a tying case, Burstein suggests, is possible adverse effect in markets for tied products.

This possible adverse effect of a tying contract arises, if indeed it arises at all, from a foreclosure theory that is neither carefully analyzed nor distinguished from other forms of "exclusionary" practices not involving separate products. Tie-ins or full-line forces, whether used as simple counting devices or the best possible proxies for consumer surplus, only appear different from direct price discrimination, multipart pricing, or exclusive dealing because of the existence of another identifiable product. But in the absence of a leverage theory, deemed implausible and not revealed, no adverse effect on competition in the "other product" markets is predictable. The case is analytically indistinguishable from the exclusionary practice example involving requirements contracts that was criticized in chapter 4.

Professor Burstein correctly identifies contracts of the type discussed as forms of vertical integration—partial mergers by contract. But their efficiency aspects deserve far more consideration than is generally recognized. As Professor R. H. Coase pointed out in an article on the subject more than thirty years ago, "the operation of a market costs something and by forming an organisation and allowing some authority . . . to direct the resources, certain marketing costs are saved. The entrepreneur has to carry out his function at less cost, taking into account the fact that he may get factors of production at a lower price than the market transactions which he supersedes, because it is always possible to revert to the open market if he fails to do this."[50] And so it is also with respect to the supply of "tied" products. The explanation of much, if not most, tying practice is the achievement of some

48. Burstein, "Theory of Full-Line Forcing," p. 63.
49. Ibid.
50. R. H. Coase, "The Nature of the Firm," *Economica*, vol. 4 (1937). Reprinted in *Readings in Price Theory* (Homewood, Ill.: Richard D. Irwin, Inc., 1952) pp. 331–51, at p. 338.

form of discrimination. And discrimination, as has been indicated, can be socially as well as privately "efficient."

In the absence of a leverage theory, against the existence of which Burstein's own analysis provides additional if not conclusive evidence, the possible countervailing effects of tie-ins on the potency of competition in tied products is most speculative. Burstein's "on the whole" approval of tie-in law turns out to be: "I think that the effects of the existing rule [a per se rule against tying] are beneficial: *it limits the potential gains of monopoly power.*"[51] This is an important subject with which his article did not deal. In the patent context, it is not at all clear that maximizing monopoly gains, even in the by no means predictable case where output is restricted, is not beneficial. For even granting output restrictions, Arrow's specific analysis of this problem (discussed in chap. 2) provided a reasoned, even though controversial, conclusion contrary to Burstein's ad hoc pronouncement.

Are Vertical Patent Contracts Entry Barring?

Three explanations have been offered in attempting to show how trade is improperly restrained when conditions of purchase are imposed on buyers. Two of these have been discussed in the patent context: (1) monopoly gaining or monopoly increasing, involving the leverage fallacy, and (2) profit maximization out of a given monopoly. A third reason, commonly urged against price discrimination, exclusive dealing contracts, and vertical mergers, is impeding potential competition by imposing barriers to the entry of new competitors.

The "barriers to entry" argument against the use of price discrimination, vertical mergers, or tying sales is again merely a variation of the leverage example. The presumption in the case of tie-in sales, for example, is that competitors are foreclosed from markets. They are said to be prevented from entering markets even though their products are as acceptable and their production is as efficient. In other words their exclusion is "arbitrary," and they are prevented from market participation on grounds unrelated to customer acceptance.

As the preceding examples of tie-in practice should indicate, however, there is strong incentive for a patentee to have "tied" products provided at the lowest possible cost. Otherwise revenue from the patent is not maximized. Moreover, neither control of the price of the

---

51. Burstein, "Theory of Full-Line Forcing," p. 93 (emphasis added).

tied product (the joint demand example) nor the counting example (price discrimination measured by rate of use) precludes the patentee from purchasing tied products from others. In fact, the purchase from others is predictable if the patentee cannot provide them more economically than outsiders. Only if the patentee could somehow achieve an alternative gain in revenue greater than this cost is there any incentive for barring the outside production of tied products. Leveraging to a second and additional monopoly over an unpatented product is the usual explanation. But, as has been stressed, neither theory nor example of how this might be done has been provided.

A variation of this leverage theory suggests that a tie-in arrangement, in which the patentee precluded all others from making an unpatented tied product during the life of the patent, might be a means of extending the effective term of the patent grant beyond its legal span by delaying the availability of an essential product necessary to the use of the patented product. If such a case should exist it would be a most unusual one, and one in which secrecy concerning the making of the tied product, perhaps the kind of secrecy involved in the Coca-Cola formula, seems hardly less legitimate than the patent on the tying product. In such case the secrecy would be the barrier to entry, not the tying arrangement. And in the event that there were no use for the secret product except joint use with a patented product, so that a tie-in might limit incentive to overcome the secrecy, this disincentive effect could not last longer than the patent. But this entry-barring case seems to be a straw man. If the tied product had the "secrecy" characteristics needed to delay but not to bar production by others, this could be anticipated by knowledge of the patent's termination. If, on the other hand, secrecy barred rather than delayed production of the unpatented product, then no tying arrangement would be called for in the first place. Perhaps restrictions upon use in patent licensing contracts could conceivably affect the availability of know-how in such manner as to delay the appearance of competitors beyond the expiration of the patent, but how this is achievable remains to be explained. And so here, as with other alleged leveraging, there is neither theory nor example.

6

More Efficient Use of Patent Monopoly Continued: Conditioning Licensees' Sales through Use of Price Restrictions

The per se rule in antitrust law, under which agreements to fix prices or to allocate territories have come to be automatically held illegal, contains the presumption that such agreements, in terms of either purpose or effect, are such as to have no redeeming justification. Here, as was indicated in chapter 1, the judgment is that so little efficiency derives from such agreements that on balance it would be a waste of legal effort to hear an "efficiency" defense. If the restrictive effect of price agreements were to be overweighed by their greater usefulness in achieving more efficient production or distribution, so that on balance trade could be shown to be expanded rather than restrained, the economic rationale for a rule against price-fixing would not exist. An evaluation of an efficiency/trade restraint trade-off would then be appropriate. Under antitrust law, however, the foregoing economic rationale for the per se rule has been lost by expansion to inappropriate areas. Ignored or forgotten is the economic rationale for the rule against the fixing of prices. Thus, from the proposition that when competing firms agree among themselves to raise prices, to lower prices, or to hold them at the same level, a search for possible consumer-benefiting efficiencies resulting from such endeavors assays so low in probability that no defense should be heard, a legal extrapolation has taken place, abetted by legal sloganeering about the per se illegality of price-fixing, so that price-fixing agreements are held to be illegal even where there is no competitive relationship among the parties to the agreements.

All buyer-seller contracts involve the fixing of a price or a price equivalent. And of course not every contract is thereby in restraint of trade and consequently illegal. But agreements between a manufacturer and his distributors or dealers to maintain the price at which the product may be sold or resold have come to be encompassed in the so-called per se rule against price-fixing, just as if they were as predictably output-restricting as price agreements among competitors. That the price so fixed involves a patented product provides no exception from antitrust law's proscription of resale price maintenance. And even in the absence of resale price maintenance, fixing the price at which a licensee may sell a patented product has been narrowed almost to extinction. But vertical price-fixing, without agreement among competitors, like other forms of vertical integration either by merger or by contract, is a means of creating consumer benefits by allocating resources more efficiently. Discussion of end-product pricing in the previous chapter provided an example of this kind of effect. Moreover, as was also indicated in the patent context, vertical price-fixing provided no obvious means of extending the scope of a proper patent monopoly to new areas.

Of the various ways a patentee can improve the effectiveness of his patent by imposing conditions on licensees, several have already been indicated. Price-restrictive licensing is another of these. Simple price discrimination and multipart pricing schemes, either directly applied or indirectly effected through tie-ins and joint-product pricing, have been shown to be means by which patentees are able to extract larger revenues attributable to the advantages afforded by the invention. Notable among these advantages was the achievement of efficient production and distribution, an advantage accruing to consumers as well as to the patentee.

Discriminatory pricing, as contrasted to single pricing, was discussed in the previous chapter as a way more customers might be served more adequately as well as more profitably. It has another advantage leading to more efficient resource allocation. Nonuniform, discriminatory price cutting can erode existing monopolies and spoil a cartel's effectiveness, again to the advantage of both patentee and consumers. Selective price cutting often is a first step in the general lowering of prices. Commissioner Elman of the Federal Trade Commission has stressed this aspect of price discrimination, especially in markets dominated by few firms. The entry of a national seller prepared to selectively lower his price in order to secure a foothold in the market may, he suggests, be the only cure for a rigid price structure characteristic of oligopoly. "In general," Elman points out, "a lack of uniformity in the prices of a national seller, competing in many geographic markets, may simply reflect the seller's flexibility in adjusting price to meet different competitive conditions in different markets. Insistence on price uniformity in such conditions could lead to high rigid prices and thereby hurt competition seriously."[1]

Tying contracts also have often been used by patentees for similar purposes. They have been found useful, for example, in evading price regulation, public or private. Buying furniture in lieu of bidding up the price of a rent-controlled dwelling is a well-known example. Leasing or selling land by a railroad, on condition that the railroad's services be used exclusively, is another example of evasion of rate regulation.

Setting prices at which licensees may sell or resell patented products is another important means by which patentees attempt, by imposing conditions of sale or resale, to exploit the advantages their patents afford. This may take the form of setting maximum prices, minimum prices, or specific prices. Alternatively, fixed or guaranteed margins or markups may be specified. Most obviously explainable in terms of the interest of a patentee, and perhaps least controversial, is the setting of maximum limits on the price licensees may charge for a patented product. This kind of case was discussed in chapter 5. It involves another example of a patentee's interest in avoiding the siphoning off of return owing to the necessary absence of effective competition among licensees. When patents can be exploited more efficiently by licensees than by the patentee, and in addition when this efficient exploitation is consistent with only a single licensee (or very few) in each market, leaving the single licensee free to raise the price would merely sanction the imposition by the licensee of a second monopoly at the expense of both the patentee and the customers. Here, a price-restrictive license setting a maximum price merely preserves a lower price and a greater output to the benefit of customers as well as to the patentee. A vertical price-fixing rule setting maximum prices or fixing maximum markups is thus a means of eliminating roadblocks to efficient distribution.

Price-Restrictive Licensing and Resale Price Maintenance

Much more controversial, in both legal and economic terms, than setting maximum prices is setting minimum prices. When a patentee

1. Elman, "The Robinson-Patman Act and Antitrust Policy: A Time for Reappraisal," 42 *U. Wash. L. Rev.* 1, 13 (1966).

sets minimum prices below which licensees are not allowed to sell, thus guaranteeing the profit margins of competing licensees and making price competition among them impossible, what may be called "the resale price maintenance dilemma" arises. Is it a device to eliminate competition among licensees, and therefore adverse to the interest of the licensor-patentee, or is it a means by which the patentee assures the provision of services without which the patent would be less valuable? The economic problem here was summarily and erroneously disposed of by the United States Supreme Court in 1911 in the *Dr. Miles* case.[2] In this early landmark case the Court ignored the possible trade-expanding (efficiency)[3] aspects of controlling licensees' prices in the interest of the original seller. The Court rested its opinion entirely upon the competition-eliminating aspects, as if the scheme were jointly imposed by resellers in an effort to protect themselves from the rigors of price competition. The *Dr. Miles* decision treated price maintenance imposed by an original seller as legally indistinguishable from a dealer cartel.[4]

Far more attention has been focused on the restrictive, anticompetitive results of price maintenance than upon its other effects by commentators as well as by courts. Moreover, there is an obscuring of the important patent policy question: whether fixing the price at which a licensee may sell or resell a patented product involves "leveraging" to additional monopoly.

In attempting to judge whether a patent is used as a screen for addi-

---

2. Dr. Miles Medical Co. v. John D. Park & Sons Co., 220 U.S. 373 (1911). Justice Hughes (at p. 407) concluded: "If there be an advantage to a manufacturer in the maintenance of fixed retail prices, the question remains whether it is one which he is entitled to secure by agreements restricting the freedom of trade on the part of dealers who own what they sell. As to this, the complainant can fare no better with its plan of identical contracts than could the dealers themselves if they formed a combination and endeavored to establish the same restrictions, and thus to achieve the same result, by agreement with each other."

Calling for the same legal conclusion for a manufacturer-imposed as a dealer-imposed resale price maintenance scheme automatically sweeps aside all possible efficiency differences between vertically imposed contracts and agreements among competitors.

3. See chapter 9 for the later development of the law on price-restrictive licensing.

4. A division of fields among licensees could conceivably be used by a patentee for the same purpose by imposing exclusive territories; but as will be indicated, the law has been more amenable to recognizing efficiency effects in such cases.

tional monopoly arising from that which is patented (that is, is not a device for maximizing reward *from the patent*), various earmarks for detection have been suggested. H. F. Furth has attempted to distinguish the "desirable" from the "undesirable" forms of price-restrictive patent licensing by a "competitive superiority" test.[5] His principal concern is to identify possible collusion among licensees. This test also signals less obvious ways a patentee may exceed the bounds of competitive superiority. Little or no attention, however, is given to possible efficiencies in distribution attributable to price maintenance not resulting from licensee collusion. The test he poses, however, is most relevant: "Every undesirable licensing arrangement is characterized by the fact that the patentee and his licensees acquire a margin of profit or a degree of control over their industry *which is unrelated to the competitive superiority of the patent.*"[6]

Furth shows that the key court decisions relating to price-restrictive licensing, irrespective of their outcome, have not faced up to the faults or merits of the practice. Also, "The various standards adduced by the Supreme Court . . . do not present an accurate picture of what the Court has been doing."[7] The criticism is well deserved. It could be extended. Not only have the courts mishandled economic effects, they have concerned themselves with technical case distinctions based upon such economic irrelevancies as "title passing" or number of licensees. Equally notable is their neglect of problems involving efficiency of distribution.

Furth views concerted action among patentees and competing licensees as the principal danger of price-restrictive licensing. This he concludes from his review of patent price-fixing cases which have reached the Supreme Court. In the first of these, *Bement* v. *National Harrow Company*,[8] involving an action by a manufacturer of patented farm machinery to enjoin one of several competing licensees from selling below prescribed prices, the Court had no trouble disposing of the case. The simple solution, easily found, was that since a patentee has the clear right to exclude others from using his patent (total

5. H. F. Furth, "Price-Restrictive Patent Licenses under the Sherman Act," 71 *Harv. L. Rev.* 815 (1958).
6. Ibid., p. 838 (emphasis added).
7. Ibid., p. 841.
8. 186 U.S. 70 (1902).

exclusion), the lesser exclusion, use at a prescribed price being an example, was within the patentee's rights.[9]

When the much-cited price-restrictive patent case *United States* v. *General Electric Company*,[10] which was later restricted but never overruled, reached the Supreme Court almost twenty-five years later, patent tie-ins[11] and vertically imposed resale price maintenance by a patentee[12] had been held to be unenforceable; and the Clayton[13] and Federal Trade Commission[14] acts, emphasizing the monopoly-creating dangers of vertically imposed restrictions, had been passed. The *General Electric* case raised two issues. The first concerned the legality of setting prices at which some 21,000 distributing "agents" of the General Electric Company had to sell lamps consigned to them. *Bauer* v. *O'Donnell*[15] had extended the per se prohibitions of resale price maintenance (applicable to a secret remedy in the 1911 *Dr. Miles* case[16]) to patented products. The Court found the distributors to be bona fide agents; therefore the resale price maintenance rule was inapplicable.[17]

9. This case was decided on this narrow ground. Not resolved here were some of the more interesting questions concerning how a prior patent pool containing eighty-five patents had been formed; nor was there anything in the opinion about possible use of a patent as a screen for industrywide price-fixing. Bement's contract with National Harrow also contained a provision that Bement would not manufacture or sell competitive harrows. No Court objection to this provision was noted. This case, decided as a patentee-imposed price case, presumably fixed in his interest as an alternative means to fixing a royalty rate, ignored the economic relevance of the fact that royalty payments were only $1.00 per harrow, and that failure to abide by the price provisions called for $5.00 per harrow damages. These were split among all licensees on the basis of their share holdings in the Harrow Company.

10. 272 U.S. 476 (1926).

11. Motion Picture Patents Co. v. Universal Film Mfg. Co., 243 U.S. 502 (1917).

12. Bauer & Cie v. O'Donnell, 229 U.S. 1 (1913).

13. An act of 15 October 1914, c. 322, 38 stat. 730.

14. An act of 26 September 1914, c. 11, 38 stat. 717.

15. Bauer & Cie v. O'Donnell, 229 U.S. 1 (1913).

16. Dr. Miles Medical Co. v. John D. Park & Sons Co., 220 U.S. 373 (1911).

17. Much later, in Simpson v. Union Oil Co. of California, 377 U.S. 13 (1964), this agency device as a means of avoiding the resale price maintenance rule was rejected. The product in Simpson was unpatented, but no more obvious difference between Simpson and a second GE case occurred to the government than existed between the early Dr. Miles and the Bauer v. O'Donnell cases. Consequently, a second General Electric case on this first issue of the old GE case is pending at this writing.

The second *General Electric* issue involved the propriety of a license granted to Westinghouse Electric Company to manufacture and sell lamps under the General Electric patents. A key condition was that Westinghouse adopt the same type of agency distribution scheme and maintain the same distributor prices fixed by General Electric. In deciding this issue for a unanimous Court, Chief Justice Taft rejected the government's contention that by the terms of the license General Electric sought to restrain and monopolize trade in electric light bulbs. The opinion did not utilize the reasoning in the *Bement* case—that the right of complete exclusion (no licensing at all) comprehended the lesser restraint.[18] Rather, the question posed was whether the price-fixing clause was, as Furth and others have indicated it to be, a most appropriate one: was it normally and reasonably adapted to secure pecuniary reward for the patentee's monopoly? As Furth has written, the following quoted language from the opinion "aptly summarizes the principle that the proper measure of the patentee's reward is his patent's competitive superiority."[19]

One of the valuable elements of the exclusive right of a patentee is to acquire profit by the price at which the article is sold. The higher the price, the greater the profit, unless it is prohibitory. When the patentee licenses another to make and vend, and retains the right to make and vend on his own account, the price at which his licensee will sell will necessarily affect the price at which he can sell his own patented goods. It would seem entirely reasonable that he should say to his licensee, Yes, you may make and sell articles under my patent, but not so as to destroy the profit that I wish to obtain by making them and selling them myself.[20]

Furth's conclusion that the foregoing quotation indicates the controlling importance of a competitive superiority test seems clear enough from the language. But much less clear, and not detailed either in the Taft opinion or in the Furth critique, is how and under what conditions protecting one's own profit from a possible price-cutting licensee is a means of maximizing patent reward. And if it is such a method, why is it any more so than a resale price maintenance agreement or a tying contract? The resale price maintenance question, the first issue of the

---

18. In a subsequent chapter I will attempt to show that no rationale for rejecting this "simple" test has been provided. And even that thoughtful and often-quoted article on this subject by Professor Thomas Reed Powell in a 1917 issue of the *Columbia Law Journal* is notable for its "question asking." A convincing "question answering" article (or court decision) is yet to appear.

19. Furth, "Price-Restrictive Patent Licenses," p. 819.

20. United States v. General Electric Co., 272 U.S. 476 (1926), at p. 490.

case, did not have to be faced because of agency:—no resale, no resale price maintenance. But the logic of Taft's language on the second issue raises most serious doubts about the validity of *Bauer* v. *O'Donnell* if not *Dr. Miles* as well. Why should General Electric's interest in being protected from price competition by its manufacturing and distributing licensee Westinghouse be any different from its interest in obtaining protection from price competition from nonmanufacturing licensees under a resale price maintenance agreement? Surely the argument that only a "manufacturing" interest deserves support is untenable. Or is it to be assumed that a patentee can maintain prices only on those activities, manufacturing or distributing, in which he himself engages? The Taft opinion seems to support the latter conclusion. And his reason seems clear—protection of higher prices and thus higher profits for the patentee *on his own activities* in making or selling the patented product. But if that is what is relevant one might then well ask, Why should General Electric, or any patentee, license Westinghouse, or any other licensee, to either manufacture or sell the product at all? Why the emphasis on *own* activities? In the absence of collusive price-fixing exceeding the "competitive superiority" of the patent over competing substitutes, the reason for any licensing must be that *others'* activities provide a more effective or a more efficient[21] means of making or marketing the patented product than if these activities were all provided by the patentee without licensing others.

Chief Justice Taft's statement that it seems "entirely reasonable" for a patentee to say to the licensee, "Yes, you may make and sell articles under my patent, but not so as to destroy the profit that I wish to obtain by making them and selling them myself,"[22] has to others, including the Supreme Court itself on resale price maintenance cases,[23] seemed "entirely unreasonable."

21. This, of course, need not be true of all levels of output. Economies of scale as well as other unique advantages of particular producers in either manufacture or distribution are relevant to a determination of licensing policy.

22. U.S. v. General Electric Co., 272 U.S. 476 (1926).

23. The legality or illegality of resale price maintenance under federal law had not been held to depend upon the competitive participation of the price maintainer in the distribution process. And the Miller - Tydings Act (act of Congress 7 August 1937, c. 690, 50 stat. 693) later legalized resale price maintenance when and only when the states provided permissive legislation, and even then only when certain competitive conditions existed. This price maintenance act has been interpreted to *exclude* its use rather than to *permit* its use when the price-maintainer participates in distribution. This legal result, not limited to unpatented products, came about because of the assumed "horizontal" price-fixing when the price-maintaining manufacturer competed with his distributors. See U.S. v. McKesson & Robbins, 351 U.S. 305 (1956).

A price-restrictive agreement, whether it is in the resale price maintenance context or in the patent licensing context, and whether the
imposer of the price restriction participates in the production or distribution of the patented product, seems to run counter to generally
accepted economic propositions. "If there is one thing which is laid
down in all the books," said F. W. Taussig at an Economic Association meeting in 1916, "it is that a decline in price leads to an increase
in the quantity demanded and sold. . . . Yet, the endeavor to keep up
resale prices would seem to be based on a contrary supposition."[24]
In speaking of a manufacturer's interest Taussig noted that once a
manufacturer set the price to his distribution trade (setting a royalty
rate to a manufacturing or distributing patent licensee would be an
equivalent), why should he concern himself with their too-low prices?
Setting the price (or royalty rate) coming to the manufacturer, Taussig
suggested, allows the manufacturer to receive the benefit of distributor
efficiency through competition. The manufacturer's interest would
seem to be, said Taussig, "that these middlemen . . . should sell as
cheaply as possible, and advertise as much as possible their cheap
sales."[25] And for the same reason Taussig might well have asked Chief
Justice Taft: Why did not General Electric encourage, rather than
discourage Westinghouse from selling patented lamps "as cheaply as
possible, and advertise as much as possible their cheap sales?" For
surely it is net receipts that should interest General Electric rather
than the sheer accounting joy of attributing profits to its own manufacturing operations. How, conceivably, could General Electric protect its own profit margin by price-restrictive licensing without also
protecting the Westinghouse margin? Sharing revenue with Westinghouse is a condition, according to Taussig's analysis, that General
Electric could avoid by eliminating the price minimums and raising
the royalty rate. General Electric, this argument goes, could then encourage Westinghouse to sell as cheaply as possible, even if this meant
the contraction of GE output or even closing down the GE production facilities.

Furth's analysis of the Court's theory in the 1926 *General Electric*
case is that if profit protection is the only function of the price-fixing
clause, "it follows that the patent's profit potential *has not been in-*

24. F. W. Taussig, "Price Maintenance," 6 *Am. Econ. Rev. Suppl.* 170
(1916).
25. Ibid.

creased. What the patentee gains by earning a royalty fee, in addition to the profits on his own sales, is offset by his surrendering a share of the total market to the licensee. "The price restrictive license," according to Furth, "changes the form of the patentee's reward, but does not increase the reward."[26]

Taussig's analysis seems to strengthen Furth's conclusion, since reward under price-fixing would not be "left the same," but would be decreased. For either Taft or Furth, the practice appears not to be a means of exploiting competitive advantage; but for Furth it becomes suspect as a collusive arrangement to eliminate competition, and presumably not a measure of competitive superiority of a patent.

The Furth conclusion is premature. As I indicated in the preceding chapter, fixing a royalty maximizes profit without exceeding competitive advantage (the Taussig case and the Furth case) only if a single product is being sold in a single market with a given demand elasticity and, in addition, if the licensees are effectively competitive. This, of course, does not preclude the possibility that the price-restrictive licensing may be a form of collusion with competitors, but it by no means makes this predictable. Once the single product, one market assumption is relaxed, setting licensee's prices or margins deserves more careful appraisal as a noncollusive means of maximizing the reward attributable to a valid patent. Vertically imposed pricing restrictions, like other forms of vertical integration, either by merger or by contract, have long suffered from the "collusion analogy" deified by the 1911 *Dr. Miles* case.

Professor Robert Bork has over the past fifteen years probed this subject both exhaustively and convincingly. His 1954 article "Vertical Integration and the Sherman Act: The Legal History of an Economic Misconception"[27] showed that the vertical integration concept "is almost entirely lacking in significance as an analytical tool for differentiating between competition and monopoly."[28] Vertical integration, he explained, adds nothing to monopoly power. "Nor does vertical integration affect a firm's pricing policy. If, for example, a firm operates at both manufacturing and retail levels, it maximizes overall profit by setting the output at each level as though the levels were independent."[29]

26. Furth, "Price-Restrictive Patent Licenses," p. 820.
27. 22 *U. Chi. L. Rev.* 157 (Autumn 1954).
28. Ibid., p. 194.
29. Ibid., p. 195.

If this conclusion holds for more formal corporate vertical integration, it seems reasonable to expect that it should hold for partial vertical integration—integration by contract, including exclusive dealing, tying, price-restrictive patent licensing, and resale price maintenance. As to the latter, in an article written in 1966,[30] and more particularly in a subsequent article in 1967 on resale price maintenance, Bork concluded that "vertical price fixing or resale price maintenance, when it is not used as a tool of a cartel among resellers or among manufacturers, can only result from the manufacturer's desire to increase efficiency, and, further, that Courts should accept that motivation as conclusive of the effect of such resale price maintenance."[31]

The efficiencies achievable from price maintenance, by patentees or others, arise when, as with many patented products, a product with no close substitutes is only useful, or more useful, when combined with some complementary product or service, which *without the price restriction*, would not be provided in the proper amounts and at prices which consumers would pay rather than do without it.[32] This is an example of the "joint demand" case, analyzed in a different context in chapter 5.

A patented product's competitive superiority is, of course, enhanced by its most efficient production, distribution, and use. In the 1926 *General Electric* case it was assumed by the Court that General Electric's patent on tungsten lamp filaments gave it a substantial edge over other lamp producers, including its major competitor, Westinghouse. The question that Chief Justice Taft posed and Furth commends is: Were the conditions of sale normally and reasonably adopted to secure reward for the patentee's monopoly? The difficulty, however, is not with the question; it is with how one finds the answer. The test for

30. Bork, "The Rule of Reason and the Per Se Concept: Price Fixing and Market Division II," 75 *Yale L. J.* 373 (1966).

31. Bork's summary in "A Reply to Professors Gould and Yamey," 76 *Yale L. J.* 731 (Mar. 1967).

32. Demand-creating activities and sales promotion efforts, fraud apart, if they increase consumer satisfaction are efficiencies of this kind. As Bork has noted ("Rule of Reason," p. 743), "When a detergent manufacturer adds bleach crystals to his product (a product complement) those consumers who prefer detergent without bleach have had their choice restricted. But if the change proves profitable to the manufacturer, we may assume that consumers as a whole are better satisfied. A law prohibiting the addition of bleach crystals would not widen the range of consumer choice but would restrict it." And so it may be with advertising.

reasonableness is not as simple as either Justice Taft or Furth supposed.

The relative shares of the lamp business in 1921 were: General Electric 69 percent, Westinghouse 16 percent, all other licensees 8 percent, and nonlicensed manufacturers 7 percent. Presumably the latter did not have patented tungsten filaments. These "high concentration" figures signal possible incentive for easy agreement, but they do not preclude other explanations.

With respect to General Electric's own manufacture (the first issue in the case), General Electric found it useful to guarantee distributor's margins, first through resale price maintenance, and later by an economically equivalent agency arrangement. There are a number of possible explanations for General Electric's adoption of this system. Bork's resale price maintenance analysis is most suggestive of explanation unrelated to horizontal combination among either producers or distributors of lamps. The evidence is strong that General Electric vertically imposed the system in its own interests on widely diverse and unorganized distributors. That it did so either to restrain its own trade in patented lamps or as a philanthropic gesture toward its distributors strains credulity. Even the most naive versions of vertical leveraging seem to be excluded, at least at the retail level. General Electric is not even in this branch of the business. Westinghouse, however, was a major competitor in the lamp business. The General Electric patent conceivably could have been used as a screen to shield a broader agreement to avoid competition between these rivals. But there was neither evidence nor finding by the Court that this was so. It seems useful, therefore, to review the Bork analysis. Possible applicability to the old *General Electric* case, although speculative because an analysis of its relevance formed no part of the argument or the opinion there, should illustrate the need for focusing on efficiency in cases of this kind.

Possible efficiencies created by price fixing, Bork indicated, include seven notable examples.[33] These examples, some of which seem plausibly applicable to the sale of lamps, raise economic questions not raised in litigated price maintenance cases. They were not raised in the 1926 *General Electric* case. When any seller, including a patentee, in the absence of a cartel agreement among competing sellers or resellers, prescribes a price or guarantees a markup for his resellers, the Bork examples indicate that such practice fosters rather than restrains trade by giving consumers more of what they want under the most favorable terms. They are thus efficient and meet a general antitrust test grounded on consumer benefit. Such a test is much stricter than Furth's "competitive superiority" test, which recognizes the validity of the patent monopoly but wants assurance that its proper scope is not extended.

Optimum Local Sales Effort: The Free-Ride Problem

For many products the provision of information, often in the form of costly personal effort, is a precondition to making sales. When these efforts cannot be identified and paid for directly, as in buying advertising in a newspaper, but rather are identified by the sale of the product, costs of these efforts must be covered by the price charged. If a first store incurred such selling cost for a customer but this customer bought the product from a second store, which sold at a cut price not reflecting the first store's selling cost, the second store could be said to be "free riding" on the first store. But for the costly efforts of the first store the second store could not have made the sale, and without being paid for its efforts (here in the form of a protected margin) the first store cannot be expected to provide the needed service.

Optimum sales effort by dealers, including lamp dealers, can be expected only when the efforts are rewarded. Sales effort is not costless. If the provision of this sales effort can be recognized and rewarded only by the dealer's sales, but competing dealers stand ready to make sales at lower prices without providing the costly sales effort, the original seller is faced with a dilemma. He would like to have the advantage of price competition among his dealers plus the sales effort. Lower prices make for greater sales. So does sales effort. But if more sales (and revenue) are generated by local sales effort than by price cuts in the absence of this sales effort, an effort forthcoming only by guaranteed dealer margins, then price maintenance becomes a precondition for providing optimum sales and service.

Although this hardly seems a credible explanation for maintaining the price of a convenience item such as 100-watt bulbs from hardware and variety stores, given a wide variety of lamps serving diverse and little-understood needs, "free-ride" possibilities should not be ignored in assessing why cut-price sale of lamps was discouraged.

Optimizing Local Sales Effort: The Uniform Product

Much national advertising stresses the high and uniform quality of the product and the related services. When the outlets through which these products and services are provided to the customers are owned by the supplier, it is not unusual that price, terms of sale, and conditions of service are closely supervised by a central authority. The best knowledge or business judgment about sales, price, and service is not always at the local level. Local autonomy in this respect varies widely. Local interest need not conform with the general interest of a company. Local price cutting at the expense of poor or infrequent service may adversely affect repeat business accruing to other localities, even when it is advantageous to a single outlet. If price and quality of service decisions are more efficiently made centrally than locally for vertically integrated organizations, why, Bork asks, should not these advantages be available to the nonintegrated? Why not integration by contract?

It seems at least deserving of consideration that a national seller of effective lighting service may have decided that efficient marketing of its products involves considerably more than getting just any light bulb to the customers at the lowest price.

Reinforcing a Market Division System

Not only does violating territorial or field-of-use limitations break down effective price discrimination, but, even without price differences, cross-selling can disrupt marketing plans, especially when exclusive distribution is called for. Selling at lower than authorized prices might be the cause of breaking down these useful (and otherwise permissible) means of distribution. Price maintenance is a possible means of inhibiting "free-riding" across territorial boundaries or across fields of use. When fixed margins are an inducement to provide the services required for effective merchandising, mere division of territories or of fields of use may need augmentation to be effective.

Territorial division among wholesale distributors is common in many trades. In some it is useful in retailing as well. General Electric "agents" have long been segregated in terms of the type of customer they serve. Commercial accounts require different kinds of service from home customers, and special prices apply to each. It seems at least possible that price maintenance might have been used by General Electric as a means of attempting to keep the "commercial" and the "home" markets separated. If so, price maintenance allows the competitive superiority test, which Furth urged should be applied in each market. And, to repeat, price discrimination can be efficient.

A Means of Transferring Information

Under many conditions setting an appropriate price requires that considerable information be obtained and analyzed. Sometimes local trade conditions may be such that this is accomplished at the outlet level. In other cases, as I have emphasized for nonintegrated as well as for fully integrated companies, this task is not performed well when left to local determination.

When the outlets through which a particular product is sold handle the product as one of a great variety of items, it is less likely that the retail dealer will have the kind of specialized knowledge and information about it that he would have were he to sell that single product or line of products exclusively. When products handled are many and diverse the individual attention given to a particular product depends upon the relative profitability of stocking it and promoting its sales rather than emphasizing other products competing for the dealer's effort or shelf space. This involves an "information problem" for the original seller and for the reselling dealer. That the product involved is patented, bears a valuable trademark, or is otherwise unique of course limits the range of very close substitutes a dealer may stock, but this by no means assures its relative advantage as a candidate for stocking, display, or promotion. In this respect the product must compete for the dealer's attention among a very wide range of alternatives. Scarce dealer display space and promotion effort are often worth bidding for, and in this process price maintenance is a means not only of assuring the dealers' profit margin but also of utilizing the often superior marketing knowledge and information of the product specialist. It seems very likely that prominent display racks for the sale of such price-maintained items as paperback books, cosmetics, or lighting supplies would involve this form of competition for dealer favor. Why this manner of doing business should be any less efficient or more reprehensible than direct leasing of the space in a retail department store by the manufacturer to promote his own sales directly neither the price-maintenance cases nor the price-restrictive licensing cases bother to reveal.

Economies of Scale in Advertising

The sale of numerous nationally advertised products can be promoted efficiently only when local advertising effort is keyed to and complements national advertising. Local and national advertising can be viewed as joint products presenting problems similar to those discussed under this heading in the previous chapter. Here there is an incentive for joint advertising action, whose efficiency could be affected adversely without some form of price protection assuring reasonable apportionment to the participants of the gains from advertising. Protecting dealer margins (price maintenance) not only allows efficient apportioning of expenses and returns, but also protects (as in the first example) nonadvertising local dealers from reaping rewards at the expense of advertising dealers, thus destroying the incentive for dealer participation in advertising promotions.

Breaking down Cartels and Controlling Local Monopolies

When both the manufacturer and the reseller possess market power, setting maximum prices, as was previously indicated, is a means of preventing the exercise of a second monopoly, to the detriment of the manufacturer and the ultimate consumers. Similar detriment to manufacturer and consumers can be avoided by the use of price maintenance under bilateral monopoly—where the customer of the first monopolists exerts his economic power as a buyer rather than a reseller.

The record of the *General Electric* case does not reveal whether Westinghouse, the principal and by far the largest of the General Electric licensees, would have been in a strong enough position to raise lamp prices against General Electric's interest. But it was clearly in the interest of General Electric that neither its own nor Westinghouse's agents do so.

Possible Fraud by a Joint Venturer

Price-fixing, as Bork has shown, using the *Screen Gems* case[34] as an example, is a means of protecting oneself against fraud by a joint venturer. And this does not eliminate any price competition that might otherwise exist. Defendant's evidence in that case convinced the Court

---

34. United States v. Columbia Pictures Corp., 189 F. Supp. 153 (S.D. N.Y. 1960). See Bork, "Rule of Reason," p. 461. Screen Gems, Inc., a wholly owned subsidiary of Columbia Pictures, was granted by Universal Pictures Company a fourteen-year exclusive license to distribute for television exhibition some six hundred Universal feature films produced before August 1948. Screen Gems would continue to be exclusive licensee for television of Columbia's features produced before this date. The Columbia-Universal contract contained a provision that Universal features should not be sublicensed for less than Columbia features of comparable quality. The government contended that these agreements were illegal because of this last provision.

that although two competing feature film makers were using a common selling agency, owned by one of them, to market the films of each at comparable prices, this did not call for a holding that the arrangement was an illegal price-fixing agreement. Rather, the price arrangement was found to be ancillary to and necessary for the achievement of distributive organization within the efficient size range. The price provisions were reasonably necessary under these circumstances to protect Universal's interest against fraudulent or discriminatory action by Screen Gems. Universal was found to have a continuing financial interest in the proceeds of distribution and insisted on a voice in the policy decisions on how its film library was to be merchandised.

A joint selling agency, of course, eliminated competition between Universal and Columbia on the films involved. But, as Bork indicates, the cost to television stations is not changed by shifting profits between Universal and Columbia. Classification in advance saved disputes afterward. An absence of a purpose or likely effect of the agreement on *general* market prices, as contrasted to the *specific* prices of the films involved, was a proper precondition to the ancillary doctrine the Court adopted.

Here in the joint-venture example, unlike the six preceding examples of possible efficiencies arising from price maintenance, there is a direct competitive relationship among the participants in the price-maintenance contract. So it was with General Electric and Westinghouse concerning the second issue in the *General Electric* case involving the patent license contract whereby Westinghouse, on the lamps it manufactured under license, agreed to adopt the same form of agency arrangement and abide by the prices General Electric established. There are close enough parallels between the *General Electric* case and the later *Screen Gems* case to suggest that Chief Justice Taft might have come to the right result not because he ignored the competition-suppressing aspects that later cases stressed but because, even if he had not, they could have been found to be ancillary to a legitimate efficiency objective.[35]

Once the efficiency aspects of the General Electric's price-maintaining contracts with its own distributor agents are recognized, together

---

35. Some antitrust scholars may find it somewhat ironic to suggest that Taft overlooked the applicability of a concept (ancillarity) which he himself is generally credited with establishing. See his landmark opinion in U.S. v. Addyston Pipe & Steel Co., 85 F. 271 (1898).

with the likely efficiencies achievable from Westinghouse's producing the patented lamps using existing facilities which General Electric would have had to duplicate, the similarity to the *Screen Gems* situation is strongly suggested. The price maintenance General Electric required of its own agents for efficiency provides the same efficiency rationale for price maintenance by Westinghouse agents, not only for the benefit of both Westinghouse and General Electric but also for the benefit of the distributing agencies of each and to consumers as well.

But is not a difficulty with this "heretical" analysis of the 1926 *General Electric* case suggested by important subsequent cases, particularly the *Masonite* case[36] in 1942 and the *Gypsum* case[37] in 1948? The difficulty, of course, involves the "industrywide" scope of the price agreement. In the *General Electric* case all but 7 percent of the lamp industry was under license to General Electric, and General Electric and Westinghouse together accounted for 85 percent of the lamp market. It must be recognized that in the *Screen Gems* case the conclusion that the prices fixed, although necessary to achieve the efficiency which was recognized, were permitted to be fixed because they were without market effect. A precondition to Court approval was the fact that the *general price level on films* was held not to be affected, at least not substantially. Market percentage (the proportion of Universal and Columbia television feature films to the total of comparable films) was low. In the General Electric case, in contrast, the proportion of price-fixed lamps was a high 85 percent. Of course, for tungsten filament lamps, acknowledged to be far superior to other lamps, the market proportion for General Electric plus its licensees is an automatic 100 percent (excluding infringement).

However appropriate a percentage-of-market criterion may be for a finding that a restraint is ancillary in nonpatent cases (or for cases involving the pooling of competing patents), this criterion, if applied generally to patent licensing arrangements, would exclude the consideration of efficiency from all patents but those of minor importance— those whose contribution over the existing cost was so slight that customers are relatively indifferent to whether or not the patent's services are made available to them. This is to say no more than that any good patent, licensed to one or to many, or not licensed at all, will have a general price effect. That, of course, is what a monopoly is.

---

36. U.S. v. Masonite Corp., 316 U.S. 265 (1942).
37. U.S. v. U.S. Gypsum Co., 333 U.S. 364 (1948).

The legitimacy of this patent monopoly makes the "no market price effect" precondition for a finding of ancillarity inappropriate for price-restrictive licensing under a valid patent. Such findings as "industry-wide control" through patents are properly reserved for the kind of test Furth urges—extension of scope or competitive superiority. Non-collusive restrictive licensing has not been shown to meet the Furth test. What is more, it does not even meet the antitrust standard (applicable to nonpatented products) once "efficiency" is given its proper role.

The efficiency presumption in the *General Electric* case is much stronger than has been recognized. This does not mean that, as in the *Gypsum* and *Masonite* cases, there were not "scope" factors whose existence should make the case go the other way.[38] The point, rather, is that the evidence required for that determination is not different from that required in the usual cartel case. There, too, evidence is often difficult to find when competitors are few. In the price-restrictive patent case the appropriate restriction to look for is restriction of the *non*patented, or the competing *other patent*.[39] Partial vertical integration by means of price-restrictive licensing or resale price maintenance, without horizontal agreement among buyers or sellers, is an unlikely hunting ground for extensions beyond Furth's "competitive superiority."

The last two chapters have stressed the economic efficiencies that are predictable from the vertical arrangements sellers make with buyers, including those that patentees make with their licensees. Foreclosure of other suppliers, although it may result from such

38. If, for example, as Telser has suggested, "it is plausible to regard General Electric and its licensed manufacturers as forming a cartel," and further, "In its own right Westinghouse owned valuable and important (competing?) patents," this indeed could have been used as evidence of "scope extension." (Telser, "Why Should Manufacturers Want Fair Trade," 3 *J. L. Econ.* 86 [Oct. 1960], at p. 100). The suggestion is, of course, that the patent licensing agreement was a screen for eliminating competition among General Electric and Westinghouse patents. That, however, was *not* the basis for the decision in the case.

39. There is substantial evidence of an industry interest and an attempt to achieve a "price stability" broader than that of the patented products in both the Masonite and Gypsum cases, but especially in the latter. Justice Douglas's opinion in Gypsum, however, is not so limited. His blanket indictment finds industrywide price-fixing patent licenses "with knowledge on the part of licensor and licensee of the adherence of others, with the control over prices and methods of distribution through the agreements and the bulletins, were sufficient to find a *prima facie* case of conspiracy." 333 U.S. 364, at p. 389 (1948).

arrangements, moreover, should not be confused with foreclosure of competitive results. Applying a less confining test to legitimate monopoly—the competitive superiority of a valid patent—economic analysis leaves no plausible rationale for the conclusion that restrictions upon use are means patentees can use to create a monopoly in an unpatented complement.

The following chapters critically analyze the cases, both before and after passage of the Clayton Act, showing how patent misuse law has become subverted by not understanding or misapplying these conclusions.

7

Legally Permissible Use Restriction in Patent Licenses before Passage of the Clayton Act

A patent allows its owner to exclude others from making, using, or vending the invention. Right to exclude others from *use* of the invention distinguishes patent owners from copyright owners. The right to exclude others from *use*, not available to copyright owners, is a right which courts have recognized as separate and distinct from that to exclude from making or vending.[1]

Divisibility of a Patentee's Right to Exclude

Not only were the rights to exclude others from making, vending, or using early recognized as separable rights under patent law, but with respect to the last right, to exclude others from use, it was never presumed that the use right was indivisible in the all-or-none sense. The divisibility of at least some uses applied to patented products sold if the stipulated uses were made explicit at time of sale. Professor Thomas Reed Powell, writing in 1917, stated that the divisibility premise most favorable to patentees was as follows:[2]

> Plainly, if the patentee sells a machine without reservation, he must be assumed to consent that the right to use the machine shall be governed

1. Thomas Reed Powell, "The Nature of the Patent Right," 17 *Colum. L. Rev.* 663 at 665 (Dec. 1917), quotes Justice Day, in Bauer v. O'Donnell, 229 U.S. 1, at p. 13, n. 10 (1913) as follows: "It is apparent that the principal difference in the enactments lies in the presence of the word 'use' in the patent statute and its absence in the copyrighted statute. An inventor has not only the exclusive right to make and vend his invention or discovery, but he has the like right to use it, and when a case comes fairly within the grant of the right to use, *that use should be protected by all means properly within the scope of the statute*" (emphasis added).
2. Powell, "Nature of the Patent Right," p. 666.

by the law of the state, and that the machine is thereby freed from the monopoly of user granted by the patent. *But if he stipulates* that he is not, by the mere sale of the machine, parting with rights under the patent law, he still retains those rights. The purchaser must then justify any use of the machine by showing that the patentee has relinquished some or all of his patent right to exclude others from using the patented machine [emphasis added].

This position is necessarily based on the assumption—and Powell was explicit about this—that "the right to exclude from use given by the patent statute is not a single, indivisible right which must be retained *in toto* or parted with *in toto*."³ And if what the patent law grants is a bundle of an indefinite number of separate rights to exclude from separate uses (including time, place, kind of use, or use with specific materials), and *if* the patentee may part with one of these rights and still retain the others, it follows, as Powell writes, that any specific right of use not permitted by the patentee remains under the protection of his monopoly.

The *A. B. Dick* case,⁴ decided by the Supreme Court in a four-to-three decision in 1912, concerned whether contributory infringement was involved by one's knowingly selling ink for use with a mimeograph machine bought under a contract specifying use only with supplies furnished by the patentee seller. The case reached the Supreme Court in 1911. It was agreed by the minority as well as the majority of the Supreme Court justices that the right of the patentee to exclude others from use was divisible in certain dimensions. These included time of use, place of use, and purpose of use.

When a patentee sells a patented machine or product, unlike the case in which the patent itself is sold, the right to exclude others from the use of the invention remains with the patentee. The purchaser of a patented product or machine, if he had the right to use it in any way not violative of law in the absence of a patent, would be in conflict with the right of a patentee to exclude others from use of the invention. And this conflict is, conceptually at least, no different for stipulated time of use, territories of use, fields of use, use with specified materials, use by purchasers at resale, or use at stipulated prices only. The essence of the patentee's claim, when rights of use are specified and unambiguously defined, as Powell has emphasized,⁵ is

3. Ibid., p. 667.
4. Henry v. A. B. Dick Co., 224 U.S. 1 (1912).
5. Powell, "Nature of the Patent Right," p. 666.

that he has never parted with his right under the patent to exclude others from the use in question. All this follows, of course, only if the premise is accepted that what the patent law grants is an indefinite number of separate rights to exclude from separate specific uses.[6] And whether or not a refusal by a patentee to permit a specific use restrains trade, either under common law or, after 1890, in violation of the Sherman Act, is not different except in degree from the situation in which the patentee licenses nobody at all but rather retains his right to exclude others from all forms and manners of use.

Need for Specific Provision for Limitation on Use after Sale

This "divisibility of use" theory of patent exploitation was rather generally accepted and was applied by courts in a wide variety of situations in early patent cases. With respect to use, however, there has long been a presumption that limitation on time or scope of use must be specifically provided for. In 1852, for example, the Supreme Court held that "a party who had purchased the right to use a planing machine [no specified limitation on the right of use was made with reference to its purchase] during the period to which the patent was first limited, was entitled to continue to use it during the extension authorized by that law"[7] [patent extension was by a special act of

6. As will be indicated, this premise has *not* been given uniform application by the courts. Except for territorial licensing, divisibility of use has increasingly been held by the Supreme Court to be illegal. Most forms of divisibility of use have not been viewed by the Court as devices for maximizing the reward attributable to the superiority afforded by a valid patent. This, as analysis in chapters 5 and 6 indicated, is mistaken. It is no less so because it is of long standing.

7. Bloomer v. McQuewan, 55 U.S. 539 (1852) at p. 550. The central question in Bloomer v. McQuewan was whether a licensee under a patent expiring in 1849, but extended for seven years by an act of Congress in 1845, had a *right of use* for the additional seven years, even though this was not specifically conveyed by the licensor. In the year 1833, during the term for which the original patent was granted, the licensee defendants in this case purchased the right to construct and *use* a certain number of machines within the limits of Pittsburgh and Allegheny counties. The circuit court decided that the licensees' right to *use* them continued. In a previous case, Wilson v. Rousseau, 4 How. 688, it had been decided that the party who had purchased and was using a planing machine during the original term for which the patent was granted had a right to continue the use during the extension. And the distinction was made there between the grant of the right to make and vend the machine and the right to use it. The right to construct and use the planing machines in the McQuewan case "had been purchased and paid for *without any limitation as*

Congress]. In 1872, however, in a case in which the time of use was
expressly stipulated by the patentee in the original conveyance, a
unanimous Supreme Court decision upheld this limitation on right
of use.[8]

The preceding two early cases, involving time dimensions on use
relating to patented machines *which had been sold,* clearly did *not* rest
on the simplistic economic notion that an act of sale gives a patentee
(or an assignee) his full and legitimate reward and that "title passing"
makes inappropriate any further claim by the patentee. This result followed only in the absence of specific reservation.[9]

In the case of *Adams* v. *Burke,*[10] decided by the Supreme Court in
1873, *implied* limitations (as contrasted to a specific provision) on the
right of use of coffin lids by an undertaker in a specific territory was
not allowed.

Justice Miller, writing for the majority, was satisfied that "the defendant, who, as an undertaker, purchased each of these coffins and
used it in burying the body which he was employed to bury, acquired
the right to this use of it *freed from any claim of the patentee,* though
purchased within the ten-mile-circle and used without it.[11] It is notable
in this case that the party from whom the defendant undertaker purchased the coffins had been assigned "all the right, title and interest
which the said patentees had in the invention . . . for, to and in a circle
whose radius is ten miles, having the city of Boston as a centre."[12]

The question in the coffin case did not involve the legality of the
territorial division among assignees for the purpose of vending coffin
lids. Rather, the question was whether the proper construction of assignment contract was such as to limit *use* within the territorial limits.

---

to the time for which they were to be used" (p. 553). Strictly, then, the Mc-
Quewan case allows a contractually *specified* division of use only by inference
(emphasis added).

8. Mitchell v. Hawley, 83 U.S. 544 (1872). In this case an exclusive right
to make and use four hat-felting machines was conveyed by the patentee in the
form of a license with both territorial and time restrictions (Massachusetts
and New Hampshire, life of the original patent) in addition to the restriction
on the number of machines. Also, the license stipulated that the licensee "shall
not, in any way, or form, dispose of, sell, or grant any license (sublicense) to
use the said machines beyond the expiration of the original term" (p. 549).

9. Mitchell v. Hawley, 83 U.S. 544 (1872) has rarely been cited by the
Supreme Court. It is one of those cases the Court is disposed to quietly forget.

10. 84 U.S. 453 (1873).

11. Ibid., p. 457 (emphasis added).

12. Ibid., p. 458.

The majority opinion, after pointing out that the right to manufacture, the right to sell, and the right to use are substantive rights and may be granted separately, went on to point out, "But, in the essential nature of things, when the patentee, or the person having his rights, sells a machine or instrument whose sole value is in use, he receives the consideration for its use *and he parts with the right to restrict that use*."[13]

The majority opinion, most narrowly read, would restrict the applicability of the foregoing language to cases in which the area of use is *implied*. Interestingly enough, *Bloomer* v. *McQuewan* is cited by the majority but no mention is made of *Mitchell* v. *Hawley*.[14] There the former case was held inapplicable to time limitations on use specifically provided for. Neither did the dissenting opinion discuss whether a specific clause in the assignment contract could bar the assignee from selling to customers outside his territory. The *Adams* v. *Burke* minority opinion, rather, stressed the impropriety of a holding under which the assignee vendor was able to confer on his vendees a right which they cannot exercise themselves.[15] It is thus possible to read *Adams* v. *Burke* as an *implied* contract case in which the implication is insufficient, thus making use subdivisions as to territory on a par with use subdivisions as to time. It is also possible to construe the decision as a "title passing" case narrowly retricted to territory of use by subsequent as contrasted to initial purchasers. Whether a patentee may protect himself or his assignees from subsequent use *by special contracts* brought home to the purchasers was not specifically decided.

A similar situation was again presented to the Supreme Court in 1895, in *Keeler* v. *Standard Folding Bed*.[16] Here the majority, after reviewing *Adams* v. *Burke* and subsequent related cases, held that "one who buys patented articles of manufacture from one authorized to sell them becomes possessed of an absolute property in such articles, unrestricted in time or place."[17] But in the very next sentence of the opinion this holding was qualified to leave the ambiguity about *implied* use just as it was after *Adams* v. *Burke*: "Whether or not," wrote Justice Miller, "a patentee may protect himself and his assignees

13. Ibid., p. 456 (emphasis added).
14. See Mitchell v. Hawley, 83 U.S. 544 (1872).
15. Adams v. Burke, 84 U.S. 453 (1873), at p. 459.
16. 157 U.S. 659 (1895).
17. Ibid., p. 666.

by special contracts brought home to the purchasers is not a question before us, and upon which we express no opinion."[18]

The dissenters in the *Folding Bed* case, however, unlike the dissenters in *Adams* v. *Burke*, the coffin lid case, made specific reference to *Mitchell* v. *Hawley*'s holding that the use limitations could be divisible in time terms if *specifically* provided for in the patent license contract. But they gave it only a passing comment to the effect that, insofar as *Mitchell* v. *Hawley* was pertinent at all, it favored the dissent.[19] The dissenting opinion in *Folding Bed* interpreted the *Adams* v. *Burke* holding (both majority and minority) as distinguishing the patentee's "divisibility rights" with respect to making and selling from those relating to the right to use. The minority opinion in *Folding Bed* focused upon the distinction of who was being sued in an attempt to distinguish *Adams* v. *Burke*. There, it was the seller of coffin lids. Here in *Folding Bed*, in contrast, the purchaser of beds was the defendant. Thus, the buyer of coffin lids in the earlier case, having bought them from one who had a legal right to *sell* them had the right to *use* them anywhere. There was, according to dissenting opinion in *Folding Bed*, no suggestion in the *Adams* v. *Burke* opinion of either the majority or the minority "that a purchaser from the assignee had or could have the right to *deal* in the patented article outside of the territory in which the purchase was made."[20] The minority also thought it relevant that a coffin lid's usefulness was exhausted by one use, whereas a bed could be reused or resold, and that this was relevant to the language in *Adams* v. *Burke* that patentee's monopoly in coffin lids, unlike beds, can reasonably be held to be exhausted after a single sale.

The rulings in both *Adams* v. *Burke* and, subsequently, in *Keeler* v. *Standard Folding Bed Company* can *not* be read as directly bearing on the question whether a licensee who has not complied with the terms of his license (for example, regarding divisibility of use) can be sued for infringement. The major "divisibility of use" cases up to 1895— *Bloomer* v. *McQuewan*, *Mitchell* v. *Hawley*, *Adams* v. *Burke*, and even *Keeler* v. *Standard Folding Bed*[21]—if they do not clearly support, at

18. Ibid.
19. Ibid., p. 669.
20. Ibid., p. 670 (emphasis added).
21. Whether a patentee may protect himself and his assignees by *special contracts brought home to the purchasers* was not before the Court in Keeler. The Court did *not* express an opinion overruling Mitchell v. Hawley. See 157 U.S. 659 (1895), at p. 666.

least do not negate the proposition that an explicit refusal of a patentee to permit particular use in time or place through a license contract is permissible under patent law. In any case, however they may be interpreted, these cases provided no convincing economic rationale for denying such rights to patentees.

Use with Specific Materials: Tie-in Sales and Patent Extension

The precise question of divisibility of use under the explicit terms of a patent licensing contract, in a different context—use only with specific materials—was presented to the Circuit Court of Appeals in the Sixth Circuit and decided in 1896 in an opinion by Judge (later Justice) Lurton and concurred in by Judge (later Justice) Taft. The case, *Heaton-Peninsular Button-Fastener Company* v. *Eureka Specialty Company,*[22] came to the court as a contributory infringement case. The defendant was the manufacturer of unpatented staples specifically produced for, and therefore of course known by the staple manufacturer to be used by the purchaser of a patented button-fastening machine, sold on condition, evidenced by a conspicuous metal label, that the machine should be used only with fasteners manufactured by the seller. Title, the notice read, was to revert to the seller on breach of this condition.

In *Button-Fastener,* unlike the earlier division-of-use cases, the question was raised whether the restriction on use (use only with material provided by the seller of the patented machine) was an illegal restraint of trade. It was alleged by the defendant in the lower court that the restriction on use imposed by the patent-owning complainant operated to create a monopoly in an unpatented article. And the judge who heard the case in the lower court said that he "was persuaded that the patentee's privilege has its limits, in the rights and interests of the public, and that it is an abuse of his privilege to so shape his dealings with his patent as to secure a monopoly upon an unpatented article."[23] A conflict between a possible patent right—exclusion of patent-licensees from particular uses—and a possible trade restraint—creation of a monopoly in unpatented staples—was resolved by the lower court by a finding that there was use of a legitimate first monopoly to create an illegitimate second monopoly. The lower court's

22. 77 Fed. 288 (1896).
23. Ibid., p. 289.

holding in *Button-Fastener* that "a monopoly upon an unpatented article" was secured was thus bottomed on "scope" grounds. The lower court in *Button-Fastener* conceived the tying of staples to the sale of the fastening machine to be a means of "leveraging" from a legitimate first monopoly to an illegitimate second. The court of appeals, however, reversed.

Judge Lurton, reading *Adams* v. *Burke* and *Mitchell* v. *Hawley* as applying only to unconditional sales, wrote: "That the complainant has attempted to state a case not within this rule is very obvious, for it charges that every sale has been under an *express restriction* as to the use of the invention embodied in the machine."[24] Moreover, according to Judge Lurton, since the right to manufacture, the right to sell, and the right to use are each substantive rights and may be granted separately or conferred together by the patentee, then if the patentee has the exclusive right to the use of his invention during the term of the patent "it would seem to follow that *any* use by another, unauthorized by the patentee, would be an infringement of his monopoly."[25]

Judge Lurton wrote "it would *seem* to follow" because he was not prepared to say that there were no limitations upon a patentee's power of contract with reference to the use of his invention by others. What, he asked, is the relationship of the patent property right, subject as is all other property to "the general law of the land," in the context of this case? The right to make and sell or use a patented invention or process, according to Judge Lurton, is not free from the restraints imposed by the general police power. *Patterson* v. *Kentucky*[26] provided Judge Lurton with an example. In this case a seller of a burning oil, condemned as unsafe by a state inspector, could not avoid conviction because the oil was patented. Also cited were public utility patent cases.[27] These cases had held that a patentee could not authorize the use of his invention by one charged with public duties and subject to regulation by law so as to relieve the licensee of an obligation to render equal service under public utility regulation. *Button-Fastener,* however, did not present this kind of public policy question

---

24. Ibid., p. 290 (emphasis added).
25. Ibid., p. 292 (emphasis added). Again, a holding subsequently reversed by the Supreme Court which later adopted the "leverage fallacy."
26. 97 U.S. 501 (1878).
27. State of Missouri v. Bell Telephone Co. 23 Fed. 539 (1885); State of Delaware v. A. Tel. & Tel. Co., 47 Fed. 633 (1891).

for Judge Lurton. His "public policy" stressed wide liberty in making contracts. Furthermore, Judge Lurton was not at all impressed by the argument that a licensing contract calling for exclusion from use of unpatented staples made by others created a monopoly of an unpatented product. "Let it be supposed," he reasoned,

that the patents owned by this complainant were so wide in character as to cheapen the process of manufacturing shoes, and to drive from competition all other modes of manufacture. Then, suppose the patentees were of the opinion that they could most profitably enjoy their inventions by retaining the monopoly of the use, and engaging in the manufacture of shoes. If content to undersell all others, they could engross the market for shoes, to the extent of their capacity to supply the demand during the life of their patents, or so long as their invention was not superseded by subsequent inventions still further cheapening the cost of manufacture. The monopoly thus secured [on *unpatented* shoes] would be the legitimate consequence of the meritorious character of their invention . . . The great consuming public would be benefited, rather than injured, for the monopoly could endure so long only as shoes were supplied at a less price than prevailed before the invention.[28]

Clearly Judge Lurton applied a "competitive superiority" test in his hypothetical case, a test which exposed the naive notion that a process patent could be deemed to create *broader* end-product monopoly by control over the conditions of the use of the process. Thus Judge Lurton, before the turn of the century, asked the same relevant economic question with respect to tie-ins that Furth was convincingly recommending for price-restrictive licensing more than sixty years later.[29]

Judge Lurton asked the economically relevant "scope" question with respect to divisibility of use: "if the patentees, by retaining to themselves the exclusive use of their invention, are able, legitimately and lawfully, to acquire a monopoly of the manufacture of shoes [the basis of competitive superiority of the patent] and destroy the shoe market for those who before had shared it, why may they not, by a system of restricted licenses, permit others to use their devices on condition that only some minor part of the shoe—the pegs, the tips,

28. 77 Fed. 288 (1896), at p. 295.
29. See chapter 6. Every *undesirable* licensing arrangement is, according to Furth, characterized by the fact that the patentee and his licensees acquire a margin of profit or a degree of control over their industry which is unrelated to the competitive superiority of the patent.

the thread, or the buttons, or the button fasteners—shall be bought from them?"[30]

For Judge Lurton, in the *Button-Fastener* case, the right of exclusive use was a divisible one and equally applicable to time, territory, complementary materials, or pricing methods. "Their monopoly in an unpatented article" (staples, and only those staples which but for the patented machine would have had no market), Lurton emphasized, "*will depend upon the merit of their patented device,* and the extent to which other clinching devices are superseded by it."[31]

This early patent-tying decision has been overruled, but its analysis, after nearly three-quarters of a century, remains to be refuted.

Licensor-Imposed Prices

The first case to reach the United States Supreme Court involving the issue of whether fixing the prices at which licensees must sell patented articles violates the Sherman Act or whether this form of licensing contract is permissible as a valid exercise of patent rights was *Bement* v. *National Harrow Company,*[32] decided in 1902. This case originated as a breach of contract suit in the New York state courts. The original plaintiff, the National Harrow Company, was a patent-holding company owned by competing harrow manufacturers making up a very high proportion of the country's spring-tooth harrow makers and owning some eighty-five patents on float spring-tooth harrows. It acquired its patents under circumstances suggesting that many of these patents may have been competing rather than complementary or mutually blocking. But it must be emphasized that the Supreme Court decided a different issue. That issue was whether a patentee could enforce on a licensee a provision concerning the price at which it could sell patented harrows, and also a provision that the licensee would not sell any harrows other than specified models covered by the license.

A unanimous Court, six justices sitting, held that as between the parties, National Harrow and Bement, these provisions did not violate the Sherman Act. The case as decided thus emphasized not its horizontal aspects but rather a vertical contract between *a* patentee and

---

30. 157 U.S. 659 (1895), at p. 295.
31. Ibid., p. 296 (emphasis added).
32. 186 U.S. 70 (1902).

a licensee. Peckham, who wrote the opinion, relied heavily upon the reasoning of Judge Lurton in *Button-Fastener* and the cases cited there. "The owner of a patented article can," Peckham wrote, "of course, charge such price as he may choose, and the owner of a patent may assign it or sell the right to manufacture and sell the article patented upon the condition that the assignee shall charge a certain amount for such article."[33]

It was also objected that narrowing Bement's manufacturing and selling rights to harrows covered by the licensed patents was in restraint of trade. Bement had agreed not to manufacture or sell any float spring-tooth harrow other than those Bement had made under its patents before assigning them to National Harrow unless Harrow had granted Bement a license. As to this objection, Peckham held: "The plain purpose of the provision was to prevent the defendant from infringing upon the rights of others under other patents, and it had no purpose to stifle competition in the harrow business more than the patent provided for, nor was its purpose to prevent the licensee from attempting to make improvement in harrows."[34]

Although Peckham's opinion in *National Harrow* utilized the "part-whole" rationale of Judge Lurton's opinion in *Button-Fastener* so that fixing a licensee's prices, like limiting his territory, limiting the time of his license, or limiting the products with which the patent could be used, is encompassed in the greater right of not licensing at all, Peckham gave the most cavalier treatment to another aspect of Lurton's opinion. Lurton had found in *Button-Fastener* that the tie-in of staples to the fastening machine did not involve a violation of antitrust law because the license contract in that case was shown to be a means of maximizing the reward due to the *competitive superiority* of the button-fastener patents and not a means of restraining trade *beyond* the scope of patents involved.

Justice Peckham thus glided with an easy glibness over the possibility that the patent pool, an escrow arrangement whereby no major competitor took a license until all others agreed to similar terms, as well as the means by which patent reward was divided among competing companies owning the National Harrow Company, was a means to broader aims than maximization of patent revenue. All of these arrangements gave the case at least a complexion of industrywide

33. Ibid., p. 93.
34. Ibid., p. 94.

horizontal price agreement in an industry which, to say the least, was not noted for an absence of price cooperation.

The Supreme Court decision in *National Harrow* established the validity of price-restrictive licensing of multiple patents.[35] Moreover, the private settlement of patent conflicts and the avoidance of infringement litigation was not then viewed as a means of using the patent pool as a screen for avoiding violation of the Sherman Act. In fact, Peckham's decision seemed to encourage this method of avoiding costly litigation. "There had been," wrote Peckham, "as the referee finds, a large amount of litigation between the many parties claiming to own various patents covering these implements. Suits for infringement and for injunction had been frequent, and it was desirable to prevent them in the future. This execution of these contracts did in fact settle a large amount of litigation regarding the validity of many patents as found by the referee. *This was a legitimate and desirable result in itself.*"[36]

That such practice might eliminate competition between competing patents, or give monopoly power through patents whose validity may have been doubtful, did not pose a serious Sherman Act question for the Supreme Court at the turn of the century. Thus Justice Peckham, by blurring the distinction between the question involving divisibility of a patentee's right to exclude others from making, vending, or using a patent and the question involving competitive superiority or scope as a measure for appropriate application of antitrust law to patent licensing practice, created an illusion of an "anything goes" patent licensing policy which did not survive the *bathtub* case[37] in 1912.

The right of inventors to apply patent licensing terms of their own choosing received additional support in 1907 in the Seventh Circuit Court of Appeals in *Rubber Tire Wheel Company* v. *Milwaukee Rubber Tire Works.*[38] This case extended beyond *National Harrow* in explicitly approving a combination of patentee and licensees to control both prices and output of a patented product. In the licensing at issue in this case the patentee authorized eighteen companies, of which the defendant was one, to make, use, and sell tires under the patent for one year; each company's share of the trade was fixed at a certain

---

35. In later years, however, as will be indicated, Supreme Court decisions have not followed this precedent.
36. 186 U.S. 70 (1902), p. 93 (emphasis added).
37. Standard Sanitary Manufacturing Co. v. U.S., 226 U.S. 20 (1912).
38. 154 Fed. 358 (1907).

percentage of the whole, the defendant's being 2 percent; two qualities of tires were to be made, with different fixed minimum selling prices per pound for each; each company agreed to pay the patentee 4 percent of its sales per month, and if in any month sales quotas were exceeded an additional royalty of 20 percent was payable on the overage; a commission of five persons supervised the transactions of all parties; all royalties over 2 percent were placed in the hands of this commission, which, after expenses, paid companies with quota deficiencies 20 percent of such deficiency; and after accumulation of a $50,000 reserve all excess was distributed among participants in proportion to their quotas.

The patent, in this interesting case, had been held invalid in a previous decision in the Court of Appeals for the Sixth Circuit. The Seventh Circuit held, however, that *except for that Circuit* [the Sixth] *and only with respect to the parties in that case,* the patent was and is valid. The Court in *Rubber Tire Wheel* saw no problem of "divisibility" of use—"Use of the invention cannot be had except on the inventor's terms. Without paying or doing *whatever he exacts,* no one can be exempted from his right to exclude."[39] The only qualification the Court imposed was that the licensee not be required to violate some law outside the patent law, "like the doing of murder or arson."[40]

Concerning whether the combination or pool among licensees to control the prices and output "of an innocuous patented article" was in violation of the Sherman Act, the Seventh Circuit found that *Bement* v. *National Harrow Company* "according to our reading was expressly excepted from the decision; and so, aided by the declaration of general principles in that and other cases, we must formulate our own answer."[41] It proceeded to do so in no uncertain terms:

Congress, having created the patent law, had the right to repeal or modify it, in whole or in part, directly or by necessary implication. The Sherman law contains no reference to the patent law . . . the necessary implication is that patented articles, unless and until they are released by the owner of the patent from the dominion of his monopoly, are not articles of trade and commerce among the several states. The evils to be remedied by the Sherman Act are well understood. Articles in which people are entitled to freedom of trade were being taken as the subjects of monopoly; instrumentalities of commerce between which people were en-

39. Ibid., p. 362 (emphasis added).
40. Ibid.
41. Ibid.

titled to free competition were being combined. The means of effecting and the form of the combination are immaterial; the result is the criterion. The true test of violation of the Sherman Act is whether the people are injured, whether they are deprived of something to which they have a right.[42]

Because none of the provisions of the contract could be seen by the Court in *Rubber Tire Wheel* to touch on "any matter outside the monopoly of the patent,"[43] the control of prices and output, the fact that licensees jointly participated in the enforcement of scheme or in the rebating of proceeds received did not deprive the public of any right. The public was not, according to the Court, "entitled to profit by competition among infringers." Here the Court, although it made no specific reference to "competitive superiority" afforded by the patent, clearly conceived its function as the application of a "scope" test. The relevant issue in assessing the applicability of the Sherman Act to patent licensing practice, according to this court, was the advantage provided by a valid patent.

Reaffirmation That Tying Does Not Leverage to New Monopoly

The same issue of licensee use restriction involving a patent tie-in, decided by Judge Lurton for the Sixth Circuit Court of Appeals in *Button-Fastener* before the turn of the century, reached the Supreme Court in the case of *Henry* v. *A. B. Dick Company*, decided in 1912.[44] The majority opinion for four justices, three justices dissenting, was written by Justice Lurton, who, as Judge Lurton, had written the earlier opinion in *Button-Fastener*. In essence he wrote the same opinion again. Here in the *A. B. Dick* case a stencil-duplicating machine, a rotary mimeograph, was sold by the patentee subject to the license restriction that it be used only with the stencils, paper, ink, and other supplies sold by the patentee. The issue was thus the same as that involved in *Button-Fastener*, in which the patented machine was sold with the license restriction that it be used only with staples sold by the patentee. Justice Lurton's conclusion was as before: "that there is no difference in principle, between a sale subject to specific restrictions as to the time, place or purpose of use and restrictions requiring

42. Ibid.
43. Ibid., p. 363.
44. 224 U.S. 1 (1912).

a use only with other things necessary to the use of the patented article purchased from the patentee."[45]

The *A. B. Dick* case, however, brought a strong dissent from Chief Justice White, in which he was joined by justices Hughes and Lamar. The essence of the dissenters' objection to the majority opinion was their conviction (an erroneous one if the previous analysis is correct) "that a patentee in selling the machine covered by his patent has *power by contract to extend* the patent so as to cause it to embrace things which it does not include."[46]

That Justice White embraced the "patent leveraging fallacy," although not unambiguously inferrable from the preceding quotation, is unmistakable in the following:

the ruling [of the majority] now made in effect is that the patentee has the power, by contract, to extend his patent rights so as to bring within the claims of his patent things which are not embraced therein, thus virtually legislating by causing the patent laws to cover subjects to which without exercise of the right of contract they could not reach, the result being not only to *multiply monopolies at the will of an interested party,* but also to destroy the jurisdiction of the state courts over subjects which from the beginning have been within their authority.[47]

Resale Price Maintenance of Patented Products

Justice Hughes, who joined Justice White in this *A. B. Dick* dissent, was the author of the previous year's majority opinion in *Dr. Miles Medical Company* v. *John D. Park and Sons Company,*[48] the resale price maintenance case critically reviewed in the preceding chapter, holding this form of vertical price-fixing illegal. Lurton distinguished this case as being inapplicable in the mimeograph case because in the latter a patented product was involved, whereas in *Dr. Miles* the product was unpatented. In his dissent in the *A. B. Dick* case, White stressed the incompatibility of the Hughes theory in *Dr. Miles* and the Lurton theory in *A. B. Dick,* pointing to the importance of using the "general law" (here evidenced by the *Dr. Miles* decision against resale price maintenance) as properly proscribing patent practice of this type. The licensing contract, therefore, patent or no patent, ac-

45. Ibid., p. 35.
46. Ibid., p. 51 (emphasis added).
47. Ibid., p. 53 (emphasis added).
48. 220 U.S. 373 (1911). See also chapter 6, Price Restrictive Licensing and Resale Price Maintenance.

cording to White "can only be maintained upon the assumption that the patent law and the issue of a patent is the generating source of an authority to contract to procure rights under that patent law not other-wise within that law, and which could not be enjoyed under the general law of the land."[49]

Concerning both issues raised by the dissent in *A. B. Dick*, use restriction by a patentee achieved by resale price maintenance or use restriction achieved through tie-in sales, the White view came to pre-vail. *Bauer* v. *O'Donnell*[50] in 1913 made the *Dr. Miles* rule applicable to patented products as White suggested; and on the tie-in issue White's minority opinion in *A. B. Dick* became his majority opinion with respect to tie-in sales in the *Motion Picture Patents* case in 1917.[51]

Justice White's dissent in *A. B. Dick* was grounded on the patent scope question—competitive superiority. So was Justice Lurton's ma-jority opinion. The narrow question before the Supreme Court in the *Dick* case was whether the acts of the defendant ink-seller constituted contributory infringement of the complainant's patents. The majority and the minority were in agreement that under no construction of the patent right can an illegal monopoly in ordinary commodities be justi-fied. The majority, finding no control over "ordinary commodities," applied "divisibility of use" precedent under *patent* law, no violation of general law, therefore infringement and also contributory infringe-ment. The minority found general law rather than patent law appli-cable, because it assumed the very point at issue, namely, that an illegal monopoly in ink was created by the licensing contract; and this, of course, deserved no patent protection.

As of 1912, then, divisibility of patent use achieved by various patent licensing devices held sway. But in the following year Justice Day's five-to-four opinion in *Bauer* v. *O'Donnell*[52] created the first notable chink in the use-divisibility armor with which the Court, up to this point, had clothed patentees. At the time the *Bauer* v. *O'Don-nell* case reached the Supreme Court, it had already been decided that an article of general use could not be price-fixed for resale. The *Dr. Miles* case involved a secret remedy. And before *Dr. Miles*, in the case

49. Henry v. A. B. Dick Company, 224 U.S. 1 (1912), p. 71.
50. 229 U.S. 1 (1913).
51. Motion Picture Patents Co. v. Universal Film Manufacturing Co., 243 U.S. 502 (1917).
52. 229 U.S. 1 (1913).

of *Bobbs-Merrill Company* v. *Strauss*[53] in 1908, Justice Day, writing
an opinion from which there was no dissent, had held that a sole right
to vend under copyright law conferred a privilege which was exhausted
by the first sale. An undertaking to limit the price of copyrighted
books for sale at retail by a notice on each book fixing the price at
retail and stating that no dealer was licensed to sell it at less than one
dollar was not permitted. Justice Day, in *Bobbs-Merrill*, specifically
mentioned the difference between the patent and copyright statutes
and disclaimed any intention to prejudge a patent case. In *Bauer* v.
O'Donnell, however, he pointed out that with respect to vending, as
contrasted to using, the sale of a patented article is not essentially
different from the sale of a book.[54] The difference in the enactments,
he pointed out, "lies in the presence of the word 'use' in the patent
statute and its absence in copyright law."[55] But Day clearly did not
view resale price maintenance as an appropriate "use" subdivision of
the type Lurton had approved in the *A. B. Dick* tie-in case. Day recognized the exclusive right of a patentee to exclude others from using
his invention, as well as his right to exclude others from making and
vending; but *Bauer* v. *O'Donnell* was not such a case for him. He
wrote, "when a case comes fairly within the grant of the right to use,
that use should be protected by all means properly within the scope
of the statute."[56] And later, "it is a perversion to call the transaction
in any sense a license to use the invention."[57] Why was not use at a
stipulated price as appropriate as use with specified materials, as in
A. B. Dick? Day provided no reasoned answer, and no written dissent
is reported. All one has to distinguish the *Dick* case is: "the title transferred was full and complete with an attempt to reserve the right to
fix the price at which subsequent sales could be made. There is no
showing of a qualified sale for less than value for limited use with
other articles only, as was shown in the *Dick* case. There was no
transfer of a limited right to use this invention, and to call the sale a
license to use is a mere play on words."[58]

53. 210 U.S. 339 (1908).
54. 229 U.S. 1 (1913), at p. 13.
55. Ibid., p. 14.
56. Ibid.
57. Ibid., p. 16.
58. Ibid.

Reversal of Tying Law: The Legal Adoption of the Leverage Fallacy

This distinction, if indeed it can be called a distinction, between use
with another commodity and use at a price lasted only until 1917.
In *Motion Picture Patents* Justice Clark, in overruling *A. B. Dick*,
wrote: "Through the twenty years since the decision in the *Button-
Fastener Case* was announced there have not been wanting courts and
judges who have dissented from its conclusions, as is sufficiently shown
in the division of this court when the question involved first came
before it in *Henry* v. *Dick Co.* . . . and in the disposition not to extend
the doctrine in *Bauer* v. *O'Donnell*."[59] The Court then went on to
espouse exactly the same kind of leveraging argument contained in
the *A. B. Dick* dissent, in spite of Justice Holmes's categorical dissent
that the majority was wrong. "There is,"

no predominant public interest to prevent a patented tea pot or film feeder
from being kept from the public, because, as I have said, the patentee
may keep them tied up at will while his patent lasts. Neither is there any
such interest to prevent the purchase of tea or films, that is made the condition of the use of the machine. The supposed contravention of public
interest sometimes is stated as an attempt to extend the patent law to
unpatented articles, which of course it is not, and more accurately as a
possible domination to be established by such means. *But the domination
is one only to the extent of the desire for the tea pot or film feeder,* and if
the owner prefers to keep the pot or the feeder unless you will buy his
tea or films, I cannot see in allowing him the right to do so anything more
than an ordinary incidence of ownership.[60]

This minority conclusion was never rebutted by the majority. As
Powell commented: "The results of an exclusion from use which is
limited in time, place or purpose are seldom likely to violate any
policy that is not violated by total exclusion from use. Cases sanction-
ing such partial exclusions as reservations of a portion of the patent
right do not permit the patentee to extend his monopoly to other
articles than the one covered by his patent. The restraint of trade

---

59. Motion Picture Patents Co. v. Universal Film Manufacturing Co., 243
U.S. 502 (1917), at p. 515.
60. Ibid., p. 520 (emphasis added). Motion Picture Patents, although decided
in 1917 after the passage of the Clayton Act, was not decided under that act.
Its impact was left aside in both majority and minority opinions.

which they render possible is less than that which would result from total exclusion."[61]

Neither the minority opinion in *A. B. Dick* by Chief Justice White nor the majority opinion in *Motion Picture Patents* by Justice Clark presents a *reasoned* analysis for overturning the "divisibility of use" rule with respect to patent licensing arrangements. Their conclusions rest on the "indefensible premise that a restriction on the use of materials with a machine is not a restriction on the use of the machine with materials."[62]

The pre–Clayton Act development of the law on price-restrictive licensing was as unstructured as tie-in law in terms of providing a reasoned decision process. And early antitrust decisions under the Sherman Act, although stressing a primary concern with price-fixing and market-division agreements, made little or no distinction between vertical and horizontal price-fixing. As has been stressed, the *Dr. Miles* opinion in 1911 had decided that vertical fixing of dealers' prices by a manufacturer was no more lawful than was horizontal price-fixing among dealers.

Price-Fixing, the Horizontal Agreement, and the Scope Problem

Price-restrictive patent licensing was approved by the Supreme Court in 1902 in *Bement* v. *National Harrow Company*, and again in 1907 by a circuit court of appeals in the *Rubber Tire Wheel* case. And both of these cases involved what has come to be characterized as "industrywide" price-fixing. The licensees whose pricing freedom was restricted under the patent license made up a substantial proportion of the industry in question. And in *Standard Sanitary Manufacturing Company* v. *United States*[63] in 1912, Justice McKenna wrote with approval of the *Bement* case, quoting that the Sherman Act "clearly does not refer to that kind of a restraint of interstate commerce which may arise from reasonable and legal conditions imposed upon the assignee or licensee of a patent by the owner thereof, restricting the terms upon which the article may be used and *the price to be demanded therefor*."[64] And as indicated by his objection the following year in *Bauer* v. *O'Donnell* to the impropriety of a patentee using

61. Powell, "Nature of the Patent Right," p. 679.
62. Ibid., p. 686.
63. 226 U.S. 20 (1912).
64. Ibid., p. 40 (emphasis added).

resale price maintenance, Justice McKenna saw no plausible distinction between price maintenance and resale price maintenance in terms of permissibility under patent licensing agreements.

Justice McKenna, however, writing for a unanimous Court, decided in the *bathtub* case that the price-fixing licensing arrangements under an assumed valid patent violated the Sherman Act. Here the patents related to a tool (for imparting enameling powder evenly to hot cast iron) used in the manufacture of unpatented bathroom fixtures. In this case each of sixteen defendants, comprising companies producing 85 percent of the enamelware produced in the United States, entered into a licensing arrangement (contingent upon their competitors' entering) with a nonproducing contracting party holding three patents transferred to it from competing producers. The government contended, and the Supreme Court found, that this case was an instance of an attempt to conceal an agreement fixing prices and interfering with competitors under the guise of a legitimate licensing arrangement for the use of patents. The licensing provisions, as well as the undisguised purpose of the originator of the scheme to eliminate cutthroat competition in the enamelware business, would have made it possible to distinguish the "use divisibility" cases. Patent scope as measured by competitive superiority was exceeded. Justice McKenna emphasized facts which showed clearly that elimination of competition from enamelware produced by nonpatented processes was both intended and effected through the license agreements; but the decision never explicitly indicated that the absence of such intent or such licensing provisions would have made the case go the other way.

McKenna's *bathtub* opinion described practices he recognized and described as being unrelated to maximizing reward to the patent owners: "What relation," McKenna asked, "has the fixing of a price of the ware to the production of 'seconds?' "[65] Seconds were imperfectly enameled fixtures largely generated by unpatented production methods. The license agreements provided that no seconds be marketed. This was thus the practical equivalent of an agreement among 85 percent of the industry not to market products competing with those produced under process patents. Moreover, the organizer of the scheme had testified, and McKenna quoted him in his opinion, that he "hoped to enable the companies to abolish ruinous competition" and to get a "revenue for each of the companies to enable them to

65. Ibid., p. 41.

make a reasonable profit."[66] And further, "On March 30, 1910, the Manufacturers' Association passed a resolution and a committee of five was constituted, to be known as the price and schedule committee, to which license agreements and resale agreements [jobbers margins were guaranteed and they in turn would not deal in seconds] should be referred. This committee was to interview the various manufacturers and obtain their consent to the agreements 'when the consent of 83% of the production' was had."[67]

With respect to the cooperation of numerous licensee competitors in formulating and supervising the scheme, the existence of an escrow arrangement calling for the licensing contracts to be in force only after a large part of the industry was signed up, and with respect to royalty rebates payable on good pricing performance, the *bathtub* case closely paralleled the scheme adopted in *Rubber Tire Wheel*. That case in turn was patterned in no small measure on what was done in the earlier *Harrow* case. The treatment of "seconds"—in effect an agreement among most competitors not to deal in products competing with the process patent—could have been used as a distinguishing characteristic, making this case, unlike the others, hinge on the fact that the agreement among competitors was unrelated to the patent or the maximization of reward under it. McKenna said as much, but he did not rest his decision on this crucial economic difference relating to the competitive superiority afforded by the patents. Rather, he threw doubt on his own rationale by not mentioning the *Rubber Tire Wheel* case at all. By hedging the basis for his decision, he offended neither the majority nor the minority in the *A. B. Dick* case, a case upon which the defendants in *Standard Sanitary* had relied most heavily in trying to get Court approval. McKenna, rather than being specific about what made for antitrust violation in *Standard Sanitary*, after pointing out that the agreements there combined the manufacturers and jobbers in very much the same manner as manufacturers and jobbers had been combined in other combinations condemned by the Court,[68] then adverted to a "necessity" test, which scarcely clarified his holding:

66. Ibid., p. 42.
67. Ibid., p. 43.
68. Specifically, in this connection, he referred to Continental Wallpaper Co. v. Voight & Sons Co., 212 U.S. 227 (1909). This case involved a combination of more than thirty formerly competing concerns which manufactured and sold more than 98 percent of all the wallpaper sold in the United States. These

The agreements clearly, therefore, transcended *what was necessary* to protect the use of the patent or the monopoly which the law conferred upon it. They passed to the purpose and accomplished a restraint of trade condemned by the Sherman law.[69]

The line between necessary patent protection and illegal trade restraint which McKenna convincingly found that the defendants had crossed was not clearly drawn. He specifically overruled no preceding case. At the same time he specifically affirmed the right of a patentee to fix the price at which licensees might sell patented products (affirming this aspect of *Bement* v. *National Harrow*). He also cast considerable doubt that the kind of industrywide arrangements involved in that case and in *Rubber Tire Wheel* could withstand judicial scrutiny if presented to the Court as Sherman Act cases in which patents were alleged to be mere guises for a combination among competitors.

The narrowest reading of the McKenna opinion, an interpretation least disruptive of permissible patent licensing practice previously affirmed by 1912, is that here for the first time the "patent scope" question was raised, and raised in a manner making it apparent that what has been described as the "competitive superiority of the patent" was exceeded. Justice Lurton, who wrote the opinions permitting the tie-ins in *Button-Fastener* and *A. B. Dick*, had done so precisely on the grounds that this was not so in those cases. He was not compelled, therefore, to dissent from McKenna's opinion in *Standard Sanitary*.

In the following year, 1913, however, when resale price maintenance of patented products was held to violate antitrust law by application of the rationale of the *Dr. Miles* case, no exceeding of "competitive superiority" in a manner different from that in *A. B. Dick* was exposed. And in 1917, in *Motion Picture Patents*, *A. B. Dick* was overruled, not by ignoring "competitive superiority" but by erroneously finding it to be exceeded.

Thus by 1917 the logic of patent misuse law was, except possibly

---

concerns, while maintaining their separate plants and identities, placed themselves under the control of a committee which decided the amount of production, patterns to be produced, prices to be charged, equalization of freight, and classification of dealers. And in this wallpaper case, as in the enamelware case, margins were guaranteed to jobbers through resale price maintenance contracts in return for which the jobbers were obliged to puchase solely from members of the combination.

69. Standard Sanitary Manufacturing Co. v. U.S., 226 U.S. 20 (1912), at pp. 48, 49 (emphasis added).

for resale price maintenance,[70] substantially rationalized on the kind of test the preceding analysis has called for. The *rule* of reason had not disappeared, but the reasoning had already become badly battered. After 1917, as subsequent chapters will indicate, judicial interpretation of permissible licensing practice has led, with few exceptions, to more and more constriction on the means by which patentees may maximize patent reward.

70. The "scope" problem did not receive explicit attention in the early resale price maintenance cases. But resale price maintenance in the drug industry and in the book industry—Dr. Miles and Bauer v. O'Donnell involved the former, and Bobbs-Merrill v. Strauss involved the latter—was then known to be widely used as a part of broader schemes involving horizontal arrangements of the sort described in the Standard Sanitary case and in the Continental Wallpaper case. (See note 68 supra, and the text at this point. See also Bowman, "Prerequisites and Effects of Resale Price Maintenance," 22 *U. Chi. L. Rev.* 825 [1955], at pp. 844–45.) Thus by 1911, when Justice Hughes wrote the Dr. Miles opinion, the close and well-known affinity of resale price maintenance with horizontal agreements among dealers and manufacturers made it easy to slip into the error that *all* resale price maintenance, vertically or horizontally imposed, was of this type. Were this so, a "scope" question, recognized or not, clearly would be involved.

8

Legally Permissible Use Restriction in Patent Licenses after Passage of the Clayton Act: Tying Cases and the "Scope" Question

---

The Shoe Machinery Cases: Similar Issues under the Sherman and Clayton Acts

In 1918, shortly after the *Motion Picture Patents* decision against the permissibility of selling a patented projection machine on condition that it be used only with designated films, the Supreme Court was faced with a similar problem involving the legality of a lease, rather than a sale, of patented shoe machines, with similar and more extensive restrictions upon use imposed upon licensees.[1] This case, like *Motion Picture Patents*, was initiated before passage of the Clayton Act. The 1917 decision in *Motion Picture Patents*, however, tested permissible use restrictions under patent law. The 1917 *Shoe Machinery* decision raised the question of permissible use restriction under antitrust law—here the Sherman Act. Justice McKenna, writing for a divided court, with two separate dissents and two justices abstaining, upheld the lease arrangement and rejected the government's contention that the Sherman Act was violated. This case, instituted before but decided after the passage of the Clayton Act, involved alleged violation of both sections 1 and 2 of the Sherman Act. This suit involved two assertions: (1) a combination and conspiracy between formerly independent shoe machinery manufacturers to monopolize the shoe machinery business, and (2) machinery lease agreements, charged to be the means by which competition was prevented and "inventive genius subjected to the designs of the combiners and conspirators, and auxiliary machines and accessories controlled and made

---

1. U.S. v. United Shoe Machinery Co., 247 U.S. 32 (1918).

subsidiary."[2] The case had been dismissed on both counts by the district court in Massachusetts in 1915.[3]

The Supreme Court affirmed the lower court on both counts over strenuous dissent. In considering the combination of formerly separate companies into the United Shoe Machinery Company, Justice Mc-Kenna, following earlier precedent of the 1913 Holmes opinion in *United States* v. *Winslow*,[4] found the combination reasonable. In *Winslow* the patented machines were found to be complementary, not competing. No competition was eliminated by the combination. "On the face of it the combination was simply an effort after greater efficiency."[5]

In regard to the leasing arrangements, Justice McKenna, having found the combination to be made up of parts which were noncompeting[6] and based on unchallenged patents, proceeded to the question whether the patent rights were lawfully exerted in the leases. In summarizing the various provisions, McKenna was unable to find any single lease clause, or all of them together, to be anything more than an appropriate means of exercising the large competitive superiority of United machines and service. Nor did he find, as the government had alleged, that the leasing provisions were coercively imposed:[7] "it is impossible to believe, and the court below refused to find, that the great business of the United Shoe Machinery Company has been built up by coercion of its customers and that its machinery has been installed in most of the large factories of the country by the exercise of power, even that of patents. The installations could have had no other incentive than the excellence of the machines and the advantage of their use."[8]

---

2. Ibid., p. 34
3. U.S. v. United Shoe Machinery Co. of N.J. 222 Fed. 349 (1915).
4. 227 U.S. 202 (1913).
5. Ibid., p. 217.
6. U.S. v. United Shoe Machinery Co., 247 U.S. 32 (1918), at p. 44: "It may be that there was a certain interchangeability in the described machines, but, in the opinion of the trial court, there was, notwithstanding, no practical competition between them."
7. Why "coercively imposed" should be a criterion for the exercise of legalized monopoly (a patent) was not explained here, nor has it been elsewhere. In economic terms all exercise of monopoly power is "coercive." Setting a single royalty rate, for example, coerces licensees into paying higher prices than they would have to pay but for the patent.
8. U.S. v. United Shoe Machinery Co., 247 U.S. 32 (1918), at p. 66. See note 7 supra. McKenna is vague indeed about coercion; but the statement— "The installations could have had no other incentive than the excellence of

Justice Day wrote a dissent vigorously at odds with McKenna's conclusions concerning both the purpose and the effect of the leasing provisions. Day posed two questions deserving consideration as to leasing. First, he asked whether certain provisions of these lease agreements violated the Sherman Act by their terms. And second, were they immune from the requirements of the act because the machinery made and leased was under letters patent?

Day's view of the lease clauses, which McKenna had viewed as normal means of maximizing reward from strong patents and superior efficiency, was that it "seems apparent" that the lease restrictions would "at least tend to monopolize an important trade in interstate commerce ... from a mere statement of their terms, having in mind their natural and necessary effect."[9]

Regarding his first question, whether the lease agreements *of themselves* should be considered within the terms of the Sherman Act, Day summarized five lease provisions: (1) the prohibitive clause (welting machine leases stating that preparatory work could not be done on the machines of others); (2) the exclusive use clause (lasting machine leases calling for all lasting to be done on United machines); (3) the additional machine clause (if metallic machines under lease become fully utilized additional United machines will be leased); (4) the product tie-in (all fastening material used with leased machines must be purchased exclusively from the lessor); and (5)[10] the cancellation provision (violating the provision of one lease may terminate all leases). Day's dissenting judgment on all of these was that they were devices "by which the purposes of the Act [Sherman Act] to protect the freedom of interstate commerce may be thwarted and monopolies promoted and created."[11] According to Day, the dominating control of the shoe machinery business by United gave a "necessary effect" to the prohibitive provisions of the leases. This suggested, although it was never spelled out in the opinion, that when a high degree of market power in an industry, or in an important segment of an industry, was achieved, a different and stricter standard was appropriate. And this stricter standard, he held, did not depend upon how the power

---

the machines and the advantage of their use"—at least suggests that his meaning of "coercion" is extracting more reward than is due to the competitive superiority of valid patents.

9. Ibid., p. 70.
10. Day lists this as (6), but no (5) is listed. See ibid., p. 69.
11. Ibid., p. 69.

was achieved. United's dominance had not been achieved by horizontal merger or by agreement among competitors as was true in the *Addyston Pipe*,[12] *Standard Oil*,[13] and *American Tobacco*[14] cases. Day placed heavy stress on the adverse effect of the lease provisions on competitors and potential competitors of United. In answering his question whether the lease agreements of themselves were within the terms of the Sherman Act, Day adopted a "fate of competitors" monopolization theory which the legislature had written into the Clayton Act in 1914, even though that act was not directly applicable to the case before him.[15] In fact, section 3 of the Clayton Act, stressing the shutting out of competitors, reads, except for the qualifying clause calling for possible lessening of competition or tendency toward monopoly, as if it were written from a model of shoe machinery practice.[16]

Day's dissenting answer to his first question adopted a hypothesis as obvious theory. The theory, although not described as such, was that full-line forcing, tie-ins, and similar licensing provisions make it so difficult for competitors to enter markets (except with a wide range of products not in the range of their production potential) that

12. U.S. v. Addyston Pipe & Steel Co., 85 F. 271 (C.C.A. 6th 1898).
13. Standard Oil of N.J. v. U.S., 221 U.S. 1 (1911).
14. U.S. v. American Tobacco Co., 221 U.S. 106 (1911).
15. Clayton Act, 38 Stat. 730 (1914) § 3. "That it shall be unlawful for any person engaged in commerce, in the course of such commerce, to lease or make a sale or contract for sale of goods, wares, merchandise, machinery, supplies, or other commodities, whether patented or unpatented, for use, consumption, or resale within the United States or any Territory thereof or the District of Columbia or any insular possession or other place under the jurisdiction of the United States, or fix a price charged therefor, or discount from, or rebate upon, such price, on condition, agreement or understanding that the lessee or purchaser thereof shall not use or deal in the goods, wares, merchandise, machinery, supplies, or other commodities of a competitor or competitors of the lessor or seller, *where the effect of such lease, sale, or contract for sale or such condition, agreement, or understanding may be to substantially lessen competition or tend to create a monopoly in any line of commerce*" (emphasis added).
The qualifying clause here italicized has been the subject of much controversy and criticism. Some would read the act almost as if this clause did not exist. The reading more compatible with the thesis of this critique is that the act, with its qualifying clause, should be read as a statutory embodiment of a very dubious economic hypothesis about the means by which competition *might* be restricted or monopoly created through practices driving or keeping competitors out of markets.
16. Justice Day, in his dissent (p. 70) cites committee reports referring to the shoe machinery licensing practice, which indicates that this identification was hardly accidental.

they should be presumptively illegal under the Sherman Act when the imposer of the conditions has a dominant position.

Moving to his second point, whether the existence of patents should change the above conclusion, his answer was at base the same as the minority opinion in *A. B. Dick* and the majority opinion in *Motion Picture Patents*, cases concerning tying arrangements. For him the restrictions went beyond the patent, and therefore the proper conclusion in any tying case should not be different under lease from that under sale.

Day's dissent was convincing to three of seven justices. It had much in common, except the conclusions reached, with McKenna's majority opinion. Each reflected strong convictions, almost religiously held, about the nature of the shoe machinery combine and its practices. Neither felt compelled to acknowledge any merit in the contentions of the other. Day, in discussing the leasing arrangements, saw nothing but foreclosure of competitors, and therefore restraint on existing and potential competition. He gave no recognition to efficiency and little or none to allowing patentees the full reward for "competitive superiority." At least not when a concern was as "great and powerful" as United. McKenna, of course, had been equally disdainful of the possible anticompetitive effects from foreclosure of competitors that Day exclusively stressed. Although this case provided a challenging opportunity for a rational resolution of the efficiency/trade restraint dilemma essential to good antitrust policy, the case did not come to grips with it, and passage of the Clayton Act, with its stress on exclusionary techniques giving rise to possible new monopoly, converted the Day minority opinion into the majority opinion in a new shoe machinery case.

In 1921 the Supreme Court again was confronted with the matter of United Shoe Machinery's leases. This time, however, the case was brought under the Clayton Act, section 3. The majority opinion, this time by Justice Day, who wrote the dissent in the 1917 Sherman Act case, carried all the participating justices except McKenna.[17] Brandeis again took no part. The issues were made up, testimony was taken, and a decree was granted by the district court enjoining the use of certain clauses in the leases. The court below[18] found that United controlled more than 95 percent of the business in the machine classes

17. United Shoe Machinery Corp. et al. v. U.S., 258 U.S. 451 (1922).
18. 264 Fed. 138.

covered by the case, that United "did not act oppressively in the enforcement of forfeiture clauses,"[19] that the machines were of excellent quality, and that valuable service and prompt repairs were provided lessees. Moreover, the validity of no patent was called into question. The central question presented was whether the exclusionary provisions of the shoe machinery leases violated section 3 of the Clayton Act because "the effect of such leases . . . may be to substantially lessen competition or tend to create a monopoly."[20]

The district court had found against United and entered a decree enjoining the restrictive use clause, the exclusive use clause, the supplies clause, the patent insole clause (*other* operations had to be performed on United machines), the additional machinery clause, the factory output clause, and the discriminatory royalty clause (lower royalty for lessees who used United's lasting machines). The district court also held that United had the right to cancel a lease for violations of its particular terms but that it could not, without violating the Clayton Act, cancel a particular lease because a lessee had violated another lease.

Although the lease clauses enjoined by the decree did not contain specific agreements not to use the machinery of a competitor, the lower court found that such was their practical effect. The likelihood that the leases may have been used to substantially lessen competition or to tend to create monopoly merely seemed apparent to the court. Justice Day wrote: "That such restrictive and tying agreements must necessarily lessen competition and tend toward monopoly is, we believe . . . apparent."[21]

Concerning the previous Supreme Court finding that the lease arrangements did not violate the Sherman Act, the Court held that a cause of action under the Clayton Act was not the same as under the Sherman Act. In the Sherman Act case the majority held that the patent rights were lawfully exerted in the leases and they were no more than an exercise of the patent monopoly. Why, asked Day, should a different answer derive from application of the Clayton Act? Day's answer was that "Congress has undertaken to deny the protection of patent rights to such covenants as come within the terms of

19. United Shoe Machinery Corp. et al. v. U.S., 258 U.S. 451 (1922), at p. 455.
20. Clayton Act, 38 Stat. 730 (1914) § 3.
21. United Shoe Machinery Corp. et al. v. U.S., 258 U.S. 451 (1922), at p. 457.

the Clayton Act."[22] And, "The patent grant does not limit the right of Congress to enact legislation not interfering *with the legitimate rights secured by the patent* but prohibiting in the public interest the making of agreements *which may lessen competition and build up monopoly.*"[23]

Day's questions concerning why these leasing arrangements, legal under the Sherman Act, should be illegal under the Clayton Act was not directly answered. His dissent in the prior shoe machinery case tried under the Sherman Act with respect to these leasing provisions indicated that he believed the provisions were illegal under either act, for precisely the same reasons. He viewed the *legitimate* rights of the patentee as being exceeded and the lease provisions as illegal under either statute. But since he carried with him all participating justices except McKenna on the proposition that leasing practices legal under the Sherman Act should be illegal under the Clayton Act, this case stands for the proposition that more strict standards of permissible patent practice are applicable under the "incipient monopoly" theory embodied in the Clayton Act than under the Sherman Act. Adverse effect on competitors of licensing provisions preventing lessees from licensing certain non-United machines or giving more favorable terms for multiple leases were not analyzed as means of extracting the maximum reward based on the competitive superiority of United's admittedly valid and valuable patents. Neither was there discussion of the possible economies of multiple machine servicing. The tendency toward monopoly was obvious to the Court.

This Clayton Act case construed the "incipiency" hypothesis of the Clayton Act so as to greatly bolster the leveraging theory of *Motion Picture Patents*. In addition it initiated a trend that continues to plague antitrust policy. It greatly strengthened the mythology, exposed in chapter 6, that an adverse effect on competitors is the presumptive equivalent of an adverse effect upon competition—almost as if the Clayton Act, particularly its section 3, had omitted the qualifying clause calling for some probability of a substantial lessening of competition or a tendency for the creation of monopoly.

The interesting economic problems involving the possible effects of use restrictions on licensees by a dominant firm with multiple and interrelated patents were not exposed by the foregoing shoe machinery

22. Ibid., p. 462.
23. Ibid., p. 464 (emphasis added).

cases. The Supreme Court did not, either by application of the Sherman Act or by application of the Clayton Act, feel compelled to assess whether United's patent licensing policy gave rise to monopoly power exceeding the "competitive advantage" of its patents. And with respect to the holding by the court that non-full-line competitors, or potential competitors, were kept from the market to the detriment of competition, the clear implication was that entry of successful and efficient competitors to United could be expected if United were to cease tying. But Day's decision in *Shoe Machinery* did not assess the probability of increased competition through new entry by firms making noninfringing shoe machines. This hypothesis, the basis for the Clayton Act's section 3, was for the Court tantamount to a conclusion.

At this time the Court still recognized the validity of merging concerns with complementary rather than competing patents or production facilities. This was because no anticompetitive result could be found from such combinations and because efficiencies were recognized. This kind of test, however, was not applied to the means by which the admittedly valid and complementary patents were exploited. Tying one patent to another patent, even when they were owned by the same company, thus came to be on the same legal footing as tying unpatented materials. That the joint exploitation of two complementary monopolies by tying them together might lead to greater output at lower prices in the manner indicated in chapters 5 and 6 was not evaluated by the contestants or by the Court. Incipient monopoly by foreclosing competitors or potential competitors was the question to which the Clayton Act directed attention. The answer was established by neither theory nor evidence. It was assumed.

Tying Cases after the Shoe Machinery Cases

Because the shoe machinery cases stressed the adverse effect of licensing practice upon competitors under circumstances in which the market position of United was so large and well entrenched, there remained the question whether the outcome of this case, as a practical or predictive matter, would be applied to concerns much less dominant, or to firms having competitors with equal or stronger market position.

Similarly unclear were questions of the possible legality of alternatives to the proscribed restrictions on the use of patents, under sale or lease. Could quality control justify a tie-in? Would the tie-in rule apply to nonpatented items if competitors were given access equal to the patentee's in supplying tied products? Would conditions of supply or the functions provided by tied products be relevant to the legality of a tie-in? What is the relationship between the use of tie-ins and the status of infringers or contributory infringers? Are tie-ins that do not violate the Clayton Act legal?[24]

After passage of the Clayton Act the restrictions on use, especially use with specified materials, became increasingly stringent. The *Carbice* case[25] in 1931, *International Business Machines* case[26] in 1936, *Morton Salt* [27] and *B. B. Chemical*[28] in 1942, the *Mercoid* cases[29,30] in 1944, *International Salt*[31] in 1947, and *Northern Pacific Railway Company* v. *United States*[32] in 1958 (a nonpatent tie-in case) indicate how the Supreme Court was unremittingly following and strengthening the "leveraging fallacy" of Justice White in *Motion Picture Patents* and the "anticompetitor is anticompetition" conclusion of Day in *Shoe Machinery.*

Function of the Unpatented Tied Product Is Immaterial

In *Carbice*, a case involving a patent for a "transportation package consisting of a protective casing of insulating material having packed therein a quantity of frozen carbon dioxide in an insulating container and a quantity of freezable product," there was no patent on the refrigerant, dry ice, or the machine for making it. Neither was the process for making or using solid carbon dioxide (dry ice) patented. The Dry Ice Corporation was the exclusive licensee of the combination patent. The circuit court of appeals had found this patent to be valid and contributorily infringed by Carbice.[33] Dry Ice Corporation did not make or sell the "transportation package." Neither did it formally license buyers of its dry ice to use the invention. Rather it obtained a royalty equivalent by selling its dry ice invoiced with a notice

24. Morton Salt v. Suppiger, 314 U.S. 488 (1942).
25. Carbice Corp. v. American Patents Corp., 283 U.S. 27 (1931).
26. International Business Machines Corp. v. U.S., 298 U.S. 131 (1936).
27. Morton Salt v. Suppiger, 314 U.S. 488 (1942).
28. B. B. Chemical v. Ellis, 314 U.S. 495 (1942).
29. Mercoid Corp. v. Mid-Continent Investment Co., 320 U.S. 661 (1944).
30. Mercoid Corp. v. Minneapolis-Honeywell Co., 320 U.S. 680 (1944).
31. International Salt Co. v. U.S., 332 U.S. 392 (1947).
32. 356 U.S. 1 (1958).
33. 38 F. 2d 62.

which required that it be used with cartons approved by Dry Ice Corporation, and that these approved cartons only be used with dry ice provided by Dry Ice Corporation. Purchase of cartons from Dry Ice Corporation was not insisted upon, and no separate royalty was charged in addition to that indirectly received from the sale of the unpatented dry ice. The patent was for a combination of which no elements were patented.

Carbice, having knowingly supplied dry ice for use in the patented combination, claimed that the situation here was indistinguishable from the tie-in of films to projection equipment, held invalid in *Motion Picture Patents*. The plaintiff, Dry Ice Corporation, attempted to distinguish that case on the ground that the unpatented refrigerant was a *necessary element* of the patented product. Moreover, to distinguish *Morgan Envelope*,[34] involving the tying of toilet paper to a toilet paper dispenser, which was held illegal, the further claim was made that dry ice was a *dynamic* element in producing refrigeration whereas paper was a *passive* element in the bathroom combination. Not surprisingly, Justice Brandeis, who wrote the opinion for the Supreme Court, was not impressed with the subtlety of these distinctions. The function and character of the unpatented product were held to be immaterial. The leverage theory of tie-ins was not reassessed. Relief was denied because Dry Ice Corporation was attempting "to employ the patent *to secure a limited monopoly of unpatented material used in applying the invention.*"[35] Brandeis thus viewed the *Carbice* case as a scope case.[36] And he seemed convinced, as justices White and Day before him had been convinced, in spite of the compelling economic arguments to the contrary by justices Holmes and Lurton, that tie-ins allowed a patentee to derive the equivalent of two monopoly revenues instead of one. "If [read *because*?] a monopoly could be so expanded," Brandeis wrote, "the owner of a patent for a product might conceivably monopolize the commerce in a large part of the unpatented materials used in its manufacture. . . . The owner of the patent in suit might conceivably secure a limited monopoly for supply-

34. Morgan Envelope Co. v. Albany Perforated Wrapping Paper Co., 152 U.S. 425, 433 (1894).
35. Carbice Corp. v. American Patents Corp., 283 U.S. 27 (1931), at pp. 33–34 (emphasis added).
36. In 1938, the rule of the Carbice case was held to be applicable whether the patent is for a machine, a product, or a process, and whatever the nature of the means utilized. See Leitch Manufacturing Co. v. Barber Co., 302 U.S. 458 (1938).

ing not only of solid carbon dioxide, but also of the ice cream and other foods, as well as of the cartons in which they are shipped."[37]

Quality Control and Tie-ins

The *International Business Machines* case,[38] decided by the Supreme Court in 1936, was a government case under section 3 of the Clayton Act to enjoin IBM from leasing its tabulating and other machines upon condition that the lessees use with the machines only tabulating cards manufactured by IBM.[39]

Appellant IBM argued that a conclusion of the district court that the tie-in tended to create a monopoly was incorrect. Two principal contentions were presented. The first was that its leases were lawful because very special cards, conforming to precise specifications, including precise electrical contacts, were essential to acceptable operations. Second, it was argued that the protection afforded by insisting on use of IBM cards could not extend monopoly. The tied cards were patented (when they had been punched). How then, IBM argued, since it already had a monopoly of the right to manufacture, use, and vend the cards separately and in combination with its sorting and tabulating machines, could IBM conceivably be creating a monopoly in the tied product? Brandeis did not attempt to answer this interesting "leverage" question. He took the alternative route to finding illegality —foreclosure. Stressing the language of the Clayton Act's section 3, "whether patented or unpatented" and citing Day's 1922 *Shoe Machinery* opinion, he found an adverse effect on competitors or potential competitors who, but for the tie-in, might be supplying cards for IBM machines. Again, as in *Shoe Machinery*, no attempt was made to spell out the competitor-competition link. Ignored was the question, Why, if IBM's cards were not competitively superior, would IBM not buy them rather than make its own whether or not card patents existed? Brandeis, like Day, in effect interpreted the Clayton Act as if it had no qualifying clause reading "where the *effect* of such lease, sale, or contract for same or such condition, agreement, or understanding may be to substantially *lessen competition* or tend to create a monopoly in any line of commerce."[40]

37. Carbice Corp. v. American Patents Corp., 283 U.S. 27 (1931), at p. 32.
38. International Business Machines Corp. v. U.S., 298 U.S. 131 (1936).
39. Two other defendants, using similar tie-ins, were involved in the government's case at the federal court level.
40. Clayton Act, 38 Stat. 730 (1914) § 3 (emphasis added).

The Brandeis opinion broke new ground, greatly narrowing a possible loophole for avoiding the strict rule against tie-ins. With the IBM decision the use of a tie-in for quality control or the maintenance of goodwill came to be greatly limited as a means of validating tying sales.

Just one year before this Brandeis decision the Seventh Circuit Court of Appeals in 1935 in *Pick Manufacturing Company* v. *General Motors Corporation*[41] decided that section 3 of the Clayton Act was not violated by GM's agreement with its dealers proscribing use in its repair of Chevrolets any parts not made or authorized by the Chevrolet division of General Motors. Pick, a supplier of competitive parts, contended that he was foreclosed from substantial business by this agreement in violation of the Clayton Act. The court, after noting that there were innumerable other markets for Pick parts, went on to stress the importance of General Motors goodwill, the difficulty of customers' knowing the true cause of improper repair, and, even after expiration of warranty, the possible harm to General Motors because "the natural result is blame of the manufacturer." The conclusion of the court of appeals was:

> We believe that the convenants complained of protect appellees in their warranties of automobiles and in their continued sale thereof with the intent to promote and preserve the goodwill of the purchasing public, essential to business success; and they do not and will not lessen competition substantially, within the meaning of the act, or tend to create monopoly.[42]

IBM made the same kind of argument with respect to using its cards with its machines that GM had successfully advanced in the *Pick* case. Although the goodwill of IBM in assuring customer satisfaction in its card-using operations seems no less important than GM's interest in automobile service, Brandeis did not attempt to spell out the difference. Nor did the Supreme Court, several months later, see fit to explain the difference when it affirmed *Pick*.[43]

Speculatively, however, several differences could have been controlling. The most obvious factual difference was the relative size of the market foreclosed. In *IBM* the court noted that the appellant made

41. 80 F. 2d 641, affirmed per curiam, shortly after the IBM decision, 299 U.S. 3 (1936).
42. Ibid., p. 644.
43. 80 F. 2d 641.

and sold 81 percent of all tabulating cards, and that its principal competitor, Remington Rand, also utilizing a tie-in, sold the remainder. The government, however, under special provisions in its lease from IBM, made large quantities of cards for its own use. Moreover, by stipulation in the IBM suit, "others are capable of manufacturing cards suitable for use in appellant's machines."[44] In *Pick*, in contrast, as the court of appeals stressed, part suppliers had innumerable alternative markets for the sale of parts. They were foreclosed only from sales to General Motors dealers, and even there only from repair of General Motors cars. It should be stressed, however, that the Brandeis decision did not rest on this distinction. But even if the relative size of the "foreclosed" market was at this time thought to be determinative in the outcome of a section 3 tying case, it was to be short-lived. In 1947, the *International Salt* case[45] effectively laid it to rest.

Another possible distinction between the *Pick* and *IBM* cases involves the court's view of the practicality of alternatives to tie-in sales as means of protecting the goodwill of the seller. "Appellant is not prevented from proclaiming the virtues of its own cards or warning against the danger of using, in its machines, cards which do not conform to the necessary specifications, or even making its leases conditional upon the use of cards which conform to them. For aught that appears," wrote Brandeis, "such measures would protect its goodwill, without the creation of monopoly or resort to suppression of competition."[46] The *IBM* case, although not completely closing the door on goodwill as a justification for tie-in sales, went a long way in that direction. The Court, believing that it had found "elimination of business competition and the creation of monopoly" to arise from tying, was not willing to make a goodwill exception, at least without evidence that goodwill alternatives were not available.

There has been no subsequent clarification by the Supreme Court indicating how much reliance can still be placed upon the *Pick* case. As has been indicated, relying upon the accessibility of alternative markets as a test of foreclosure under a tie-in has for practical purposes been erased by subsequent decisions. On the other hand, a possible narrow exception, although never passed upon by the Su-

44. International Business Machines Corp. v. U.S., 298 U.S. 131 (1936), at p. 139.
45. International Salt Co. v. U.S. 332 U.S. 392 (1947).
46. International Business Machines Corp. v. U.S., 298 U.S. 131 (1936), at p. 140.

preme Court, may be found in a First Circuit Court of Appeals decision in 1961.[47] In the *A. O. Smith* case it was the manufacturer's policy not to sell its unloaders unless they were to be installed in concurrently purchased or already owned silos of its own manufacture. But because of very special circumstances, in which silos made by others had been permitted but were found unsatisfactory because of special unloading problems, the holding was that the Clayton Act was not violated. Here, unlike the situation in *IBM*, or indeed in *Pick*, there was direct evidence that there was no practical substitute for the tie-in as a means of achieving quality control. Moreover, it is worth noting that the defendant from 1951 to 1957 had sold eighty unloaders to thirty-six customers who did *not* use silos provided by the patentee. It must be concluded that the protection of goodwill is a very narrow exception under tie-in law.

Tie-ins Bar Infringement Suits Even against Noncompetitors

Morton Salt v. *Suppiger*,[48] decided by the Supreme Court in 1942, involved a patent infringement suit. The patent infringed covered a machine for depositing salt tablets in containers used in the canning process. The patentee's practice was to license its machines only on condition that the salt deposited be bought from the patentee. A seller of an infringing unpatented salt-depositing machine contended that his infringement should not be enjoined because the patent was being used to restrain trade in the sale of salt tablets in competition with the patentee's tablets. Granting summary judgment, the district court dismissed the complaint on this ground. The Seventh Circuit Court of Appeals reversed because it could not find a violation of the Clayton Act. It did not appear to this court that this method of use restriction lessened competition or tended to create a monopoly in salt tablets.

Rather than to overturn this finding by the court of appeals with respect to the "competitive effect" prerequisite to violation of the Clayton Act, Justice Stone, writing for an undivided Court, held that whether the Clayton Act was violated did not have to be decided. Rather, the question was "whether a court of equity will lend its aid to protect the monopoly when respondent *is using it as the effective*

---

47. Dehydrating Process Co. v. A. O. Smith Corp., 292 F. 2d 653 (1961).
48. 314 U.S. 488 (1942).

means of restraining competition with its sale of an unpatented article."[49] But *restraining of competition* was precisely what the Seventh
Circuit found not to exist under the Clayton Act. Where, it might seem
reasonable to question, in view of past patent tie-in cases, was a more
stringent rule against this kind of use restriction to be found? The
Supreme Court's ingenious answer implies that misuse under patent
law is a stricter standard than is provided by the Clayton Act's section
3, an interesting view of trade restraint, considering that a primary
purpose of the Clayton Act was to reach anticompetitive practices not
reachable under either patent law or prior antitrust law.

This case did *not*, Justice Stone took pains to point out, turn on the
fact that the alleged infringer competed with the patentee in the sale
of salt tablets. For purposes of this case the Court assumed that "the
petitioner was doing no more than making and leasing the alleged
infringing machines."[50] But the Court went on to point out, citing the
Motion Picture Patents and *Carbice* cases, that an exclusive right,
including the right of excluding others from use, affords no immunity
not within the grant. *Morton Salt*, then, being a "leverage" case involving the suppression of competition in an unpatented product and
viewed as exceeding the scope of the patent grant, need meet no more
test than that tying existed. There is a public interest. "Where the
patent is used as a means of restraining competition with the patentee's
sale of an unpatented product, the successful prosecution of an infringement suit even against one who is not a competitor in such sale
is a powerful aid to the maintenance of the attempted monopoly of
the unpatented articles, and is thus a contributing factor in thwarting
the public policy underlying the grant of the patent."[51]

The patentee argued that competition in supplying salt was not at
issue, and that the doctrine which withholds the aid of courts of equity
from a patentee because he is using the right asserted contrary to the
public interest is a limited one. It is limited to those cases where the
patentee seeks to restrain contributory infringement by the sale to
licensees of a competing unpatented article. The respondent in *Morton
Salt* wanted previous cases distinguished because he sought to restrain
the petitioner from a *direct* infringement involving the manufacture
and sale of the salt-tablet depositor.[52] But the Court, viewing the tie-in,

49. Ibid., p. 490 (emphasis added).
50. Ibid., p. 491.
51. Ibid., p. 493.
52. Ibid., p. 492.

as had courts before it, as an obvious means of creating a limited monopoly in an unpatented product, had no difficulty in barring the prosecution of an infringement suit even against one who is not a competitor of the patentee in the sale of the unpatented tied product. The adverse effect on the public interest is enough, Stone held, regardless of whether a particular defendant suffers from the misuse. This "public interest effect," Stone held, thus made it unnecessary to decide whether the patentee had violated the Clayton Act.

In effect, then, irrespective of whether either competitors or competition in the tied product is shown to be adversely affected, irrespective of whether the competitive superiority of the invention is exceeded, and irrespective even of a showing of a tendency toward lessening of competition or monopoly creation as called for by the Clayton Act, a patent tie-in comes to be so conclusively anticompetitive that neither direct nor contributory infringement actions can be enforced by patentees who utilize this means of use restriction.

In *B. B. Chemical* v. *Ellis*,[53] a companion case to *Morton Salt* in 1942, the Supreme Court also held that the owner of a *method* patent who authorizes manufacturers to use it only with materials furnished by the patentee may not enjoin infringement by one who supplies the manufacturer with materials for use in the patented method. That alternative means of extracting a reward from a valid method patent were not available to the patentee was not of significance to the Court. Since it had already been settled that all tie-ins enlarge or extend a monopoly, it is without significance that it is not practicable to exploit the patent right otherwise.[54]

The Mercoid Cases and Contributory Infringement

Each of the foregoing tying cases involved the use of the patent for a machine or process "to secure a partial monopoly in supplies consumed in its operation or unpatented materials employed in it." This is how Justice Douglas characterized these cases in 1944 in his *Mercoid Corporation* v. *Mid-Continent Investment Company*,[55] decision: "But we can see no difference in principle where the unpatented material or device is an integral part of the structure embodying the pat-

53. B. B. Chemical v. Ellis, 314 U.S. 495 (1942).
54. Ibid., p. 498.
55. Mercoid Corp. v. Mid-Continent Investment Co., 320 U.S. 661 (1944), at p. 665.

ent."[56] *Leeds and Catlin,*[57] decided in 1909, had been authority for the conclusion that one who sells an unpatented part of a combination patent for use in the assembled machine may be guilty of contributory infringement. But, wrote Douglas in commenting on this case in his *Mercoid* opinion, "The protection which the Court in that case extended to the phonograph record, which was an unpatented part of the patented phonograph, is in substance inconsistent with the view which we have expressed in this case . . . [and] must no longer prevail against the defense that a combination patent is being used to protect an unpatented part from competition."[58] The contributory infringer can, according to *Mercoid,* thus stand in no better position than the direct infringer in *Morton Salt.*

In *Mercoid Corporation* v. *Minneapolis-Honeywell Company,*[59] a companion case, Minneapolis-Honeywell had licensed five of its manuturing competitors under a combination patent on a system of furnace control. There were no patents on the parts. The licensees were granted a nonexclusive right to make, use, and sell a "combination furnace control" (defined as a thermostatic switch usable under the combination patent and designed in one unit to control the fan and limit circuits). Royalty payments to Minneapolis-Honeywell were based on sales of the combination furnace controls.[60] Minneapolis-Honeywell, in this second *Mercoid* case, tried on several occasions to induce Mercoid to take a license on the same terms as others. These attempts were unsuccessful, and so Minneapolis-Honeywell brought an infringement suit.

Neither Minneapolis-Honeywell nor Mercoid sold or installed the "system" in furnaces. Neither, therefore, practiced the invention. They were competitors in supplying the unpatented switch used in the combination. These switches, as the circuit court of appeals had held, had "no other use than for accomplishing the sequence of operations of the Freeman patent."[61] This court also concluded that although the con-

---

56. Ibid.
57. Leeds & Catlin Co. v. Victor Talking Machine Co. (no. 2), 213 U.S. 325 (1909).
58. Mercoid Corp. v. Mid-Continent Investment Co., 320 U.S. 661 (1944), at p. 668.
59. 320 U.S. 680 (1944).
60. The licenses also established minimum prices for the sale of controls. Cases covering such practice are discussed in chapter 9.
61. Mercoid Corp. v. Minneapolis-Honeywell Co., 320 U.S. 680 (1944), at p. 683.

trol was unpatented it served "to distinguish the invention" and to mark the "advance in the art" achieved by the Freeman patent.[62] Accordingly, the appeals court had held that "the patent laws permit and the anti-trust laws do not forbid the control over the sale and use of the unpatented device which Minneapolis-Honeywell sought to achieve through its licensing agreements."[63]

The Supreme Court reversed. "The legality of any attempt to bring unpatented goods within the protection of the patent is measured by the anti-trust laws not by the patent law," Justice Douglas held. He then went on to say, citing his companion *Mercoid* v. *Mid-Continent* opinion: "the effort here made to control competition in this unpatented device plainly violates the anti-trust laws, even apart from the price-fixing provisions of the license agreements."[64] To Douglas and five concurring justices it was obvious that there was "control" and that the control was illegal on the authority of *Morton Salt*.

Toward the Per Se Illegality of Tie-ins

In 1947 the Supreme Court specifically held tying arrangements to be illegal per se. In *International Salt Company, Inc.* v. *United States*,[65] Justice Jackson held that it was violative per se of section 1 of the Sherman Act and section 3 of the Clayton Act for the lessor of a patented machine to require lessees to use only the lessor's unpatented products with them. The amount of salt involved in International's leasing contracts amounted to about $500,000 in 1944. This amount of business affected by these contracts, the Court held, "cannot be said to be insignificant or insubstantial."[66] "Under the law, agreements are forbidden which 'tend to create a monopoly,' " wrote Jackson. And then, without explaining how this tendency might take place, he had no difficulty in assuming that the tendency, however slight or however incipient, pointed in only one direction—toward a monopoly. "It is immaterial that the tendency is a creeping one rather than one that proceeds at a full gallop."[67]

62. Ibid.
63. Ibid., p. 684.
64. Ibid.
65. 332 U.S. 392 (1947).
66. Ibid., p. 396.
67. Ibid.

International argued that because its lessees were protected from noncompetitive prices for salt, the tie-in arrangement did not have the adverse effect on competition called for by the Clayton Act. If a lessee were offered salt of equal grade at a price lower than International's, unless the lessor was willing to meet this price, the lessee was not bound by the tying restriction according to the agreement. The argument did not impress the Court. "We do not think this concession relieves the contract of being in restraint of trade, albeit a less harsh one than would result in the absence of such a provision."[68] On this, the main issue involving trade restraint and tendency toward monopoly, there was by now wholehearted agreement on the Supreme Court.[69]

Although International Salt was the "dominant" seller of salt in the United States, as the opinion of the Court indicated, clearly the opinion provides no basis for assuming this was important to the outcome of the case. Rather, as has been stressed, only $500,000 worth of salt was "controlled." The holding was that this was "not insubstantial."

Any lingering doubt about the possible legality of tie-in sales was laid to rest by Justice Black in *Northern Pacific Railway Company* v. *United States*[70] in 1958. "Indeed 'tying agreements serve hardly any purpose beyond the suppression of competition,' " he wrote, quoting Justice Frankfurter.[71] Black went on to write, stressing not only that an adverse effect on a competitor is an adverse effect on competition but in addition that leveraging to new monopoly is involved in tying, "They deny competitors free access to the market for the tied product, not because the party imposing the tying requirements has a better product or a lower price but because of his power or leverage in another market. . . . They are unreasonable in and of themselves whenever a party has sufficient economic power with respect to the tying product to appreciably restrain free competition in the market for this tied product."[72]

How much this "power over the tied" need be is evidenced by the nature of the tying product in the case at issue. Northern Pacific had extensive landholdings. These unique parcels of land were the "tying

---

68. Ibid., p. 397.
69. Ibid., p. 402. Justice Frankfurter, with whom justices Reed and Burton joined, dissented only with respect to relief.
70. 356 U.S. 1 (1958).
71. Standard Oil Co. of California v. U.S., 337 U.S. 293, at pp. 305–6.
72. Northern Pacific Railway Co. v. U.S., 356 U.S. 1 (1958), at p. 6.

product" in this case. Without bothering to mention what proportion of what relevant economic market these holdings composed, and it surely was small indeed, he then went on to the evidence about the existence of power. The answer? Circular but simple. "The very existence of this host of tying arrangements is itself compelling evidence of the defendant's great power, at least where, as here, no other explanation has been offered for these restraints."[73]

The development of the law with respect to tying practice has been a one-way street. Its signpost was misdirected by Justice White in *Motion Picture Patents* in 1917. His leveraging fallacy was received as gospel. Were it true, as succeeding justices assumed, much of the subsequent law would have been unobjectionable. But by parlaying a leverage fallacy with an unproved, incipient monopoly hypothesis (arising from an assumed identity between effect on *competitors* and effect on competition) the Court has since 1917 consistently applied faulty economics leading to the wrong answers to the questions it has asked.

73. Ibid., pp. 7–8. But there was other explanation for the restraints. The tie-in involved preferential shipping over the Northern Pacific. There was minimum rate regulation. The equivalent of a rate reduction through favorable land terms could explain the tie-in without "power in land."

9

Legally Permissible Use Restrictions in Patent Licenses after Passage of the Clayton Act: Price Restrictive Licensing and Territorially Restrictive Licensing

---

Price Restrictive Licensing

Price Restrictive Licensing and Agreement among Competitors

In the preceding chapter the cases dealing with attempted restrictions on use through tying provisions in patent licensing contracts involved what the court saw as improper monopoly-extending, or competitor-disadvantaging imposed by the patentee upon the licensees. No agreement among any competitors or potential competitors was prerequisite to the outcome of these tying cases. The restraints alleged were vertical—"imposed" upon the licensees by the licensor. Previous critical analysis of the tie-in law rests on this fact. As has been stressed, neither economic nor legal analysis has been able to explain or describe how vertical arrangements create monopoly or restrain trade. And none of the cases reviewed in chapter 8 were shown to do so.

Price-restrictive licensing, however, gives rise to the possibility of horizontal agreement among competitors of a kind not involved in tying cases. Analysis in chapter 6 with regard to price maintenance exposed the question, Does price-fixing by a patentee merely exploit the advantage of the patent by its vertical imposition, or does it provide a guise for eliminating competition among noninfringing competitors?

An early example of an agreement among competitors involving products not covered by the patent was illustrated in the *Standard Sanitary* (*bathtub*) case in chapter 7.[1] There the noninfringing patent substitute was the unpatented imperfectly enameled "seconds."

---

1. Standard Sanitary Mfg. Co. v. U.S., 226 U.S. 20 (1912).

The important price-restrictive patent case *United States* v. *General Electric* of 1926,[2] discussed in chapter 6, was decided as a vertical price-fixing case. There was no allegation that either Westinghouse or the other smaller licensees agreed to eliminate competition in competing products. The question at issue was whether a patent owner, General Electric, could license others to make or sell the *patented* product at designated terms of sale, including price. Justice Taft's answer in 1926 was yes. There was no dissent.

This same question previously had been answered in the same way by Justice Peckham in *Bement* v. *National Harrow* in 1902.[3] "The owner of a patented article," Peckham then held, "can, of course, charge such price as he may choose, and the owner of a patent may assign it or sell the right to manufacture and sell the article patented upon the condition that the assignee shall charge a certain amount for such article."[4]

The Taft opinion in *General Electric* allowed the pricing of the licensee's product because this practice (the title-passing question apart) was "reasonably adopted to secure the pecuniary reward" to the patentee.

The major objection to licensee price-fixing—that it can be used as a screen to legalize mutually advantageous price agreements not related to providing the patentee with pecuniary reward due to the competitive superiority of his patents—was not at issue in either the *Bement* or the *General Electric* case.

In the cases concerning price-restrictive licensing after *General Electric*, emphasis has increasingly been upon the conspiratorial aspects of mutually advantageous price-fixing arrangements, and decreasingly upon whether the "conspiracy" is related to the elimination of competition not measured by competitive superiority.

The Department of Justice has long been attempting to undo the *General Electric* decision. As Gerald Gibbons has summarized aptly, "Price-fixing cases in the patent context received high priority in the Justice Department and between 1939 and 1948 the Supreme Court decided nine cases concerning this subject."[5]

2. U.S. v. General Electric Co., 272 U.S. 476 (1926).
3. 186 U.S. 70 (1902).
4. Ibid., p. 93.
5. Gerald R. Gibbons, "Price Fixing in Patent Licenses and the Antitrust Laws," 51 *Va. L. Rev.* 273 (1965), at p. 274. The nine cases referred to by Gibbons are: Interstate Circuit, 1939; Ethyl Gasoline, 1940; Univis, 1942; Sola Electric, 1942; Masonite, 1942; MacGregor v. Westinghouse, 1947; Katzinger,

The Narrowed Scope of Permissible Price-Fixing after General Electric
Interstate Circuit, Incorporated, v. *United States*[6] was decided by the
Supreme Court in 1939. Although this case involved copyrighted films
rather than patented products, the case has had great impact on price-
restrictive patent licensing law (and in a broader context upon antitrust conspiracy law in general because of the standards it set by inference for the establishment of "conspiracy in restraint of trade"). In this
case the appellants argued that distributors of films protected by the
Copyright Act were free to license these films for exhibit subject to
restriction (including admission prices in exhibition houses) "just as a
patentee in a license to manufacture and sell the patented article may
fix the price at which the licensee may sell it."[7] *Bement* and *General
Electric* were cited as the authority for this argument. But after noting
that *Interstate* also forbade its licensees to show other films with its
own, and that this was illegal under the line of tying cases beginning
with *Motion Picture Patents,* the Court went on to say that it was
equally illegal to set "the admission price which shall be paid for an
entertainment *which includes features other than the particular picture
licensed.*"[8]

The inclusion of nonlicensed films in the admission price, however,
was not essential to a finding that overall the Interstate Circuit arrangements were illegal. There was more than a vertical price-fixing arrangement between the copyright owner and his licensees; horizontal
agreement among *competitive* distributors was also found. But the
Court drew no "scope" distinction between horizontal and vertical
agreement. It analogized price control to tying. Controlling price over
an area broader than the single copyrighted film thus became another
application of the "leveraging" fallacy. This led to a further narrowing
of the *General Electric* rule. Unless the price fixed was strictly limited
to a product covered by the patent, it now seemed reasonable to forecast, price control would not be permissible. And, as it was held with
respect to tying one patented article to another patented article in
Shoe Machinery, so it was with respect to fixing prices of two products

---

1947; Line Material, 1948; and Gypsum, 1948. They indicate the result of Thurman Arnold's assistant attorney generalship and the erosion of the General
Electric doctrine.
  6. 306 U.S. 208 (1939).
  7. Ibid., p. 228.
  8. Ibid. (emphasis added).

used together, irrespective of whether or not both were patented or copyrighted.

Since going to a movie inevitably includes the comfort of the seats, the cleanliness of the rest rooms, the convenience of the location, and the possibility of obtaining well-buttered popcorn at reasonable prices, all of which, as much as multiple film features, are encompassed in the admission price, the *Interstate Circuit* case seems to effectively prevent any control of admission prices.

That the price-restrictive licenses, along with clearance provisions concerning first- and second-run showings, were a means of exploiting the competitive superiority of a unique and valuable copyrighted film did not impress the majority. As Justice Roberts emphasized in his dissent, this fixing the prices charged by first-run and subsequent-run theaters and the provision for "clearances" between the showing of first-run and subsequent-run pictures "is a perfectly natural procedure and one obviously required to protect the value of the first-run license."[9] Roberts thus viewed the price provision as a legitimate means of maximizing the reward, not of broadening the scope, of a legitimate monopoly. His view convinced justices McReynolds and Butler, but it did not prevail. The dissent ignored the agreements the majority found between Interstate and its competitors, but the majority, on the other hand, did not distinguish these from those which Interstate *imposed* on its "downstream" distributors and exhibitors. *Interstate Circuit* did not overrule *General Electric*. It did limit the application of price-restrictive licensing to the precise object covered by the patent or copyright.

Industrywide Jobber Licensing: The Ethyl *Case*

The *Ethyl* case,[10] in the following year, confirmed *Interstate*'s limitation on the right of a patentee to fix licensees' prices. Here again there was substantial evidence indicating the use of patents as a screen for broader price-fixing than that reasonably ascribable to the competitive superiority of the legal monopoly. But again the Court did not make the distinction. Rather, it relied heavily on the precedent of tying cases

9. Ibid., p. 238. A "perfectly natural" procedure protecting the first-run license is perhaps a rather obscure way to describe a use restriction when joint products are marketed. But however stated, a serious objection to the majority opinion is invited. It was grounded on the unfounded assumption that two monopolies are somehow created by this method of exploiting one.

10. Ethyl Gasoline Corp., et al., v. U.S., 309 U.S. 436 (1940).

and resale price maintenance cases, thus submerging once more a scope analysis.

The Ethyl Gasoline Corporation was the owner of patents on a fluid compound containing tetraethyl lead, which, when added to gasoline, increased the efficiency of high-compression combustion engines. This corporation manufactured the patented fluid and sold it to refiners and to jobbers of gasoline. At the same time it licensed them to use the patents under specified conditions. Refiners were licensed to manufacture and sell, and jobbers were licensed to sell, gasoline containing the patented fluid. Their sales, however, were limited to other licensed refiners or to jobbers who were also licensed by Ethyl. Sales to retail dealers or consumers were permitted if certain health and safety requirements were met. Minimum octane-rating differentials were set and the licensees were required to set a certain fixed price differential over their best nonpremium grade of commercial gasoline. Ethyl charged no separate royalty but received its return from the sale of the tetraethyl fluid.

This licensing system was very broad. Practically all refiners and some 11,000 of 12,000 gasoline jobbers in the United States were under license. Ethyl generally required each licensed jobber to purchase all his treated fuel from a single supplier and in some instances refused to license jobbers who wished to switch sources of supply. Moreover, it was found to be "an established practice of appellant to investigate the business ethics of licensed jobbers in order to ascertain whether *they maintain the marketing prices*, policies and practices prevailing or ostensibly prevailing in the industry."[11]

This licensing arrangement, its broad operation throughout the oil industry, and especially the method by which it was policed suggested strongly that more than just the price differential of the patented product was being supervised. The scheme, it might have been found, inhibited price competition in all gasoline whether or not it contained the patented tetraethyl fluid. Appellant Ethyl Gasoline Corporation licensed 123 refiners, including every major oil company except the Sun Oil Company, a company not generally doing business through jobbers. These refinery company licensees refined 88 percent of all gasoline sold in the United States, and the gasoline processed by them under license agreements with Ethyl composed 70 percent of gasoline sold. The very breadth of the licensing system, plus the fact that the

---

11. Ibid., p. 454 (emphasis added).

11,000 licensed jobbers were generally required to apply for their licenses *through the refiners* from whom they expected to purchase motor fuel, was explained by the appellant as a means of closely supervising health regulations relating to a poisonous lead substance. But refiners who, under the terms of their license contracts, sold gasoline at a prescribed differential between "regular" and "ethyl" gasoline were also in a position to use their supervision of jobber licenses so as to conform jobber pricing practice to a possible interest of the refiners in avoiding competition among themselves. Although appellant Ethyl argued that "the restraints upon the sale of the patented fuel by the refiners, and the restrictions placed upon the jobbers, are all reasonably necessary for the commercial development of appellant's patents and for insuring a financial return from them,"[12] it is not unreasonable to suppose that licensee refiners found them equally or more useful as a screen for supervising all gasoline prices irrespective of the importance of the Ethyl patents. Why, for example, would it be in the interest of the patentee to insist that a jobber procure a new license before changing his source of supply among refiners? The licensee refiners, as a group, *if* they were using the *Ethyl* patents as a screen for stabilizing prices and eliminating interbrand price competition, would find their recommendation about a necessary license from Ethyl a means of policing price-cutting jobbers who otherwise would have alternative sources of supply. The Court found it a "long established practice of appellant to refuse to grant licenses to jobbers who cut prices or refuse to conform to the market policies and posted prices *of the major refineries or the market leaders* among them."[13] And if policing of price-cutting jobbers by licensee refiners were part of the value received by refiners from their patent licenses, refiners not dealing through jobbers would find a license under the Ethyl patents less valuable. One major refiner, the Sun Oil Company, did not take a license. Perhaps it was happenstance that this company did not generally do business through jobbers. The *Ethyl* decision, however, did not turn on the fact that the Ethyl patents were a screen for industrywide price-fixing of unpatented gasoline. The case was easier to decide on a narrower issue, resale price maintenance. And this obviated, of course, a careful appraisal of whether the licensing arrangements in the *Ethyl* case exceeded in

12. Ibid., p. 451.
13. Ibid., p. 450 (emphasis added). It is also notable that Standard Oil Co., N.J., owned 50 percent of the Ethyl Corporation, the owner of the tetraethyl lead patents.

scope what would have reasonably been attributable to the competitive superiority afforded by patents acknowledged to be valuable.

Nevertheless, in the *Ethyl* case the Court was not unmindful of the scope question. But Justice Stone got to this question only after going through the now-familiar rigamarole about title passing and how "by its sales to refiners it [Ethyl Corporation, the patent owner] relinquishes its exclusive right to use the patented fluid . . . by authorized sales of the fuel by refiners to jobbers the patent monopoly over it is exhausted."[14] Also, the Court noted, "Agreements for price maintenance are . . . , without more, unreasonable restraints within the meaning of the Sherman Act because they eliminate competition."[15] And by 1940, of course, this legal conclusion had become as applicable to vertical as to horizontal agreements. Stone did stress the primary refiners' interest: "The extent to which appellant's dominion over the jobbers' business goes beyond its patent monopoly, is emphasized by the circumstances here present that the prices and market practices sought to be established *are not those prescribed by appellant-patentee, but by the refiners.* . . . Such benefits as result from control over the marketing of treated fuel by the jobbers accrue primarily to the refiners. . . . The licensing conditions are thus *not* used as a means of stimulating the commercial development and financial return of the patented invention."[16] This conclusion, that the patentee did not benefit his licensees in such manner to maximize return from his patents, is certainly suggestive, but it is scarcely determinative for a conclusion that the patents were a screen for restraining competition in noninfringing products. In the 1912 *Standard Sanitary* case, where the prices of unpatented "seconds" were controlled, it was at least arguable that this made the difference. But by 1940, when *Ethyl* was decided, it was clear that this kind of finding was not needed. *Ethyl*'s outcome was predestined by the line of resale price maintenance cases beginning with *Dr. Miles* in 1911 and extended to patented products in *Bauer* v. *O'Donnell* in 1913.

Price Maintenance Further Limited: The Univis *Case*

In 1942 the Supreme Court decided another resale price maintenance case involving patented products.[17] The result was consistent with, but

14. Ibid., p. 457.
15. Ibid., p. 458.
16. Ibid., pp. 458–59 (emphasis added).
17. U.S. v. Univis Lens Co., 316 U.S. 241 (1942).

went beyond, the result in *Interstate Circuit,* in which the setting of theater admission prices was proscribed. Stone again wrote the majority opinion for an undivided Court. The licensing scheme assailed by the government was the use of patents on spectacle lens blanks to control the price of the finished, further fabricated product of which they were an essential part. Three classes of licenses were issued: (1) licenses to wholesalers authorizing them to purchase blanks from Univis Lens Company, to finish them by grinding and polishing, and to sell them to prescription licensees only at prices fixed by the licensor (a patent-holding corporation formed by Univis Lens Company, which owned a majority of its stock); (2) licenses to finishing retailers who purchased blanks from the lens company, and in addition to grinding and polishing, adjusted frames and supports and sold these finished products at prices set by the licensor; (3) licenses to prescription retailers without facilities for grinding or finishing lenses, who prescribed and adjusted glasses for their customers. Prescription retailers were licensed to sell finished lenses only to consumers at prices prescribed by the licensor.

The Univis Lens Company, the sole manufacturer of the patented unfinished lens blanks, paid a royalty of 50¢ a pair to its patent-holding corporation when rough lens blanks were sold. The policy of the licensing corporation was to issue licenses only to qualified licensees with "high standards of practice," and instructions to its field representatives were that "price cutters" were not to be licensed.[18]

The district court[19] held that without licenses the lens-finishing step would infringe the patent, and it concluded, on the precedent of the *General Electric* case, that the licensor could condition his licenses upon maintenance by the licensee of his prescribed retail price.[20] The district court, however, held the prescription retailer licenses unlawful because their restriction upon the *resale* of the finished product was not within the patent monopoly and therefore was prohibited by the Sherman Act. Moreover, the resale price maintenance agreements regarding finished lenses, which were a different product from the lens blank, were not within the exception to the Sherman Act created by the Miller-Tydings Act.

On appeal to the Supreme Court the question raised by the government was the propriety of the price maintenance of lenses by the

18. Ibid., pp. 245–46.
19. 41 F. Supp. 258 (1941).
20. U.S. v. Univis Lens Co., 316 U.S. 241 (1942), at p. 247.

wholesalers and retailers who performed grinding and finishing operations. The Supreme Court assumed, for purpose of the decision, that the patent was not fully practiced until the grinding and finishing operations were performed, and then went on to decide that the price of the finished lens could not be controlled anyway. The lower court and the appellee were relying upon the *General Electric* case. The Supreme Court found no occasion to reconsider *General Electric* because: "The Court in that case was at pains to point out that a patentee who manufactures the product protected by the patent and fails to retain his ownership in it can not control the price at which it is sold by his distributors."[21] Title passing was crucial. Moreover, the Supreme Court further held, "Whether the licensee sells the patented article in completed form or sells it before completion for the purpose of enabling the buyer to finish and sell it, he has equally parted with the article."[22]

Univis, unlike *Interstate Circuit* or *Ethyl*, exposed no plan which could be utilized to restrain competition beyond that attributable to the competitive superiority of the patents. Nor was there any evidence that a dominant position by Univis in the lens industry had anything to do with the outcome of the case. The arrangement was one of partial vertical integration through contract. Whatever may have been the rationale for adopting the scheme, the absence of economic rationale for the decision is amply demonstrated by the precedent relied upon by the Supreme Court. "The first vending of any article manufactured under a patent puts the article beyond the reach of the monopoly which that patent confers";[23] and "Agreements for price maintenance of articles moving in interstate commerce are without more, unreasonable restraints within the meaning of the Sherman Act."[24]

In *Sola Electric Company* v. *Jefferson Electric Company*,[25] decided by the Supreme Court in the same year as the *Univis* case, the right of a licensee to challenge the validity of patent as a counterclaim to a suit for infringement was allowed when the patentee was employing

21. Ibid., p. 252.
22. Ibid. And as to the Miller-Tydings exception: "We find nothing in the language . . . or in its legislative history, to indicate that its provisions were to be so applied to products manufactured in successive stages" (ibid., p. 253).
23. Ibid., p. 252, citing among other cases, Morton Salt Co. v. Suppiger Co., 314 U.S. 488 (1942).
24. Ibid., citing among other cases, Ethyl Gasoline Co. v. U.S., 309 U.S. 436 (1940).
25. 317 U.S. 173 (1942).

price-restrictive licensing. The lower court had held the licensee estopped. In overruling the district court, the Supreme Court pointed out that since vertical price-fixing would be illegal were the patent invalid, it would be against public policy not to allow the test irrespective of state law.[26] This result, the Court noted, was consistent with the *Morton Salt* case[27] involving a parallel problem in which a tying contract was involved.

Agreements with Licensees Who Are Competitors: The Masonite *Case*

The *Masonite* case[28] was also decided in 1942. Once again, as in the *Ethyl* case, there was strong if ambiguous evidence that the Masonite patents were licensed in a way that provided a screen for elimination of competition in noninfringing products. The question presented by this case was whether the appellees, including principal competitors in the sale of hardboard, had combined to restrain trade or commerce in violation of sections 1 and 2 of the Sherman Act. The bill to enjoin the alleged violations of the act had been dismissed by the district court on the authority of *General Electric*.

Masonite had hardboard patents which the district court had found to be "fundamental and basic." Masonite manufactured hardboard under license for its principal competitors, some of whom had patents of their own and some of whom did not. Sale was not, however, made to those "competitor-distributors." The distributors sold under agency agreements.

The district court characterized this agreement as "true agency," thus distinguishing this case from recent price-maintenance cases and bringing it under the *General Electric* rule. Justice Douglas, however, was not to let this case be decided on a narrow "title-passing" issue. "We assume in this case," he wrote, "that the agreements constituted the appellees as *del credere* agents of Masonite. But that circumstance does not prevent the arrangement from running afoul of the Sherman

26. Subsequently, in 1947, the Supreme Court in Edw. Katzinger Co. v. Chicago Metallic Manufacturing Co., 329 U.S. 394 (1947), and in MacGregor v. Westinghouse Electric Manufacturing Co., 329 U.S. 402 (1947), held that an invalid price-fixing provision was not severable. Rather, it was held that the same logic of Sola renders the entire license agreement invalid. Hence a licensee could challenge the validity of the patent, *despite a covenant not to challenge.* These 1947 cases were decided by bare majorities.
27. Morton Salt Co. v. Suppiger Co., 314 U.S. 488 (1942).
28. U.S. v. Masonite Corp., 316 U.S. 265 (1942).

Act."[29] Then, ambiguously in terms of the competitive superiority of Masonite's patents, he discussed the patent scope question in a manner that embraced as indistinguishable the precedent of vertically imposed restrictions in tying cases (*Morton Salt*) and the precedent of the cases involving horizontal agreement eliminating competition beyond that provided by the competitive superiority of a valid patent (*Standard Sanitary* and *Ethyl*).

Douglas did not completely proscribe the use of the agency device by a patentee as a means of controlling the use of a valid patent; but he narrowed it so as to bring into question the validity of the very license (the Westinghouse license) which the *General Electric* case approved. For Douglas the legitimate use of the agency device to fix prices was quickly exhausted. Douglas wrote in this connection: "if it may fairly be said that that distribution *is part of the patentee's own business* and operates only to secure to him the reward for his invention which Congress has provided,"[30] then a patentee who employs such an agent is not enlarging the scope of his patent privilege. Perhaps this is mere dictum; but he went on to write, "And when it is clear, as it is in this case, that the marketing systems utilized by means of the *del credere* agency agreements are those of competitors of the patentee,[31] and the purpose is to fix prices at which competitors may market the product,[32] the device is, *without more*, an enlargement of the limited patent privilege and a violation of the Sherman Act."[33]

No agreement or understanding to abandon competing products was found. Although the record at least suggested this, the evidence was not deemed relevant. "The power of Masonite to fix the price of the product which it manufactures, and which the entire group sells and with respect to which all have been and are now actual or potential competitors, is a powerful inducement to abandon competition."[34]

Justice Douglas did not explain why "an inducement to abandon competition" would not be involved, actually or potentially, by any licensee who found a patent worth paying for, whether or not the

29. Ibid., p. 277.
30. Ibid., p. 279 (emphasis added).
31. Westinghouse, it should be remembered, was a competitor of General Electric and was so recognized in the 1926 General Electric case.
32. Note that "the product" seems clearly *not* to refer to noninfringing competitive products in this context.
33. U.S. v. Masonite Corp., 316 U.S. 265 (1942), at p. 279.
34. Ibid., p. 281.

patent was licensed with price-restrictive provisions. In this case, however, licensed competitors were "industrywide." And although the situation bore strong earmarks of an industrywide understanding not to sell unpatented or other patented substitutes, as in the bathtub case, *Masonite* went much further than *Standard Sanitary*. It cast serious doubt upon the permissibility of licensing an appreciable segment of an industry while maintaining the price of the patented product—agency or not.

If this case could be said to turn on whether the agreements were more than "patentwide" as measured by their competitive superiority, it was only because Douglas seemed to believe that this was conclusively inferable from the fact that the agreements were "industrywide." And, of course, the better the patent, the more likely it is that it would be widely adopted, especially if production or distribution were efficiently conducted by multiple firms.

Cross-Licensed Patents and Price-Fixing: The Line Material *Case*

In 1948 the Supreme Court again was faced with the question of distinguishing or overruling *General Electric*. This 1948 case, *United States* v. *Line Material Company*[35] almost, but not quite, sounded the death knell of the price-restrictive licensing the *General Electric* case had supported. But the Court became so divided on a rationale for deciding this case that Justice Reed, in an attempt to carry a widely divided court, wrote an opinion turning on cross-licensing. Four of eight justices were unwilling to overturn the *GE* case. Prior price-restrictive license cases, irrespective of how one might evaluate the economic effect of the decision, at least had the minor merit of being consistent with previously decided cases. The *Line Material* case, however, was a tour de force in terms of either logic or precedent. Reed carried the Court only with respect to the outcome. In trying to justify his decision and still carry the Court, he distinguished *General Electric* by stressing that two patentees had come together in *Line Material*.

These patents were *not* competing, however. One company, Southern States Equipment Corporation, possessed a patent covering a fuse to break electric circuits when current became excessive. The release mechanism in the Southern patent, however, was complicated and expensive. A separate company, Line Material, invented a superior and cheaper improvement which could not be used without infringing

35. 333 U.S. 287 (1948).

Southern's dominant patent. The efficiency of these inventions could not be enjoyed by either the patentees or the consuming public without being used together. For purposes of efficient exploitation or use they were mutually blocking. Consequently, Line and Southern exchanged licenses (royalty free) and Line was allowed to issue price-restrictive licenses to other manufacturers. A principal licensee, the General Electric Company, vigorously opposed the price restriction in the Line Material license, as it also had opposed the price restriction in a prior Southern Equipment Corporation license.

There were energetic efforts to find or create competing substitutes for these patents. General Electric accepted a price-restrictive license only because it was preferable to doing without the use of the patents. There was no record, as there was in *Masonite*, that licensees might have been in league to use the dropout fuse licensing scheme jointly as a screen for eliminating noninfringing competition in the circuit-breaker industry.

The crux of the *Line Material* opinion was the existence of the cross-license. Price restrictions under any cross-license under this decision were considered to be per se illegal, whether the patents so licensed were complementary, supplementary, mutually blocking, or competing. Reed was, at least, unequivocal about what this decision covered: "when patentees join in agreement as here to maintain prices on their several products, that agreement, however advantageous it may be to stimulate the broader use of patents, is unlawful *per se* under the Sherman Act."[36] A more arbitrary and unprincipled per se rule would be difficult to construct. And as yet no commentator or critic has been able, on an economically rational basis, to explain why, if the *General Electric* decision was right, was not the *Line Material* decision wrong.

Joint Ownership of Conflicting Patents and Price-Fixing:
The New Wrinkle *Case*

In 1952 the rule concerning price-restrictive licensing in the context of a cross-license, formulated in *Line Material*, was applied to pooled patents assigned to a holding company. In *United States* v. *New Wrinkle, Incorporated*,[37] however, the pooled patents did not complement each other as they did in the *Line Material* situation. In *New*

36. Ibid., p. 314.
37. 342 U.S. 371 (1952).

Wrinkle two competing companies had been in litigation in regard to certain patents covering manufacture of wrinkle-finish enamels, varnishes, and paints. Each company claimed it controlled the basic patents on wrinkle finish, and each contended that the other's patents were subservient to its own. Rather than continue costly litigation, the parties resolved the conflict by pooling the patents in a jointly owned patent-holding company, which in turn set minimum price schedules for its licensees. After twelve of the principal producers of wrinkle finishes had subscribed to the minimum prices prescribed in the license agreements, the minimum price schedules became operative, and subsequently more than two hundred, or substantially all, manufacturers of wrinkle finishes in the United States signed similar agreements.

Two very important questions—first, the validity and scope of the patents pooled and, second, the possible suppression of competition in the sale of noninfringing wrinkle finishes—were not explored by the Court because of the easier solution provided by the *Line Material* precedent. The first question poses a serious and continuing question irrespective of whether the pooled patents are price controlled. Settling conflicting claims avoids the risk to each of the contesting parties that neither patent will be held valid, or that the claims of each will be so limited that outside competition can operate without danger of infringement. On the other hand, if it can be assumed that the only question is not validity or scope of the claims, but merely which party will prevail over the other, then the so-called pool has no effect (other than who gets the reward) different from that which would occur were there no conflict.

The question whether the patents were a screen for a price agreement covering noninfringing wrinkle finishes does not, of course, depend upon whether a single patent or pooled patents are involved. And the fact that price-fixing is "industrywide" may be a necessary precondition, but it is not a sufficient one for testing competitive superiority. Exceeding competitive superiority depends upon the ability of the industry to collusively fix prices or restrict output of unpatented products or products produced under competing patents. This "screening" to achieve the broader restraint has been described as a cartel activity. And cartels consisting of very large numbers are fragile instruments for trade restraint. There were more than two hundred licensees in the paint industry in *New Wrinkle*. So again in *New Wrinkle* there were problems appropriately resolvable under patent-misuse or antitrust law by the application of a scope test. It was not applied. The issue was no longer even being argued by litigants when the *New Wrinkle* case was tried. Rather, patent defendants in price-restrictive antitrust suits continued to lose the case distinction game they played with the government over what was left of the *General Electric* doctrine.

Toward the Demise of the General Electric *Rule*

Perhaps all that is left of permissible price-restrictive licensing now is to a single licensee. And whether price-restrictive licensing is industrywide is, of course, not necessarily related to the number of licensees. (Mr. Gibbons has summarized the state of the law with respect to industrywide price-restrictive licensing: "While there was some indication in various opinions in the late 1940's that industry-wide or multiple price-restrictive licenses might be illegal, this rule has been neither accepted nor rejected by the Supreme Court."[38])

In 1956, the Third Circuit Court of Appeals decided the *Newburgh Moire* case.[39] The case was a suit for infringement of patents relating to improvements in imparting moire pattern effects to textiles. Of five moire finishers in the industry two had price-restrictive licenses from the plaintiff. The court, in reviewing *General Electric* and the cases following it which went the other way, pointed out that a distinguishing characteristic, and for it a controlling one, was that in the 1926 *General Electric* case there was only a single licensee who was price-restricted, whereas in the subsequent cases a substantial number, usually most of the industry, were included. Finding a plurality of price-fixed licensees to be distinguishing (for economic reasons not divulged) the court held that the moire license plan was illegal because more than a single licensee was involved.

In 1960, the *Newburgh Moire* holding on the illegality of multiple licenses with price-fixing provisions was followed by the United States District Court in Pennsylvania.[40] The Supreme Court refused to hear appeal.[41]

In *United States* v. *Huck Manufacturing Company*[42] the United States district court in Michigan was confronted with the legality of

---

38. Gibbons, "Price Fixing," p. 299.
39. Newburgh Moire Co. v. Superior Moire Co., 237 F. 2d 283 (1956).
40. Tinnerman Products, Inc., v. George K. Garrett Co., 185 Fed. Supp. 151 (E.D. Pa. 1960).
41. *Cert. denied*, 368 U.S. 833 (1962).
42. 277 Fed. Supp. 791 (E.D. Mich. 1964).

price-restrictive licensing to a single licensee. In this case, although only one licensee was involved, the licensor and the licensee were "the only producers of a general line of lockbolts."[43] Since a particular form of lockbolt was the subject of the licensed patent in question, this made the single license "industrywide." The lower court could see no basis for distinguishing the *General Electric* case. It therefore dismissed the government's case. This holding was narrowly affirmed by an equally divided Supreme Court in 1965.[44] Single-licensee price-fixing made it by a hair.

Territorial Limitations

In the early cases reviewed in chapter 7, involving licensee restrictions on the right to use an invention, no distinction was made by the courts concerning the propriety of controlling use with other materials (tying), use or sale at a price (price-restrictive licensing), or use or sale in particular territories (territorial-restrictive licensing). But beginning in 1917, tying arrangements were increasingly proscribed by court interpretation until they become almost automatically illegal; and price-restrictive licensing, although approved for a longer period when the noninfringing products were not included, later also became most severely restricted even when the prices fixed did not involve the patent as a "screen" for broader price-fixing. The law with respect to territorial use restriction, on the other hand, remained almost exactly as it was, at least until 1967 when the Supreme Court decided the *Schwinn* case.[45] The patent law (§ 261) does set forth that a patentee may convey an exclusive right under his patent "to the whole or any specified part of the United States." This language, relating to conveying an exclusive territorial right, however, was not extended to purchasers from licensees. This was the holding in the 1895 *Folding Bed* case, previously discussed.

Title passing, rather than competitive considerations, long has been relevant to purchasers from licensees whose sales territories are geographically limited. This rule has been considered to be applicable not only to licenses to make *and* vend, but also merely to vend. Thus, if

43. No other licenses for Huck's "general line" lockbolts were granted, but exclusivity was not written into the contract.
44. 382 U.S. 197 (1965).
45. U.S. v. Arnold, Schwinn & Co., 388 U.S. 365 (1967).

a patentee manufactured all of a patented product himself, he might, for example, with impunity sell his patented product through jobbers or wholesalers whose licenses to vend restricted their sales territory to particular geographic areas. In 1967, however, the Supreme Court decision in the *Schwinn* case, although involving an unpatented product, held that section 1 of the Sherman Act was violated by franchising territorially exclusive wholesalers if, but only if, title to the product passed to the wholesaler.[46]

Just as the economically frivolous resale price maintenance rule, erroneously equating vertically imposed prices with agreed-upon prices among competing dealers, was applied to patented and unpatented commodities alike—first in *Dr. Miles* with respect to a secret remedy in 1911 and then to a patented product in *Bauer* v. *O'Donnell* in 1913, as was indicated in chapter 7—so, one might predict, may this newer but equally frivolous rule regarding title passing, adopted for the vertically imposed territorial franchising of unpatented products in the *Schwinn* case, soon be held applicable to patented products. Thus one of the last signs of permissible use restriction, territorial licensing, is being turned toward that legal junk-heap which has long been the repository of other forms of use restriction.

---

46. In the Schwinn case the government charged, among other things, that Schwinn had violated section 1 of the Sherman Act by requiring its retail outlets to adhere to prices it established for its products, and by allocating exclusive marketing territories to its wholesalers. The district court found that retail prices had not been set except in states where valid fair trade (resale price maintenance) laws were enforced. This finding was not appealed. But as to division of fields among the wholesalers Justice Fortas held:
"We conclude that the proper application of § 1 of the Sherman Act to this problem requires differentiation between the situation where the manufacturer parts with title, dominion or risk with respect to the article, and where he completely retains ownership and risk of loss . . . . [W]e are not prepared to introduce the inflexibility which a *per se* rule might bring if it were applied to prohibit all vertical restrictions of territory and all franchising . . . . But to allow this freedom where the manufacturer has parted with dominion over the goods—the usual marketing situation—would violate the ancient rule against restraints on alienation and open the door to exclusivity of outlets and limitation of territory further than prudence permits." [388 U.S. 365 (1967), at p. 378 et seq.]

10

Patent Pools

In the preceding cases concerned with the problems of permissible licensing practice, the combination of separate patents, whether by cross-license or by pooling, was not the central issue under review. Except for price-restrictive licensing, evidenced in the last chapter by the Supreme Court decisions in the *Line Material* and *New Wrinkle* cases, most of the problems exposed did not deal with accumulation of patents or distinguish what was permissible in licensing one or multiple patents. The problem of patent accumulation, the aggregation of several or numerous patents under single ownership or control, is conceptually indistinguishable from the merger problem under antitrust law. The central question concerning the propriety of combining patents is not different from that involved in combining other properties. Merging of patents, like merging of other assets, may be horizontal, vertical, or conglomerate. And in each case the same economic questions deserve consideration. A central issue in any pooling of assets is whether competition among the merged resources is eliminated or whether more efficient use of the merged resources results.

Combination or pooling of patents is a frequently used means of eliminating the competition among them. This result, however, arises only when the patents are competing or potentially competing. Just as in the general merger case, so in the patent merger case; it is the horizontal merger, the merger of competing companies or competing patents, which raises the economically relevant antitrust problem. Antitrust law has had somewhat less success with the problem of mergers, even mergers among competitors, than it has had with agreements not to compete. This is because formal mergers, unlike the loose agreements under which the parties remain independent, display conflicting tendencies: trade restraint and efficiency. And the law with

respect to horizontal mergers, it should be remembered, weighs the
trade-restraining aspects of mergers more heavily as the relative market position of the merger participants increases. Loose associations
of competitors (price or division of market agreements), on the other
hand, are not usually assessed in these terms. A per se rule against
cartels has been rationalized by a "no efficiency" presumption.

A pool of competing patents can be more readily analogized to a
loose association than to a horizontal merger. This, of course, depends
upon one's evaluation of the pool's efficiency-creating potential. A
pool of competing patents is difficult to distinguish from the cartel in
this respect. If this is so, there is presumptively a strong case for treat-
ing a pool of competing patents as an illegal arrangement in restraint
of trade. Thus, for example, if it were established that there were two
nonconflicting competing processes for making the same product, each
patented and separately owned, their combination would eliminate
user alternatives and raise the user's cost of production above that
measured by the "competitive superiority" of either of the patents.
If, on the other hand, as in the *Line Material* case, one patent was
subservient to the other, an improvement patent unusable without
infringing the basic patent, then combining or pooling them eliminates
no user alternative. In terms of possible trade restraint, this case is
indistinguishable from a vertical merger. The two patents combined
in *Line Material* could not restrict output or raise price any more than
if the two were exploited separately.[1]

The pool of patents in the *New Wrinkle* case gave rise to a different kind of problem—the problem of identifying the nature of the
relationship (competitive or noncompetitive) of the patents pooled.
Pooling is a means of resolving conflicting claims, as that case demonstrates. Patent litigation is costly. It is costly to the parties involved
and also to the community. Not litigating, on the other hand, can be
cost-saving to the parties but costly to the community if invalid claims
are established or if competition between valid but competing claims
is eliminated. Conceptually, a trade-off[2] between savings in litigation
cost against the loss from trade restraint is called for; but, unfortunately, a relative measure of the two countervailing factors seems

    1. See chapter 6, note 27. The reference is to Bork, *Vertical Integration and
the Sherman Act: The Legal History of an Economic Misconception.*
    2. The nature of this trade-off is similar to that described by Williamson in
"Economies as an Antitrust Defense," 63 *Am. Econ. Rev.* 18 (March 1968).
See particularly his figure 1 at p. 21.

dependent upon incurring the cost of litigation, and after that cost is sunk the issue has been mooted.

In patent pooling cases the courts have occasionally been disposed to explore the nature of patents pooled or, as when companies merge, to appraise the market position of the merged properties relative to the rest of the market. The important *Standard Oil of Indiana* case in 1931 was such an instance.[3] Sometimes the courts have looked for behavior indicating whether the purposes of the parties were monopolistic.[4] In other cases, they have scarcely looked at the pool at all, taking it as a part of a bygone scheme. Especially did this characterize the early cases involving alleged use of patents to monopolize an industry. *Bement* v. *National Harrow, Standard Sanitary*, and *United Shoe Machinery* all involved the use of acquired or pooled patents, but the acquisition of patents was not the issue in these cases.[5]

Were it possible to clearly and definitively classify the relationship between patents into two mutually exclusive categories—competing and noncompeting—the problem of evaluating the propriety of patent pooling would be greatly simplified. But the relationship that patents bear to each other is not often an either/or matter. The relationship of patented processes or products can be competing, complementary, or blocking, or a little of each.[6]

Because of the recognized need for resolving problems of technological interdependence as well as the legal problem of mutual exclusiveness, both courts and commentators have recognized a valid need for the interchange or the pooling of complementary or blocking patents as the only feasible alternative to a waiver of valid patent rights.[7]

3. Standard Oil Co. (Indiana) v. U.S., 283 U.S. 163 (1931).

4. The early Sherman Act cases involving merger adopted both approaches simultaneously. A monopoly-gaining theory involving aggressive behavior and market-share theory were utilized simultaneously in Standard Oil Co. of N.J. v. U.S., 221 U.S. 1 (1911), and in U.S. v. American Tobacco Co., 221 U.S. 106 (1911).

5. In U.S. vs. Winslow, 227 U.S. 202 (1913), discussed in chapter 8 at note 4, however, the merger of companies owning complementary shoe machinery patents was approved.

6. See Gilbert Goller, "Competing, Complementary and Blocking Patents: Their Role in Determining Antitrust Violations in the Areas of Cross-Licensing, Patent Pooling and Package Licensing," 50 *J. Pat. Off. Soc'y*. 723 (Nov. 1968).

7. See, for example, *Report of the Attorney General's National Committee to Study the Antitrust Laws* (1955) at p. 242: "Patent interchange may thus promote rather than restrain competition."

Gasoline Cracking Patents

The valid reasons recognized for patent pooling, however, merely point up the need for careful scrutiny of the relationship between patents, especially when, as in the *Standard Oil of Indiana* case, major competitors combine their patents. In this case, on the basis of an extensive report by a master to whom the case had been referred by the district court, there was a review of seventy-three patents and seventy-nine license contracts. "The master found that the primary defendants had not pooled their patents relating to cracking processes; that they had not monopolized or attempted to monopolize any part of trade or commerce in gasoline; and that none of the defendants had entered into any combination. He recommended that the bill be dismissed for want of equity."[8]

This suit, which had been brought by the government in 1924, did not reach the Supreme Court until 1931. The issues to which most of the evidence had been addressed in the trial court had been eliminated by the time the case reached the Supreme Court. The violation of the Sherman Act before the Supreme Court rested substantially on the purpose and effect of three contracts entered into by the primary defendants. These primary defendants were Standard Oil Company of Indiana, the Texas Company, and the Standard Oil Company of New Jersey. Each was a large producer of cracked gasoline. A fourth defendant, Gasoline Products Company, was solely a patent-licensing concern. Each of these concerns had secured numerous patents covering its particular cracking process, and, "since the phenomenon of cracking *was not controlled by any fundamental patent*, other concerns had been working independently to develop commercial processes of their own."[9]

Beginning in 1920, conflict developed among the four companies concerning the validity, scope, and ownership of issued patents. One infringement suit was begun; cross-notices of infringement, antecedent to other suits, were given; and interferences were declared on pending applications in the Patent Office. The primary defendants asserted that it was solely these difficulties which led them to execute the three principal agreements which the government had attacked as an illegal combination to control the cracking art.

---

8. Standard Oil Co. (Indiana) v. U.S., 283 U.S. 163 (1931), p. 166.
9. Ibid., p. 167 (emphasis added).

The three contracts under attack were a 1921 contract between Standard of Indiana and the Texas Company, a 1923 contract between the Texas Company and the Gasoline Products Company, and a 1923 contract among Standard of Indiana, the Texas Company, and Standard of New Jersey. Under these contracts, which differed only slightly in their terms, each primary defendant was released from liability for infringement of the patents of others, each acquired the right to use the patents of the others for its own process, each could license independent concerns releasing its licensees from past and future infringement claims from patents held by other primary defendants, and each was to share in some fixed proportion the fees received under the multiple licenses. Royalties were fixed by the agreement in the first contract, but this provision had been eliminated before the lower court's decree.

The government contended that the three agreements constituted a pooling of royalties from their several patents and that thereby competition among them in the commercial exercise of their respective right to issue licenses was eliminated, thus eliminating competition in royalty rates among the patents. The restraint of trade thus charged arose out of the making and effect of the provision for cross-licensing and for division of royalties. The contractual arrangements, it was alleged, enabled "the primary defendants, *because of their monopoly of patented cracking processes*, to maintain royalty rates at the level established originally for the Indiana process."[10]

The foregoing contention by the government, that the agreement allowed royalty rates to be maintained at the level originally established by Standard of Indiana, is consistent with alternative explanations. If the patents of any of the primary defendants were basic and the others subservient, or if they were mutually blocking, then maintenance of the royalty rate(s) could have followed as readily as if the patents had been competing. In the latter case only, however, is competition eliminated. A "competitive superiority" test in which the market sets the value of each individual patent is not exceeded unless the patents are effective substitutes. Resolving this issue is crucial to a finding that monopoly, or restriction of competition, in the business

10. Ibid., p. 174 (emphasis added). It was also contended that the agreements to maintain royalties violated the Sherman Act because the fees charged were onerous. This contention about the reasonableness of the rates, however, was held to be without legal significance.

of licensing cracking processes resulted from the execution of these agreements.

Justice Brandeis characterized the pooled patents as competing. He wrote, "In the case at bar, the primary defendants own *competing patented processes* for manufacturing an unpatented product."[11] And the rest of the opinion, although wrong in terms of economic analysis, is consistent with a conclusion that when he wrote *competing* he meant what economists mean by the term—that the pooled patents were substitutes for each other. Were this not so, it is difficult to understand why he felt compelled to stress that cracked gasoline in the years in question made up only 26 percent of total gasoline (the *wrong* market if the patents were worth anything), or why he emphasized the master's finding that "the defendants were in active competition among themselves and with other refiners; [and] that *both kinds of gasoline* were refined and sold in large quantities by other companies."[12] Moreover, Brandeis, in answering the government's contention that the agreements were made in bad faith, cited with approval the master's ruling "that it was not necessary to determine whether any of the *competing* process patents actually infringed another."[13] The lower court had held that the patents were adequate consideration for the cross-licensing agreements and that the violation charged could not be predicated on patent invalidity.

Two commentators, one a lawyer and the other an economist, have addressed themselves to the question of whether the pooled patents in this case were competing or noncompeting. And each views this issue as crucial in evaluating the correctness of the Brandeis opinion. Gilbert Goller, in a 1968 article in the *Journal of the Patent Office Society*,[14] stresses noncompetitiveness. Goller, in the third section of this article, after pointing out the overlapping nature of patent interrelationships involving competing, complementary, and blocking patents, attempts to rationalize the legal outcome in the case. Brandeis's opinion in this case, he contends, does not delineate his view of the nature of the patent interrelationship involved. Goller writes, "Its often-quoted statements approving patent interchanges when blocking, complementary or infringing patents are involved, are general in nature and

11. Ibid., p. 175 (emphasis added).
12. Ibid., p. 178 (emphasis added).
13. Ibid., p. 180, n. 19 (emphasis added).
14. Goller, "Competing, Complementary and Blocking Patents."

superficially do not appear to be directed specifically to facts in the case."[15] His contention is that Brandeis's use of the phrase *"competing patented process"* was completely unintentional. Goller recognizes these as "troublesome" words, as indeed they are. He says there are two possible ways of explaining them. The first explanation, he contends, is a problem of "full context."[16] The following quotation is said to provide this context:

> In the case at bar, the primary defendants own competing patented processes for manufacturing an unpatented product which is sold in interstate commerce; *and agreements concerning such processes are likely to engender the evils to which the Sherman Act was directed.*[17]

Goller's interesting contention is that the above statement should not be read as it is written because "in support of it" Brandeis cites *United States* v. *International Harvester Company.*[18] Because the court in that case held that a merger of five dominant harvester companies was in itself a violation of both the first and second sections of the Sherman Act, Goller suggests that "the words in *Standard Oil* could be considered as merely characterizing the competitive nature of the patents and their owners in order to point out the danger of a violation that exists and the extra scrutiny which is necessary when competitors combine."[19] This explanation of Brandeis's use of the word *competing* is then, alternatively, accepted by Goller as meaning what it says but not saying enough. The case is thus alleged to stand for what the court *realized* but would not say. Goller's alternative explanation of the case is to take Brandeis at his word that patents were competing, but at the same time to recognize that the Court realized (without saying so) that the patents were also complementary, blocking, or infringing, and that the interchange was approved because of these latter characteristics.[20]

In addition to the question of the credibility of this "rule of the well-hidden reason," there is still the unanswered question of why or when, if patents are competing, even though they are also in some respects complementary and mutually blocking, the elimination of

15. Ibid., p. 731 (emphasis added).
16. Ibid.
17. Ibid. (emphasis added).
18. 214 Fed. 987 (D.C. Minn. 1914). App. dismissed, 248 U.S. 587 (1915).
19. Goller, "Competing, Complementary and Blocking Patents." pp. 731–32.
20. Ibid., p. 732.

competition between them should be sanctioned. This question is analogous to that involved in determining the propriety of any horizontal merger—the problem of weighing efficiency against trade restraint. When this kind of question is relevant, as it often is when patents are accumulated, there is strong reason to weigh these effects and not to adopt a per se rule.[21] Neither Goller's comment nor Brandeis's opinion is at all convincing that the anticompetitive aspects of the pool in the *Standard* case should not have made this case go the other way.

John S. McGee has made an insightful and relevant economics analysis of the *Standard Oil* cracking case.[22] Except for renumbering of footnotes, and the figure he devised, McGee's analysis of this case is reproduced verbatim as a model of the relevance of economic analysis to a legal issue.[23]

McGee's Analysis of the "Cracking" Patents Case:[23-1]

This opinion is a masterpiece of its kind: it simultaneously misleads about fact, and misfires logically. To what extent these deficiencies are due to defects in legal tactics, the record, or judicial economics is not clear.[23-2] In any case, before analyzing the decision it will be useful broadly

21. The still-current and frequently cited authority (see, for example, Phillip Areeda, *Antitrust Analysis* [Boston: Little Brown & Co., 1967], p. 377) with respect to patent accumulation is: "The mere accumulation of patents, no matter how many, is not in itself illegal." (Automatic Radio Mfg. Co. v. Hazeltine Research, Inc., 339 U.S. 827 [1950], at p. 834.)

Section 7 of the Clayton Act was amended in 1950 with the purpose of establishing stricter standards for merger approval. The impact of this amendment, applying as it does to the acquisition of assets and not excluding patent assets, deserves mention as potentially important counterauthority. The act of 29 December 1950 amends the first paragraph of section 7 of the Clayton Act to read:

> That no corporation engaged in commerce shall acquire, directly or indirectly, the whole or any part of the stock or other share capital, and no corporation subject to the jurisdiction of the Federal Trade Commission *shall acquire the whole or any part of the assets* of another corporation engaged also in commerce, where in *any line of commerce* in any section of the country, the effect of such acquisition may be substantially to lessen competition or tend to create a monopoly. [64 Stat. 1125, 15 U.S.C. sect. 18; emphasis added.]

22. John S. McGee, "Patent Exploitation: Some Economic and Legal Problems," 9 *J. Law Econ.* 135 (Oct. 1966), at pp. 150–60.

23. The "Cracking" Patents Case section is presented with the permission of the author and the *Journal of Law and Economics*.

23–1. Standard Oil Co. v. United States, 283 U.S. 163 (1931).

23–2. Fortunately, there are other comprehensible sources. I have relied

to trace the evolution of thermal cracking processes through about the middle twenties.[23-3]

When the Standard Oil Co. (N.J.) was dissolved in 1911, Standard Oil (Indiana) was left with a large Midwest market and little or no crude oil of its own. Kerosene had been king, but was being dethroned by gasoline. Primitive distillation techniques sharply limited the output of the more valuable and lighter petroleum fractions, including kerosene and gasoline. The automobile revolution was under way. With it, the demand for gasoline would soar. And Midwest fuel oil markets, not favored by large maritime demands, were constrained by moderate coal prices. Furthermore, crude oil was relatively expensive.

The stage was thus set for a technique that could economically extract more gasoline from a barrel of crude oil by converting cheap fuel oil into relatively dear gasoline, or by substituting capital and an idea for crude oil. The Burton process, a classic text-book response, was invented by employees of the Standard Oil Co. (Indiana), a company of the sort and in the area most likely to profit from it. Whereas some cracking, inadvertent and otherwise, had been observed long before Burton's discoveries, his was the first commercial process for breaking down fuel oils under high temperatures and pressure. Patented in 1913, even the unimproved Burton process doubled gasoline yields and reduced gasoline costs by perhaps twenty-eight percent.[23-4] The new process used as raw material the residual oils left after kerosene and lighter fractions had been distilled out of crude oil.

The Indiana Company exploited the process through discriminatory non-exclusive licensing, as well as production on its own account. Licensees paid 25 percent of cracking profits, as defined by the licensor.[23-5] Royalties per barrel thus varied amongst licensees, and none was to sell Burton-cracked gasoline within Indiana's marketing territory.

The Burton process was profitable. Enos estimates that it earned about $150,000,000 for Indiana Standard, of which over $26,000,000 in royalties alone were earned through 1924.[23-6] Nevertheless, it was a "batch"— as contrasted with continuous—process, and, as such, doomed. Though

---

upon Enos, Petroleum Progress and Profits (1962); Beaton, Enterprise in Oil: A History of Shell in the United States (1957); McKnight, A Study of Patents on Petroleum Cracking, With Special Reference to Their Present Status (1938).

23–3. This paper therefore stops short of catalytic cracking, which revolutionized the industry again.

23–4. Enos, Id., at 42. Contrary to the glib summary of the Court, cracked gasoline was not at first equivalent to straight-run distilled motor fuel, and sold at a substantial discount. But relatively simple treatments soon brought it into public favor. Indeed, though this had no importance in an era of low-compression engines, much later it was recognized that cracked gasoline had better anti-knock characteristics.

23–5. Enos, Id., at 45. Although any dollar payment can of course be expressed as so much per barrel of charging stock, the opinion is somewhat misleading on this point.

23–6. Enos, Id., at 309.

available data probably overestimate the share of specific processes, Burton units accounted for 100 per cent of cracked gasoline output from 1913 through 1919; over 90 per cent through 1922; and only about 9 per cent by 1929.[23-7]

In 1920 and 1921, about ten rival cracking processes were introduced.[23-8] Although the Court's opinion seems to say that important patent conflict began in 1920, that is incorrect. One of the newer processes was based on various patents of Jesse A. Dubbs and his son, Carbon Petroleum Dubbs, some of whose design features and patents were at least tenuously related to an application made in 1909, four years before Burton's.[23-9] As we will later see, Dubbs' patents were used to attack the Burton process as early as 1915 in an action that was settled in 1931. It seems especially curious, therefore, that the opinion never even mentions either the Dubbs process, which later became very important, or the company that owned it.

The Dubbs process had several advantages. It was continuous; and, with C. P. Dubbs' "clean circulation" feature, reduced coke deposits, broadened the range of usable feedstocks, lengthened the productive run, yet brought gasoline yields almost within reach of the Burton-process. Although the first commercial unit using the Dubbs and Trumble patents, which were controlled by Universal Oil Products Company (UOP), was completed in 1921, it was not until 1922 that satisfactory performance was actually achieved.[23-10] With the improvements and increased capacities that followed, the Dubbs process became full-blown by 1926.

From the beginning, UOP's policy of patent exploitation differed somewhat from that of Standard (Indiana). Licenses were, generally, non-discriminatory,[23-11] reckoning royalties in terms of barrels of feedstock charged to the cracking units rather than a percentage of profits, and included yield guarantees, technical assistance, and defense against infringement suits. UOP, unlike Indiana, was solely a research and licensing concern.

Standard Oil (N.J.) had been an early licensee under Burton patents. Royalty costs and technical limitations under the Burton process—including infeasibility of using the heavy and high-sulphur cracking stocks most cheaply available—encouraged Jersey Standard to develop its own process.[23-12] What emerged was called the Tube and Tank process, which was employed in a small unit by 1920. It was very similar to the Dubbs process.[23-13] Jersey's contributions to it were buttressed in 1921 by buying certain Ellis patents. The first two Jersey licensees, commencing in 1921,

23–7. Enos, Id., at 285.

23–8. Enos, Id., at 60. Most turned out to be impractical.

23–9. Enos, Id., at 60–69.

23–10. Enos, Id., at 77–81. McKnight, Id., at 17–19.

23–11. Shell companies came to enjoy lower royalty rates, for which there are various possible explanations. Shell contributed the important Trumble patents. A Shell subsidiary had been the first licensee.

23–12. Enos, op. cit. supra note 34, at 100–101.

23–13. Enos, Id., at 109.

paid substantially less per barrel of feedstock than was being charged for
either the Burton or Dubbs process; but they also realized substantially
lower gasoline yields.[23-14] As practiced, these processes differed somewhat
in their tolerance for feedstocks; relative employment of capital, labor and
fuel; and output of the middle distillates (including kerosene) and heavy
fuel.[23-15] Although variable costs, including royalties, were closely comparable under the Burton and Tube and Tank processes, the rate of return
on new capital was significantly higher under the latter.[23-16]

There is little doubt that each of the processes so far discussed, and
perhaps a few others as well, was workable and potentially valuable. They
were also close substitutes. Their legal validity, and the degree of inde-
pendence in their exploitation thus became questions of very substantial
monetary interest. It will be recalled that one of Jesse Dubbs' early patent
applications, covering emulsion-breaking, which started work on what
came to be much improved Dubbs cracking processes, antedated Burton's
application by four years. When this early application, much altered,
ripened into a patent in 1915, UOP used it to attack Indiana Standard's
Burton process. Some refiners thought the suit would quickly invalidate the
Dubbs patents. They were wrong. It was not until fifteen years, 22,000
pages of transcript, and $3 million to $4 million dollars, later that the
suit was settled. In January, 1931, the Shell, California, Indiana, Texas,
and New Jersey companies together bought UOP and its Dubbs patents.[23-17] The Gasoline Products Company, owner of the Cross patents,
also became party to an agreement not to sue one another or their licensees for patent infringement.[23-18]

In the meantime, there had been other cracking patent pools. In 1921,
the Texas and Indiana companies pooled their patent resources, thus
combining the Burton and Holmes-Manley processes; and, in 1923, the
Gasoline Products (Cross) and Texas (Holmes-Manley) companies came
to terms with respect to their processes.[23-19] Perhaps too many reasons
have been given for these agreements.[23-20] One of them was presented by
Mr. Brandeis: "The primary defendants [the Indiana, Texas, New Jersey,
and Gasoline Products companies] assert . . . that their sole object was to
avoid litigation and losses incident to conflicting patents." Unless by

23–*14*. In 1921 gasoline yields a little over 14.2% of charge stock were
realized. Maximum Burton yields were above 30%. The first Tube and Tank
licensees paid 10 cents per barrel of feed stock; proposed Dubbs royalties were
15 cents; and, expressed in terms of feed stock, Burton royalties averaged
around 17 cents. Enos, Id., at 111.

23–*15*. Enos, Id., at 112.

23–*16*. Enos, Id., at 113.

23–*17*. Enos, Id., at 89. Apparently each subscribing company got a paid up
license under U.O.P. patents. Beaton, Enterprise in Oil: A History of Shell in
the United States 257 (1957).

23–*18*. Enos, op. cit. supra note 34, at 68.

23–*19*. Enos, Id., at 115.

23–*20*. E.g., Enos, Id., at 114–118.

"losses" they meant to include foregoing potential monopoly returns on the patents themselves, there were various alternative ways to avoid costs and pains of litigation. They might have agreed to dedicate all patents, or to license and sublicense royalty-free all around. It is probably sufficient that litigation costs money and that any patentee can lose patent suits in any of several ways: all or several competing patents may be held to be valid and not infringed, which tends to reduce the worth of each of them; one's own patents may be scuttled while others' are upheld; and patents covering one or more valuable processes—whoever may have claimed them—might be found to be invalid (for example, because of prior discovery), but the process freely opened to all. Furthermore, even if it were wholly certain that all competing patents would be upheld, it may easily pay for their several owners to reach some kind of agreement with respect to them.

Among other things, the Government attacked the three early patent agreements, one of 1921 (the Indiana and Texas companies); and two of 1923 (Texas and Gasoline Products companies; and the Indiana, Texas, and New Jersey companies). The Court finds that "the royalties to be charged were definitely fixed in the first contract; and minimum sums per barrel, to be divided between the Texas and Indiana companies, were specified in the second and third.[23-21] Nevertheless, it is able to conclude that:

> There is no provision in any of the agreements which restricts the freedom of the primary defendants individually to issue licenses under their own patents alone or under the patents of all the others; and no contract between any of them, and no license agreement with a secondary defendant executed pursuant thereto, now imposes any restriction upon the quantity of gasoline to be produced, or upon the price, terms, or conditions of sale, or upon the territory in which sales may be made.[23-22]

Conclusion indeed! If nonnegligible royalty rates are fixed in licenses under which substantial production actually takes place, output and price effects *have* thereby been accomplished.[23-23] The real question is whether after 1923 there continued to be agreement in fixing royalties. For, it is clear, once the agreement to share royalties was reached, it would have been eminently sensible and relatively easy to agree to maximize the amount of royalties to be shared. If the cross licensing arrangements defined a broad homogeneous technological field, any part of which manufacturers could choose to use once they took out a license, terms offered by any licensor to any new licensee would tend to equality no matter what he called the technique actually used. But if the various processes were clearly identi-

23–21. Standard Oil Co. v. United States, 283 U.S. 163, 168 (1931).
23–22. Id., at 170.
23–23. A similar error is made by Mr. Hughes in Appalachian Coals, Inc. v. United States, 288 U.S. 344 (1933). Hughes found that the exclusive sales agency planned would fix coal prices for the collieries who owned it, but that "no attempt was made to limit production." Id., at 367.

fiable, and if a licensee actually used and paid for only one of them, royalty rates could differ even though there were perfect collusion. Furthermore under certain circumstances, with symmetrical sharing, joint participants might be induced to maximize joint shares even though there were no explicit agreement about royalty rates. What would be required is that deviationist behavior lose more by reducing a firm's share in royalties from others' patents than it would gain on royalties from its own.

Unfortunately, data on thermal cracking royalties are fragmentary and ambiguous. According to one authority, the basic UOP (Dubbs) royalty rate was 15 cents per barrel of charge from 1922 through 1933, whether UOP was "fighting" the other major patent holders or—after 1931—was owned by them![23-24] The royalty rate for the New Jersey (Tube and Tank) process was reportedly 10 or 12 cents per barrel of charge in 1922, and, as in the case of the other processes, was reduced in 1934, 1938, and in the 1940's.[23-25]

In 1934, in the Great Depression, UOP reduced royalties to ten cents per barrel; and, in 1938—with aging Dubbs patents and the spread of the new catalytic cracking processes—to five cents. By 1944, when thermal cracking was in decline, and catalytic cracking was taking over the field, the rate fell to three cents.[23-26]

The Government not only claimed that defendants were not competing with their patents, but that the royalties they set were oppressive. Brandeis concluded that both claims failed. In the Court's view, "the allegation that the royalties charged are onerous is, standing alone, without legal significance . . ." Significant or not, the allegation was put to a casual empirical test: ". . . the continued operations of the licensees, their increasing production and the absence of complaint on their part tend to disprove the charge.[23-27] Whatever economic significance "onerous" may have, the Brandeis test for it is nonsensical. For, as the theory has already shown, rationally exploiting even the strongest patent by licensing will always produce those results, especially pronounced when—as with gasoline—demand is growing rapidly.

Thus the decision comes to center on two key concepts: "domination"

23–24. Enos, op. cit. supra note 34, at 311. Royalty discounts (1924 or 1926) for very large users are discussed by Enos at 90; and in Beaton, op. cit. supra note 34, at 253 (1957). Enos' royalty data for Standard (Indiana) end with 1924. The original type of Burton units stopped operating in 1917; the improved Burton-Clark units stopped in 1931. Enos, Id., at 56.

23–25. Enos, Id., at 111, 245, 304, 126–128. Compare at 322, which gives a royalty of 12 cents in 1922.

23–26. Enos, Id., at 91, 214, 286, 311. Beaton op. cit. supra note 34, at 258, says U.O.P.'s royalty rate fell to ten cents in 1932, rather than 1934.

23–27. Standard Oil Co. (Indiana) v. United States, 283 U.S. 163, 172, and n. 7 (1931).

and "industry."[23-28] The first problem is to discover which "industry" is the relevant one; the second, to judge whether defendants "dominated" it. Both involve questions of fact and economic logic. In both respects, I think the Court was wrong. It may be argued, somewhat ingenuously, that no more facts can be pulled out of a record than were placed into it; that what goes into it is influenced by the vision and skill of the adversaries; and that the Supreme Court inherited a record that may have been flawed and stale.[23-29] Deficiencies in logic are harder to rationalize.

First, consider the questions of fact. The Court held that in 1924 and 1925, the New Jersey, Indiana, Texas, and Gasoline Products companies ". . . owned or licensed . . . only 55 per cent of the total cracking capacity, and the remainder was distributed among twenty-one independently owned cracking processes.[23-30] Judging from Enos, the 55 per cent figure may be substantially incorrect or importantly misleading. In 1927, for example, processes of the four defendant companies accounted for about 67 per cent of the total cracking capacity; UOP's Dubbs process—never even mentioned by the Court—for almost 13 per cent; and "other thermal processes" (perhaps including coking and other highly remote substitutes) for about 20 per cent.[23-31] Although Indiana and UOP were at that time in legal contest, there is no evidence that they were competing vigorously in royalty rates. On the hypothesis that those suits were simply to determine or alter the company *shares* of maximum joint proceeds, it would not be far-fetched also to count in UOP. After 1931, it is mandatory, since UOP had been bought. That would raise the group share of total capacity to around 80 per cent. As a share of cracked gasoline output in 1927, processes of the Texas, New Jersey, Indiana, and Gasoline

23–28. If combining patent owners effectively dominate an industry, the power to fix and maintain royalties is tantamount to the power to fix prices. And,

> Where domination exists, a pooling of competing process patents, or an exchange of licenses for the purpose of curtailing the manufacture and supply of an unpatented product, is beyond the privileges conferred by the patents and constitutes a violation of the Sherman Act. The lawful individual monopolies granted by the patent statutes cannot be unitedly exercised to restrain competition.

Id., at 174.

23–29. Suit was brought in June 1924. The final decree of the District Court was entered on January 20, 1930. The Court, or someone else, does appear to have done some research to supplement the trial record. Id., at 176, n.11.

23–30. Id., at 175.

23–31. Enos, op. cit. supra note 34, at 286. I suspect, too, that closer investigation might reveal a geographic component to explain some of the "other . . . processes." For crude oil types and prices and product prices varied geographically. As a consequence, some of the "other thermal processes" may have been confined to certain areas and perhaps were ineffectual substitutes elsewhere.

Products companies may have accounted for around 65 per cent. According to the same source, the four defendants produced or licensed around 70 per cent in 1925.[23-32] In any case, the combined shares and methods of exploitation did produce nonnegligible royalty rates and royalty incomes, in both instances probably much higher than noncooperative pricing of five close substitutes would have permitted.[23-33]

Whereas the Court's arithmetic is suspect, its economics is simply wrong. For it concluded that the relevant "industry" was neither cracking patents nor cracked gasoline, but *all* gasoline. As Brandeis put it:

> The output of cracked gasoline in the years in question was about 26 per cent of the total gasoline production. Ordinary or straight run gasoline is indistinguishable from cracked gasoline and the two are either mixed or sold interchangeably. Under these circumstances the primary defendants could not effectively control the supply or fix the price of cracked gasoline by virtue of their alleged monopoly of the cracking process, unless they could control, through some means, the remainder of the total gasoline production from all sources. Proof of such control is lacking.[23-34]
>
> In the absence of proof that the primary defendants had such control of the entire industry as would make effective the alleged domination of a part, it is difficult to see how they could by agreeing upon royalty rates control either the price or the supply of gasoline, or otherwise restrain competition.[23-35]

On the Court's theory, it would be even more "difficult to see" how between 1913 and 1920, with a patent monopoly but with relatively smaller importance of cracked gasoline to the total, Indiana Standard was able to earn millions of dollars in royalties. If Figure *1* cannot correct the Court's myopia, it at least reveals it. Consistently with the Court's view, assume that gasoline refining is a competitive industry. S_9 would be its supply curve if there were no cracked gasoline. D is the demand for gasoline, and P_9 would be the price of gasoline. With cracking, C_0 would be the maximum achievable supply of cracked gasoline if zero royalties were charged for the process. The new total supply, on the same assumption, would at each price sum the cracked and straight-run gasoline supplied. S_0 is that potential supply, which presumably would be approximated if there were a large number of patentees competing vigorously in licensing economically identical processes. The price, with competition in licensing and production, would be P_0. Gasoline sales would total Q_0, of

23–32. Id., at 285. See also at 119, for much higher shares, which "may be overestimated. . . ." Compare 283 U.S. at 176, n.11.

23–33. This assumes that a non-collusive "oligopoly" of five would not produce pure monopoly outcomes; and that court tests, if completed, would not have given all power to one patentee.

23–34. 283 U.S. at 176–177.

23–35. Id., at 179.

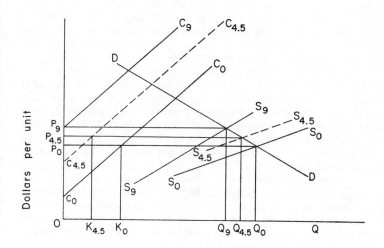

Fig. 1*a*. (From McGee)

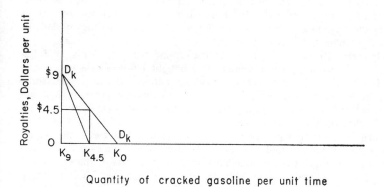

Quantity of cracked gasoline per unit time

Fig. 1*b*. (From McGee)

which K_0—in this example roughly one-third—would be cracked. Figure *1* B shows a derived demand for cracked gasoline. It was derived from a few propositions and simplifying assumptions. Given a fixed demand curve for all gasoline, the gasoline price is determined by the total supply of gasoline, cracked plus straight-run. Given a fixed supply curve for straight-run gasoline, significant variations in the supply of cracked gasoline will change the price of *all* gasoline.[23-36] And, whether because there is collusion amongst patentees or only one patentee, changes in the royalty rate will change the supply of cracked gasoline. At a zero royalty rate, C_0 is that supply curve. At a royalty rate of zero, the gasoline price will be P_0, and K_0 cracked gasoline will be sold. Hence the K_0 quantity in Figure *1* B. At a royalty rate of $9 per unit of gasoline produced, zero cracked gasoline will be produced even at a price as high as P_9, which is as high as it *can* go unless final demand rises or the supply of straight-run gasoline should fall. Thus, the quantity of cracked gasoline sold and the demand for patents to produce it depend upon the royalty charged. For royalties between zero and $9, interdependency of *total* gasoline supply and the supply of cracked gasoline must be recognized explicitly. In this simple example, assuming zero marginal cost of patent licensing, the maximizing royalty would be $4.50, which yields a cracked gasoline supply function of $C_{4.5}$ and sales of $K_{4.5}$. A large number of competing patentees would obtain essentially zero royalties under the same circumstances, and the price of *all* gasoline would be significantly lower. And note that these fairly substantial effects occur in this example *even though cracked gasoline is about one-sixth* (not 26 per cent) of all gasoline sold.

Of course, I have not proved that the defendants (and others) in the *Cracking Patents* case conspired to fix royalty rates, though theory and facts suggest it. I *have* demonstrated that it would pay to do so under similar circumstances, even though patents govern a minority share of some larger total "market." The Court did not think that was possible, even if there *were* collusion. In short, there is a market for patents as well as the "product." The Court chose to look at the wrong market, or at the right one in the wrong way.

In January, 1931, the Court, of course, found for defendants. In January, 1931, a group of major refiners had bought UOP. These two events consolidated the principal thermal cracking patents. By this time, some of the basic patents had expired. Nevertheless thermal cracking had not yet played out its string. It may be useful briefly to note some developments following the 1931 decision.

A further, somewhat puzzling, agreement occurred in 1937: the Texas, Indiana, New Jersey, and Gasoline Products companies—all of them parties to earlier agreements, and the first three members of the group that acquired UOP in 1931—plus Atlantic and Gulf, granted UOP rights to all their cracking patents.[23-37] Thereafter, UOP could license under all major thermal cracking processes. According to McKnight,

23–36. The simplest assumption will do: S_9 is, then, either the supply function applicable when factors are bought by both sectors at constant supply prices; or one describing one of two wholly independent sectors.

23–37. Beaton, op. cit. supra note 34, at 258, who reports that all subscribers to the 1931 purchase of U.O.P. had gotten paid-up licenses. Not so puzzling is the presence of Atlantic and Gulf, neither of which apparently had much, if any, patent strength in the field. Each paid $3 million, and got licenses under U.O.P. patents. Even so, it is not clear whether or to what extent they were

The most important immediate effect of the agreement is probably the acquiring, by Universal, of licensing rights under the Behimer patents owned by the Texas Company. One of the less commendable results . . . is that the monopoly possessed by Universal since 1921 by virtue of Dubbs ["clean circulation"] patent 1,392,629 [issued October 4, 1921] is extended at least to 1949 under Behimer patent 1,883,850, and that any possibility of a court test of the validity of the latter patent is practically eliminated.[23-38]

---

buying immunity from suits for past practices, paying damages, buying rights thought to be valuable in the future, or pooling profits.

McKnight's account differs somewhat; but still leaves areas of mystery. "Unexplained" animosity developed between U.O.P. and the four major patent adversaries with whom it had made peace in 1931—three of whom had participated in its purchase! After 1931 visible litigation centered on Winkler Koch, an engineering firm that had made some installations alleged to infringe various GPC, Indiana Standard, and U.O.P. patents. Winkler Koch won suits involving Indiana, and GPC; but lost—in Universal Oil Products Co. v. Winkler Koch Engineering Co., 6 F. Supp. 763 (1934), aff'd, 78 F. 2d 991 (1935)—to U.O.P., certain of whose Dubbs and Egloff patents were upheld. Whether these or similar suits had anything to do with the "animosity" is not clear to me. According to McKnight, however, some kind of litigation amongst the old rivals was approaching trial in 1937, when the new agreement was made. Under it, he says, U.O.P. paid an undisclosed amount for nonexclusive patent rights from the Texas, Gasoline Products, Indiana, New Jersey, Atlantic, and Gulf Companies. McKnight, op. cit. supra note 34, at 113–114. See also 128–29, describing certain important Behimer patents not issued till 1932, "When the matter claimed therein was already old in the art." McKnight concludes that the 1937 agreement effectively forestalled court tests of these patents, which may suggest a more specific explanation of both the "animosity" and the agreement itself.

To add still another possibility to what is already too many, the so-called Cross process of Gasoline Products Company suffered some patent damage on November 18, 1936. Gasoline Products Co., Inc. v. Champlin Refining Co., 86 F. 2d 552 (1936). The much earlier agreement probably reflected Cross process patent weakness. As McKnight puts it, "It is hard to see how the Ellis patents [related to New Jersey Standard's Tube and Tank process], with their early date, should not have dominated the subject matter of the Cross patents if the owners of the former had chosen to press their claims. They did not so choose, selecting rather to pool their rights with those of the Cross interests, thus escaping the expense and hazards of litigation." McKnight, Id., at 83.

According to Beaton, a 1944 Supreme Court opinion, Universal Oil Products Co. v. Glove Oil & Refining Co. 322 U.S. 471 (1944), invalidated crucial C. P. Dubbs ("clean recirculation") and Egloff ("selective cracking") patents, practically eliminating U.O.P.'s patent position. Beaton, op. cit. supra note 34 at 258. But both previously had been upheld in Universal Oil Products Co. v. Winkler Koch Engineering Co., 6 F. Supp. 763 (1934), aff'd, 78 F. 2d 991 (1935), cited by McKnight, op. cit. supra note 34 at 20.

23–38. Id., at 113–114. In 1931, an earlier settlement had been reached so far as overlaps between certain Dubbs and Behimer patents. The Dubbs claims on a hot-oil pump were relinquished in favor of those of Behimer; and Behimer

As is often true, however, it was premature to talk of indefinitely extending monopoly power through improvements on old processes. What
happened was the development of catalytic cracking, which in a relatively
few years wiped out thermal cracking.

Glass Containers: The Hartford-Empire Case

Perhaps the case which more than any other is pointed to as an example of industry cartelization achieved through pooled patents is
the *Hartford-Empire* case.[24] The plan of action and the trade-restraining effects alleged by the government and found by the Court in this
case were so all-embracing that no simple abstract can expose the
numerous areas where patent and antitrust law conflicted. Patents were
accumulated by internal development, by purchase, and by pooling.
Competing and conflicting patents were pooled or cross-licensed
through settlement of litigation. Divisions of fields of use were
assigned among the participating companies, and these fields were
protected by the pooled patents of the participants. Moreover, through
a trade association the closely cooperating members were found to
have assigned and policed production quotas among themselves and
used various means of discouraging increases in production by outsiders. Justice Roberts, who wrote the majority opinion, concluded:

> In summary, the situation brought about in the glass industry, and
> existing in 1938, was this: Hartford, with technical and financial aid of
> others in the conspiracy, had acquired, by issue to it or assignment from
> the owners, more than 600 patents. These, with over 100 Corning con-
> trolled patents, over 60 Owens patents, over 70 Hazel patents, and some
> 12 Lynch patents, had been, by cross-licensing agreements, merged into a
> pool which effectively controlled the industry. This control was exercised
> to allot production in Corning's field to Corning, and that in restricted
> classes within the general container field to Owens, Hazel, Thatcher, Ball
> and such other smaller manufacturers as the group agreed should be
> licensed. The result was that 94% of the glass containers manufactured
> in this country on feeders and formers were made on machinery licensed
> under the pooled patents.[25]

Given this situation the Court had so little difficulty in distinguish-

---

claims on clean circulation gave way to those of Dubbs. Enos, op. cit. supra
note 34, at 71. See also McKnight, at 127, for an assertion that as late as
1938, operating even a typical 1922 unit might infringe Behimer!
   24. Hartford-Empire Co. v. U.S., 323 U.S. 386 (1945).
   25. Ibid., p. 400.

ing the *Standard Oil* cracking case that it found detailing these differences unnecessary except in the most general terms—"It is clear,"
Roberts wrote, "that, by cooperative arrangements and binding agreements, the appellant corporations, over a period of years, regulated
and suppressed competition in the use of glass making machinery and
employed their joint patent position to allocate fields of manufacture
and to maintain the prices of unpatented glassware."[26]

The *Hartford-Empire* arrangement differed from that in *Standard
Indiana* principally in terms of its all-inclusiveness. In each case patents were pooled and exploited in such manner that competition among
them could have been found to have been eliminated. But in the *glass
container* case there were found to be assigned territories and maintained prices for unpatented as well as patented glassware. This, however, was not a distinction made by the Court in explaining why the
cracking pool was legal and the glassware pool was illegal. The illegality of the Hartford-Empire scheme was all too obvious to the entire
court. It found that Hartford-Empire, the most important supplier of
machinery to the industry, had conspired with major glass container
manufacturers as well as with the industry's trade association to monopolize container machinery patents, glass container machinery, and
the trade in glass containers as well.[27]

---

26. Ibid., pp. 406–7.
27. The economic grounds for so sweeping a conclusion has not gone unchallenged. In a detailed analysis of the glass container industry in general, and
the Hartford-Empire case and its case record in particular, James A. Brown,
Jr., wrote a dissertation on this subject in 1966. ("Antitrust and Competition in
the Glass Container Industry," Ph.D. diss., Department of Economics, Duke
University, Durham, North Carolina.) Brown's examination of the trial record
led him to the conclusion that this record did not entirely support the courts'
findings. Why, it was posited in Brown's thesis, would a company with Hartford's strong patent control need to cooperate with other glass container manufacturers or utilize a trade association in order to earn the greatest return from
its patents? His conclusion, summarizing a careful economic analysis, was
(pp. 322 et seq.) that Hartford and several leading container manufacturers,
all of whom held machinery patents, entered into complicated cross-licensing
arrangements, the result of which was that Hartford was able to consolidate
its patent control of the *gob feeder* and thus to collect production royalties on
about two-thirds of domestic glass container output. Owens-Illinois Glass Company, under the terms of its cross-licensing agreement with Hartford, automatically received a portion of Hartford's income, and produced most of the
remaining one-third of the glass container output on its patented *suction* machines. Owens, the country's largest manufacturer of glass containers, and
nonmanufacturing Hartford, along with Hazel-Atlas Glass Company, the industry's second largest firm, which also supplied patent rights for a share of

When it came to the question of what relief would be appropriate,
however, the Court was sharply divided. This division concerned what
was necessary and proper to restore competition in this industry. The
Court evidenced a reluctance to dissolve the pool which was un-
matched by a reluctance to regulate the industry's behavior.[28] The
government requested dissolution of Hartford-Empire, the principal
patent holder. The decree of the district court reserved but did not
deny this relief. The Supreme Court overruled this part of the lower
court decree. It was too drastic. Also, it seems reasonable to infer, it
was potentially too disruptive and too complicated to serve the interest
of licensees. Regulation of licensing at nondiscriminatory, reasonable
rates was an easier alternative. There was case precedent for proscribing bad behavior, as well as for attempting to stimulate *competition* by
fostering the interests of *competitors*. In addition, although it was not
made explicit in the opinion, the complicated interrelationships among
the patents pooled and the potential difficulties foreseeable in attempting to reopen previously settled conflicting and competing claims must
surely have impressed the Court. The long, complicated history of
patent acquisition involving technical subject matter did not lend itself
to easy prediction about the results of depooling in an industry so long
controlled.

In attempting to fashion adequate relief, District Judge Kloeb, after
finding that the defendants "far exceeded the rights conferred upon
them by the patent grant,"[29] concluded that "no half-way measures

---

Hartford's income, were the principal (and only significant) participants in
this patent-sharing scheme.

Thus the Brown conclusion does not deny, but rather affirms, the Supreme
Court finding with respect to the elimination of competition among competing
machinery patents. What it does cast great doubt upon is that these patents,
once pooled, were exploited not in the interest of the patentees, but rather in
the interest of licensees. With respect to licensing practice, for example: "Hartford did not cooperate with ordinary container manufacturers [i.e., those without
important patents] to restrict output and to limit competition in the industry"
(p. 323). And with respect to the Glass Container Association: "this study
located no evidence to substantiate the courts' findings that Hartford cooper-
ated or conspired with GCA to help enforce the quota system. In this instance,
the licensees acted independently of Hartford and even contrary to Hartford's
best interests, as economic theory demonstrates" (pp. 223–24).

28. Justice Roberts delivered the majority opinion. Three justices, Douglas,
Murphy, and Jackson, did not take part. Justices Black and Rutledge dissented
with respect to the adequacy of the relief.

29. United States v. Hartford-Empire Co., 46 F. Supp. 541 (D.C., N.D. Ohio
1942) at p. 619.

will suffice."[30] The government, as has been indicated, had requested the dissolution of Hartford-Empire. Judge Kloeb wanted to avoid that step if possible, but recognizing that alternatives might not be effective, stated that if his alternatives did not work that he would order dissolution. To make sure that a dissolution remedy would remain open he held it "absolutely necessary that the receivers (immediately to be appointed) take over the management of Hartford forthwith."[31] Funds from each licensee were to be earmarked and set aside pending appeal.

The permanent steps which Judge Kloeb decreed in fashioning relief, however, were directed at abuses. The court viewed as the greatest abuse the licensing and lease system. "It is through the licensing and lease system that Hartford retains control over and dominates the industry."[32] Although the court recognized that such a system "may be perfectly legal and just if properly used," the deliberate abuse in this case and the danger that it would continue to be misused called for the conclusion "that this entire system must be abolished."[33] Automatic machinery was to be put on the basis of outright sale to anyone at reasonable prices. The machinery patents and patent applications[34] controlled by any of the defendants were to be free of royalty to any manufacturer of machines. All present licenses were to be canceled and machinery was to be sold to existing licensees at *reasonable rates.*

The Supreme Court, not without vigorous dissent, thought even contingent dissolution of Hartford-Empire unnecessary and inappropriate. It ordered that the receivership which Judge Kloeb had established "be wound up and the business returned to Hartford."[35] With respect to the lower court's decree that machinery be sold rather than leased and that machinery manufacturing be licensed royalty-free to machinery makers, the Supreme Court held: "we think they go beyond what is required to dissolve the combination and prevent future combinations of like character."[36] And, after pointing out that Hartford had reduced all royalties to a uniform scale and eliminated output restriction as well as field of use provisions, the Court found that

30. Ibid., p. 620.
31. Ibid.
32. Ibid., p. 621.
33. Ibid.
34. Including all patent rights relating to the suction machine feeders, forming machines and lehrs.
35. Hartford-Empire Co. v. U.S., 323 U.S. 386 (1945), at p. 411.
36. Ibid., p. 414.

future misuse was appropriately protected by court injunction.[37] Furthermore, since no reward was to be available to Hartford for the use of its valid patents under the District Court's decree, the Supreme Court found this confiscatory. It was not impressed by the government's argument that Hartford might, with the Court's consent, sell its patents and thus get some revenue. At the suggestion that some of Hartford's patents were improperly obtained, and some were awarded a priority to which the invention was not entitled, the higher court concluded that "avenues are open to the Government to raise these questions and to have the patents cancelled." But if, as the Court went on, "as we must assume on this record, a defendant owns valid patents, it is difficult to say that, however much in the past such defendant has abused the rights thereby conferred, it must now dedicate them to the public."[38]

The decree below was thus so substantially modified as to effectively overrule the lower court's whole theory of relief. Moreover, although "fair pricing" of a public utility character was called for in the decree proposed by Judge Kloeb (reasonable pricing of machine sales), the revised decree by the Supreme Court relied almost entirely on "reasonable fee fixing" to achieve its aims. Patent licensing in the glass container industry became a regulated industry, much as if it were a natural monopoly.[39]

Neither the majority nor the minority opinions of the Supreme Court placed any significant emphasis on the shortcomings of regulatory relief. Rather, disagreement related primarily to the monopoly-maintaining potential of lease versus sale and the impropriety of an appeals court's second-guessing a better-informed trial court. And more generally, there was emphasis on judicial disagreement about the relative priority of antitrust over patent law. The continuing controversy about where patent rights end and antitrust laws take over was discussed in the relief context without any more rational clarification of the "scope" question than earlier decisions had exhibited.[40]

37. But see Brown, "Antitrust and Competition in the Glass Container Industry," in which an economic study of the record casts considerable doubt as to whether the method of licensing was anything more than a profit-maximizing device.

38. Hartford-Empire Co. v. U.S., 323 U.S. 386 (1945), at p. 415.

39. See chapter 12 regarding compulsory licensing.

40. Mr. Brown has summed up the policy implication of this question: "Only one of Hartford's cross-licensing transactions, the 1924 agreement with Owens, seems to have diminished traditional economic competition significantly. There

The *Hartford-Empire* case presented a clear and unequivocal example of patent pooling giving rise to output-restrictive activity considerably beyond that measured by the competitive superiority of the individual patents. How much more probably cannot be assessed.[41] Had each successive patent acquisition or cross-license been currently reviewed in terms of whether the patents joined were competing or noncompeting, perhaps the frustrating experience of fashioning either divestitory or regulatory relief could have been avoided. But whether it could or could not, this does not detract from the importance of asking the right questions—and asking them at the right time. The patent omelet which was the *Hartford-Empire* case did not lend itself to unscrambling.

Incandescent Lamps, Bulbs, Tubing, and Cane

In the 1926 *General Electric* case the acquisition, cross-licensing, or pooling of patents was not at issue. Later, however, in an antitrust action brought by the government and reaching the district court in 1949, the government charged General Electric, International General Electric, Westinghouse, Corning, N. V. Philips, Hygrade Sylvania, and others with a conspiracy to monopolize and restrain interstate and foreign trade in the incandescent electric lamp industry in violation of sections 1 and 2 of the Sherman Act.[42] Violation of the Clayton Act was also alleged, but attention is here limited to the patent-pooling aspects of the case. Specifically alleged in this connection was acquiring and maintaining monopolies of (1) patents relating to incandescent electric lamps, and (2) patents relating to glass bulbs, tubing and cane."[43]

The government complained that agreements and cross-licenses between General Electric and Corning were contrived to establish in them the control of the manufacture and sale of glass for electrical

---

was no patent conflict between Hartford's gob-feeding process and Owens' suction process, and the two firms appear to have agreed, at least tacitly, not to license these alternative processes in competition with one another . . . probably the main, and perhaps the only, [logical] concern of the antitrust litigation." (Brown, "Antitrust and Competition in the Glass Container Industry.")

41. Principally, however, measured by the competition eliminated between gob-feeding and suction-feeding. See note 40, supra.

42. U.S. v. General Electric Co. et al., 82 F. Supp. 753 (D.C. N.J. 1949).

43. Ibid., p. 766.

purposes which they divided in two fields. Corning's field was the sale of glass parts; General Electric's was for the manufacture and sale of incandescent electric lamps.[44] The government further alleged that "in order to bring patent rights and licenses of other glass companies within the field created by General Electric and Corning, and in order to prevent competition Corning entered into agreements with the Hartford-Empire Company . . . [and] by virtue of its agreements with Corning, General Electric secured the benefits of the agreements with Hartford."[45] To substantiate this last contention a 1927 letter from Corning's attorney was quoted:

> I have studied as best I could the Corning-Hartford-Empire agreement, and as I interpret it Hartford-Empire gets no rights in machines that Corning develops in the field of bulbs or mold blown articles usable in conjunction with electricity, and therefore there is no reason why Corning could not enter into a further agreement with General Electric to pool their future inventions.[46]

The government further alleged that exclusive licenses of Philips's patents to Corning were a part of a conspiracy from which General Electric also benefited. Here the government argued that neither General Electric nor Corning would be troubled by competition from the large Netherlands producer N. V. Philips. The government also contended that the "real purpose of these agreements was to keep Philips out of the United States glass market and that General Electric actively participated with Corning in accomplishing this purpose."[47]

In its patent licensing it was General Electric's policy to obtain "the beneficial use of the patents of its domestic licensees."[48] Similar arrangements with respect to foreign patents were derived through arrangements made abroad by its subsidiary, International General Electric. Regarding these arrangements the court noted: "Since the main buttress of its position in the incandescent electric lamp industry was patents, it followed the conscious policy of funneling into its control all patents held by its licensees and touching any phase of the industry. . . . The [nonexclusive] license includes the right to sublicense for the life of the patent. It [General Electric] was thus placed in the

44. Ibid., p. 786.
45. Ibid., p. 789.
46. Ibid.
47. Ibid., p. 797.
48. Ibid., p. 815.

position of rendering impotent any possible advantages to which one of its licensees would normally be entitled as the owner of the patent."[49]

Judge Forman's conclusion about the patent-accumulation aspects of the case left no doubt of its illegality under the Sherman Act. The patent accumulation was an attempt to monopolize. He wrote:

In this present case, General Electric regimented an industry by, among other things, its acquisition of patents to perpetuate a control over the incandescent electric lamp long after its basic patents expired to maintain a dominant position rendering it possible for it to eliminate competition and maintain an industrial monopoly of the type recognized by the Transparent-Wrap case to be an eventuality violative of the antitrust laws. Its aggregation of patents into its control permitted General Electric to monopolize patents and by so doing it violated § 2 of the Sherman Anti-Trust Act.[50]

Final judgment was not passed until 1953,[51] after the government and the defendants had offered numerous suggestions for implementing the opinion in this many-faceted case. With respect to patents and technology, the district court provided that the defendant's patents on incandescent lamps and lamp parts be dedicated to the public. Lamp machinery patents held by General Electric, as well as its other lamp machines and lamp parts patents issued in the previous five years, were to be licensed at reasonable royalties. Relief called for royalty-free licensing. It thus clearly exceeded that allowed by the Supreme Court in *Hartford-Empire*. In fact it was strongly contended by the defendants that royalty-free licensing was foreclosed by that decision. Concerning this Judge Forman, citing the more recent *National Lead* case,[52] held that royalty-free licensing cannot always be precluded because it may be confiscatory. His holding, quoting *National Lead*[53] was:

While it has been contended that because of the decision in this Court in Hartford-Empire . . . the District Court was not free in the present case to require the issuance of royalty-free licenses, we feel that, without reaching the question of whether royalty-free licensing or a perpetual injunction against the enforcement of a patent is permissible as a matter

49. Ibid.
50. Ibid., p. 816.
51. U.S. v. General Electric Co., 115 F. Supp. 835 (D.N.J. 1953).
52. U.S. v. National Lead Co., 332 U.S. 319 (1947).
53. Ibid., p. 338.

of law in any case, the present decree represents an exercise of sound judicial discretion.

"Sound judicial discretion" in this respect in *Hartford-Empire,* in *National Lead* or in *General Electric* is difficult to distinguish. Each of these cases is characterized by the fact that more was involved than an attempt to maximize the reward due to the superiority afforded by valid noncompeting patents. The schemes in each of these cases involved either the elimination of competition between patents or utilizing patents as a screen for creating broader monopoly. The restriction thus effected was greater than the sum of the restrictions afforded by the individual patents. This kind of "scope extension" might have provided a rationale for allowing royalty-free licensing and in this respect overruling *Hartford-Empire.* It did not. Royalty-free licensing has not been recommended solely for "scope extension" reasons. Neither has it been reserved for cases where competing and noncompeting patents are so inextricably intermixed that divesture is unworkable. Consequently, royalty-free licensing by "sound judicial discretion" remains open to wide speculation and great uncertainty.[54] It continues to be urged by the government in a wide variety of situations, and it is often utilized in consent judgments.[55]

54. Those who minimize the precedent-setting value of royalty-free licensing by judicial discretion can point to the fact that Westinghouse and Corning, in 1942 and 1946 respectively, before Judge Forman's ruling, had already accepted consent decrees which provided for royalty-free licenses. (See Vaughan, *United States Patent System,* p. 122.) But National Lead, cited by Forman, is the leading precedent for the Supreme Court decision allowing royalty-free licensing.

55. See chapter 12.

11

Legally Permissible Use of Accumulated Patents

In the *Line Material* and *New Wrinkle* cases (discussed in chapter 9) price-restrictive licensing was prohibited because separately owned patents had been combined by cross-license or assignment. This prohibition, it will be recalled, was held applicable even though the patents were noncompeting. In *Line Material*, for example, the patents cross-licensed were basic patents and improvement patents. In the pooling cases, analyzed in chapter 10, the patents combined bore a wide variety of relationships, not always identified, but the evidence in each case was strong that competition among patents was eliminated. Also notable was the elimination of competition in unpatented products. But when patents were pooled, and the pooled patents were found to be used as a part of a scheme to cartelize an industry, as they were in the *Hartford-Empire* case and in the 1949 *General Electric* case, the courts adopted regulatory relief strongly conditioned by previous misuse cases in which patent pooling or cross-licensing was not involved. A question does arise, however, about stricter standards of misuse being applicable when patents are pooled than when they are not. The *Line Material* cross-license resulted in the proscription of only one form of misuse—price-restrictive licensing. In *Hartford-Empire*, which involved an industrywide pool, on the other hand, not only were divisions of fields agreements[1] also struck down, but compulsory licensing of *all* patents was called for.

In his 1949 *General Electric* decision, Judge Forman found that one of the means the General Electric Company had used "to perpetuate a

---

1. Long-standing precedent with respect to division of fields is afforded by the Addyston Pipe case (U.S. v. Addyston Pipe and Steel Co., 85 F. 271 [C.C.A. 6th 1898]).

control over the incandescent electric lamp after its basic patents expired"[2] was the requirement that General Electric's licensees license back all improvements or new inventions in the field covered by the patents licensed. These license-back contracts were nonexclusive by their terms. But Judge Forman held that even this form of licensing-back, at least in the incandescent lamp case, involved an improper extension of the scope of the original patents. He did not, however, explain how this scope extension was expected to work. He merely quoted language from the *Transparent Wrap* case,[3] a case which approved an assignment-back provision in a patent license.

Permissibility of Agreements to Assign Back Improvements: The Transwrap Case

The provision of the agreement in *Transwrap,* around which the controversy in that case turned, was a covenant to assign to the licensor any improvement patents applicable to the licensed packaging machine.[4] No pool of patents, however, was involved in *Transwrap.* The patent license agreement at issue in that case granted the licensee an exclusive license to manufacture and sell in the United States, Canada, and Mexico a patented machine under patents then owned or later acquired by the licensor, subject to the condition noted that the licensee assign back improvements. The license agreement contained a formula by which royalties were to be computed and paid. It was subject to termination for specified defaults. The parties operated under this agreement for several years when the licensor ascertained that the licensee had taken out certain patents on improvements on the machine in breach of the agreement to disclose and assign. Since this did not occur, the agreement was terminated. The licensee then instituted action asking that the provision regarding the improvement patents be declared illegal and unenforceable and that the licensor be

---

2. U.S. v. General Electric Co., et al., 82 F. Supp. 753 (D.C. N.J. 1949), at p. 816.

3. Transwrap Corp. v. Stokes Co., 329 U.S. 637 (1947).

4. The relevant provision in the Transwrap case (ibid., p. 639) reads: "If the licensee shall discover or invent an improvement which is applicable to the Transwrap Packaging Machine and suitable for use in connection therewith and applicable to making and closing of the package . . . it shall submit the same to the Licensor, which may, at its option, apply for Letters Patent for the same."

enjoined from terminating the agreement. The district court held the provision valid. The court of appeals, in a divided decision, reversed, citing the line of patent tie-in cases beginning with *Motion Picture Patents* and continuing through *Mercoid*. The circuit court of appeals viewed the contested provision as a means of achieving a monopoly over that which "is not embraced in the invention."[5] The logic, or illogic, of leveraging to a second monopoly by exercise of the first, typical of tie-in law, was for the court of appeals indistinguishable from a grant-back.

Justice Douglas, who wrote the majority opinion reversing the court of appeals, was faced with the problem of refuting the holding by the court of appeals that: "If the restraint is lawful because of the patent, the patent will have been expanded by contract. That on which no patent could be obtained would be as effectively protected as if a patent had been issued. Private business would function as its own patent office and impose its own law upon licensees."[6] It had been further noted by the court of appeals that "since all improvement patents would not expire until after expiration of petitioner's patents on the machine, the arrangement put respondent at a competitive disadvantage."[7]

Douglas, in overruling the court of appeals, wrote an opinion pointing up three "difficulties" with the opinion of the circuit court of appeals. These "difficulties," interestingly enough, turn out to be remarkably similar to the kind of difficulties inherent in patent tie-in decisions critically analyzed in chapter 8. In particular, Douglas's analysis of the "scope" problem with respect to licensing-back provides a useful but unutilized guide for reassessing the "leverage fallacy" increasingly characterizing the Supreme Court's tie-in decisions since 1917.

The first of the three difficulties Douglas saw with the circuit court of appeals' opinion related to what Congress wrote into the patent statute with respect to assignability of patent rights. He quoted the following language:

> Every application for patent or patent or any interest therein shall be assignable in law by an instrument in writing, and the applicant or patentee or his assigns or legal representatives may in like manner grant

5. Ibid., p. 640.
6. Ibid., p. 641.
7. Ibid.

and convey an exclusive right under his application for patent or patent to the whole or any specific part of the United States.[8]

The statute, as Douglas stressed, "does not limit the consideration which may be paid for the assignment *to any species or kind of property.*"[9] And "we see no difference whether the consideration is services or cash, or the right to use another patent."[10]

Douglas's point is well taken. But it might be added that equally appropriate remuneration would, by this analysis, also include any other form of noncash payment including use with patentee's materials. Indeed, why restrict any use, if the competitive superiority of individual patents accumulated, through either license or assignment, is not exceeded? Clearly, Douglas was not holding that the language he quoted sanctioned the assignment of *competing* patents into a pool. And neither, as he later specified, was he holding that a different rule is appropriate for licensing-back agreements than for assigning-back agreements. But his holding in *Transwrap* was based on the scope of a patent's superiority. By his logic it thus might be said to be applicable to all use-restrictive licenses including tying contracts not involving leveraging. His rule applied to licensing agreements as well as to outright assignments. His language seems clear on this: "the freedom of one who assigns a patent is restricted to the same degree whether the assignment is made pursuant to a license agreement or otherwise."[11]

Since a patent is a species of property giving the patentee or his assignee the exclusive right to make, use, and vend the invention or discovery, and since that exclusive right is the essence of the patent privilege, it is, Douglas held, "for purposes of the assignment statute, of the same dignity as any other property which may be used to purchase patents."[12]

Douglas's conclusion that patents may be paid for in a variety of ways without violating patent law was recognized as being only a partial answer to the position taken by the circuit court of appeals. His second "difficulty" involved the holding (like the holdings in

8. Ibid., p. 642, citing R.S. § 4898, 35 U.S.C. Supp. V § 47.
9. Ibid. (emphasis added).
10. Ibid.
11. Ibid., p. 643.
12. Ibid.

patent tie-in cases) regarding the divisibility of the right to exclude. The court of appeals had pointed out that the power to refuse a license does not mean that a patentee has the power to license on such conditions as he may choose. But why not? Douglas now concedes to the appeals court opinion that if leveraging to a second monopoly is involved that "would enable the patentee not only to exploit the invention but to use it to acquire a monopoly not embraced in the patent."[13] Douglas, about as unequivocally as critics of tie-in law could wish, now calls for a competitive superiority test. Applying this test to the current case (without distinguishing patent tie-in cases except to note that Congress has not made illegal the acquisition of improvement patents by the owner of a basic patent),[14] Douglas writes: "It is, of course, true that the monopoly which the licensor obtains when he acquires the improvement patent extends beyond the terms of the basic patent. But . . . *that is not creating by agreement a monopoly which the law otherwise would not sanction.* The grant of the improvement patent itself creates the monopoly."[15] The holding seems both clear and correct—no leverage, no illegality. Douglas then goes on to write: "On the facts of the present case [as on the facts of the *Line Material* case which went the other way?] the effect on the public interest would seem to be the same whether the licensee owns the improvement patent."[16]

In this kind of test, one recommended in this study for much more general application, a judicial line-drawing is made possible between permissible patent licensing practice and activitity that violates antitrust law. All patents, as Douglas recognizes, create monopoly. Combining patents, whether by license-back or by other means, however, is appropriately tested by the same scope standard.

Douglas's third "difficulty" is actually a reservation suggesting the appropriateness of a "rule of reason" by which licensing-back is to be tested in such manner as *not* to lend approval to schemes by which "as patents are added to patents a whole industry may be regi-

---

13. Ibid.
14. Ibid., p. 642. But where, Douglas might be asked, if the absence of a statutory prohibition is pertinent, is the statutory prohibition of any use-restrictive licensing? See chapter 7 for the development of this court-made law.
15. Ibid., p. 646 (emphasis added).
16. Ibid.

mented."[17] The cases he cites in his third point in this connection
include cases similarly identified in preceding chapters: *Standard Sanitary*, *Masonite*, *Ethyl Gasoline*, and *Hartford-Empire*, among others.[18]

The Applicability of the Transwrap Rule to "Industrywide" Agreements

It was this third section of the Douglas opinion in *Transwrap* that
Judge Forman used to justify his condemnation of the license-back
arrangements imposed by the General Electric Company upon its
licensees in the 1949 *General Electric* case. This was because the
assignment-back approved in *Transwrap* was distinguishable from a
license-back as a part of broader arrangement to control an industry
by acquiring all sources of patent competition.

The Douglas rationale for deciding whether a license-back provision
is a valid exercise of a patentee's rights under patent law or a violation
of antitrust law was grounded in the kind of test in which *monopoly*
exploitation of the superiority afforded by the patent could be recognized and distinguished from monopoly arising from the combination
of patents with competing patents or with unpatented substitutes.

Transwrap's Logic Subsequently Ignored

No leverage to new monopoly was found in *Transwrap*. This laudable
conception of a rule of reason has not, however, been extended and
applied to comparable situations in later cases. In fact the leveraging
fallacy, typical of tie-in law, is still being applied with undiminished
rigor to a wide variety of restrictions on use. An example is provided
by the Supreme Court opinion in the *Brulotte* case[19] in 1964. Douglas,
the author of the foregoing *Transwrap* opinion, there found that the
Thys Company had unlawfully misused its patent monopoly by contracting with purchasers of its patented hop-picking machines for
"royalty" based on use beyond the patent term. Douglas held, "A
patent empowers the owner to exact royalties as high as he can
negotiate with the leverage of that monopoly. But to use that leverage
to project those royalty payments beyond the life of the patent is

17. Ibid.
18. Douglas, however, also includes in this section Clayton Act cases, particularly the IBM case. See ibid., pp. 647–48.
19. Brulotte v. Thys Co., 379 U.S. 29 (1964).

analogous to an effort to enlarge the monopoly of the patent by tieing the sale or use of the patented article to the purchase or use of un-patented ones."[20]

How paying "machine royalties" over a period longer than the life of the patent could conceivably be the equivalent of extending the effective life of a patent, the majority opinion again did not reveal. But a dissenting opinion by Justice Harlan exposed the absence of leveraging to additional monopoly. Harlan not only exposed the lever-age fallacy, he also indicated how, by legal draftsmanship, future licensors could achieve precisely the same result without this "techni-cal" legal violation. "Installment of a patented, coin-operated washing machine in the basement of an apartment building without charge ex-cept that the landlord and his tenants must deposit 25 cents for every use," he analogized, "should not cause patent misuse."[21] Harlan's economic analysis of the licensing provision at issue is both terse and true:

> Assume that a Thys contract called for neither an initial flat-sum pay-ment nor any annual minimum royalties; Thys' sole recompense for giv-ing up ownership of its machine was a royalty payment extending beyond the patent term based on use, without any requirement either to use the machine or not to use a competitor's. A moment's thought reveals that, despite the clear restriction on use both before and after the expiration of the patent term, the arrangement would involve no misuse of patent lever-age. Unless the Court's opinion rests on technicalities of contract drafts-manship and not on economic substance of the transaction, the distinction between the hypothetical and the actual case lies only in the cumulative investment consisting of the initial and minimum payments independent of use, which the purchaser obligated himself to make to Thys. I fail to see why this distinguishing feature should be critical.[22]

The *Brulotte* v. *Thys* case stands as warning to those who by analogy would extend *Transwrap*'s relevance beyond the narrow confines of the licensing-back question.

The licenses contested in the *Brulotte* case listed twelve patents. Seven of these were incorporated in the hop-picking machines sold to Brulotte and licensed for specified use. All of these patents had expired by 1957, at which time the petitioner, Brulotte, ceased making the payments he had contracted to make with the seller and licensor,

20. Ibid., p. 33.
21. Ibid., p. 36, n. 1.
22. Ibid., pp. 35–36.

thereby occasioning this legal action. The decision in *Brulotte* does
not rest on the existence of multiple patents. Since all of the patents
had expired when the licensee stopped payment, a literal reading of
the majority opinion does not decide the question whether only partial
payment is required when one or several of multiple patents expires.
In effect, multiple patents were treated as one. But the theory of the
case, standing as it does for the proposition that extending payments
beyond the expiration of a patent is a means of converting a seventeen-year monopoly into a longer one (time leverage), seems logically
extendable to the proposition that a similar time extension is involved
if the payment is not proportionately reduced when one of several
patents expires. To take an extreme example, if Brulotte, rather than
waiting until all the patents embodied in the hop-picking machine
had expired completely to discontinue his payments, had reduced his
payments by one-seventh when the first of the seven patents had expired, why would this not also be permissible by application of the
theory of the case?

A question arises, however, about the applicability of this foregoing part-whole deduction from the logic of the *Brulotte* decision.
The question concerns possible conflict with a 1950 decision by the
Supreme Court in *Automatic Radio Company* v. *Hazeltine.*[23] There
some 570 patents and 200 patent applications were licensed in a block
at a minimum annual payment, but with a single royalty rate applicable whether a licensee used all of the patents or only one of them.
In a footnote reference to this case in his *Brulotte* opinion, Douglas
attempted distinction based on use by farmers and use by manufacturers without indicating what this difference was. The Hazeltine situation is, he wrote, "not apposite here for the present licensees are
farmers using the machines, not manufacturers buying the right to
incorporate patents into their manufactured products."[24]

If this distinction is meant to convey a conclusion that leveraging
to new and improper monopoly is accomplished through "time extension" imposed upon farmer licensees by extracting payments after
patents have expired, but is not involved in charging manufacturers
for patents never used, the distinction, to put it most generously,
deserves a somewhat less cryptic explanation. As I will indicate in the
next section, which is concerned with block licensing, the *Hazeltine*

23. 339 U.S. 827 (1950), subsequently discussed infra at note 27.
24. Brulotte v. Thys Co., 379 U.S. 29 (1964), at n. 5.

decision rested on a finding that no leveraging to new monopoly was involved. Convenience to both licensor and licensee in the marketing of a very large number of patents and prospective patents was also stressed in that decision. After the decision in *Brulotte* it seemed predictable that there would be danger in relying heavily on *Hazeltine* for licensing multiple patents in blocks at a single rate.

Block Licensing

Use or misuse of patents which are jointly licensed (whether pooled or otherwise accumulated) involves block booking. In the *Paramount Pictures* case,[25] a case involving copyrighted films decided by the Supreme Court in 1948, the motion picture defendants had been charged with violating sections 1 and 2 of the Sherman Act by a comprehensive scheme involving, among other things, pooling copyrighted films and booking them in blocks, thus depriving customers of the right to select the particular films they wanted on the basis of individual evaluation.[26] The analogy to tie-in law seemed clear. The issue had already been decided in the post–Clayton Act *Shoe Machinery* case—conditioning the granting of a license under one patent upon the acceptance of a different license is illegal. The tie-in cases often involved foreclosure of competitors from supplying the tied products. When, however, the tied product is also patented, selling the products together is no more a means of foreclosing competitors than is selling them separately. And sometimes licensing patents in "blocks" is efficient.

The question of the permissibility of licensing multiple patents under a single license, as I explained in the previous section, was at issue before the Supreme Court in *Automatic Radio Company* v. *Hazeltine*,[27] in 1950. Hazeltine was a patent-holding and research company. It neither manufactured nor sold products. Hazeltine Research, Incorporated, it should be remembered, held 570 patents and 200 patent applications. How these had been accumulated was not at

25. U.S. v. Paramount Pictures, 334 U.S. 131 (1948).
26. For an economic explanation of why any rational profit-maximizing businessman would use this method of sale, see Alchian and Allen, *University Economics* (Belmont, Calif.: Wadsworth Publishing Company, 1967), p. 127, n. 17. See also George Stigler, *The Organization of Industry* (Homewood, Ill.: Richard D. Irwin, 1968), p. 165.
27. 339 U.S. 827 (1950).

issue in the case. The question was the legality of the practice of licensing in a block the patents and applications relating to the manufacture of radio broadcasting apparatus. The licenses at issue called for a minimum fee of $10,000 a year or, if higher, a royalty of 1 percent of all radio receiver sales, patented or unpatented. In this case the Supreme Court majority, in an opinion written by Justice Minton, rejected the precedent of the tie-in cases. The reason was explicit. Leveraging to a second monopoly was what made tie-ins illegal. "That which is condemned as against public policy by the 'Tie-in' cases is the extension of the monopoly of the patent to create another monopoly or restraint of competition—a restraint not countenenced by the patent grant. . . . The principle of those cases cannot be contorted to circumscribe the instant situation."[28]

The royalty, as administered (all patents together and based on total sales), created no new monopoly. Neither did it restrain any competition beyond the limited grant. And "the mere accumulation of patents, no matter how many, is not in and of itself illegal."[29] The Court then went on to explain how a licensee was not disadvantaged. "Petitioner cannot complain because it must pay royalties whether it uses Hazeltine patents or not. What it acquired by the agreement into which it entered was the privilege to use any or all of the patents and developments as it desired to use them. If it chooses to use none of them, it has nevertheless contracted to pay for the privilege of using existing patents plus any developments resulting from respondent's continuous research."[30]

A narrow reading of *Hazeltine* leaves unanswered the legality of licensing patents in blocks, when competing patents of separate companies or noncompeting patents of competing companies are pooled or cross-licensed. Moreover, as was stressed by Judge Leahy in *American Securit Company* v. *Shatterproof Glass Corporation*[31] in 1957, the Supreme Court in Hazeltine "stated it was *not* confronted with the contention that the licensor *refused* to grant a license under one or more of its patents unless a license was taken under all."[32] This last distinction, resting on the nonexistence of coercion, is, as Judge Leahy contended, the reason the precedent of "tie-in" cases was not applied

28. Ibid., pp. 832–33.
29. Ibid., p. 834.
30. Ibid.
31. 154 F. Supp. 890 (D.C. Dela. 1957).
32 Ibid., p. 894.

in *Hazeltine.* Although resolving the permissibility of block licensing (or for that matter any other form of licensing) on the basis of whether a licensee is "coerced" would seem to place practically all monopoly-maximizing activity by a patentee in jeopardy, Judge Leahy's interpretation was subsequently adopted by the Supreme Court in *Zenith Corporation* v. *Hazeltine* in 1969.[33]

Judge Leahy, however, did not rely solely on the existence of coercion for his conclusion that block licensing of patents by Securit was illegal. Any exercise of monopoly power, whether by exploitation of a valid patent or otherwise, involves coercing one's customer into doing what he would not have to do were there no monopoly. Emphasizing coercion merely detracts from the "scope" issue. It cannot resolve whether the licensing practice in question makes for monopoly power greater than that afforded by the competitive superiority of the patents whose use is allegedly coerced.

Judge Leahy's opinion in *Securit,* although accurately forecasting the Supreme Court's attitude on the relevance of coercion, in the alternative relied upon Securit's violation of a consent decree it had entered in 1948 in settlement of an antitrust case brought by the government. That decree had outlawed the very practices at issue in this private litigation. Leahy wrote two opinions in the same case. Only the first involved coercion. The second concluded, "plaintiff's standard form of license agreement violates the terms of the consent

33. 395 U.S. 100 (1969). In this case the court of appeals, citing Automatic Radio Mfg. Co. v. Hazeltine Research, Inc., held in part that conditioning the grant of a patent license upon payment of royalties on unpatented products was not misuse. The Supreme Court reversed this holding. Citing the Brulotte case, the Supreme Court found the patentee seeking "to extend the monopoly of his patent to derive a benefit not attributable to use of the patent's teachings" (p. 136). Automatic Radio v. Hazeltine, however, was not overruled. There, said the Court, "The percentage royalty was deemed an acceptable alternative to a lump-sum payment for the privilege to use the patents" (p. 137). Total-sales royalties may not be coerced. The Supreme Court's holding on this issue was: "But we do not read *Automatic Radio* to authorize the patentee to use the power of his patent to insist on total-sales royalty and to override protestations of the licensee that some of his products are unsuited to the patent or that for some lines of his merchandise he has no need or desire to purchase the privileges of the patent" (p. 139). But as Justice Harlan indicates in his dissent, "What the Court does not undertake to explain is *how* insistence upon a percentage-of-sales royalty enables a patentee to obtain an economic 'benefit' not attributable to use of the patent's teachings, thereby involving himself in patent misuse" (p. 144). The leveraging fallacy prevailed again. What seems to be left of the total-sales royalty doctrine of the 1950 Hazeltine case is consensual approval by licensor and licensee.

decree rendered by the Ohio Court, and defendant, here, may assert the violation of that decree as a defensive shield to ward off the infringement action of plaintiff in this court."[34]

As the prior consent judgment to which *Securit* was a party suggests, although the question has not been faced by the Supreme Court, when competing patents are pooled and jointly managed, as they were in *Hartford-Empire* and *General Electric*, and especially when, as in *Standard Sanitary*, the patents screen trade restraints in unpatented substitutes, it seems most improbable that the *Hazeltine* precedent would turn out to be controlling. Of course, it could be argued with good reason that how patents had been accumulated should be immaterial to the propriety of licensing in blocks. Block booking, in either case, extends monopoly or does not extend monopoly. When competing patents are merged monopoly is extended. It is not necessarily retracted by banning block licensing. And, as I will attempt to indicate in the next chapter, patent relief is not often nicely fitted to the cloth of the trade restraint.

Resolution of the efficiency/trade restraint dilemma inherent in patent pooling has not been resolved by the courts. Rather, it has been papered over with the regulatory relief of compulsory licensing in an attempt to cure abuses.

34. American Securit Co. v. Shatterproof Glass Corp., 154 F. Supp. 890 (D.C. Dela. 1957), at p. 897.

12

Relief from and Corrections for Patent-Antitrust Conflicts

As with other legal obligations, the effectiveness of patent law and antitrust law, or the effectiveness of the resolutions of conflict between these laws, depends in very large measure upon the sanctions imposed for their violation. Clarity, coherence, and consistency of the legal rules to which these sanctions are applied are of course preconditions to effective relief. This is so whether the relief is meant to undo existing violations, prevent future specific violations, or deter violations which are difficult to detect.

Relief from What?

In appraising antitrust and patent law, and the appropriate spheres of each in resolving the conflicts between them, a primary economic consideration, efficient resource allocation, has provided the yardstick used in this study. The temporary monopoly a patent system provides has been accepted not as an ideal means of allocating resources (it misallocates them in the short run, as does all monopoly), but as a feasible if imperfect means, in the long run, of stimulating the production of the kind and amount of information consumers want. This conclusion about the net advantage from a patent system, whose rewards, it is assumed, are best attained from temporary monopoly, has been and continues to be a subject of honest controversy among capable and impartial analysts. Critics, however, have not been successful in convincing the legislature that an alternative would be preferable. Neither a non-market-oriented reward system nor a system involving withdrawal of special protection for invention has gained legislative favor. And whether or not an "on balance" conclusion about the desirability of an incentive patent system is accepted, if we take the system as given, short-run monopoly is its key characteristic. Temporary monopoly has its shortcomings. Consequently there is, properly, concern that this monopoly be kept within the confines of the invention it has been designed to promote.

This problem of keeping the patent monopoly within bounds has given rise to considerable controversy and criticism. An appropriate measure of a patent's scope, it has been concluded, is the "competitive superiority" of the patented idea over the next best substitute. For the most part, neither the legislature nor the courts have undertaken the task of providing a better alternative. Although the presumption is often dodged, it has not been disclaimed.

The courts, and particularly the Supreme Court, however, have with increasing strictness contracted the scope of permissible patent use and expanded the definition of patent misuse. And this has paralleled increasingly stringent antitrust law relating to vertical contracts. There are those who would ascribe judicial proscription of use-restrictive licensing to lack of sympathy with the patent system itself, relying as it does on a monopoly grant. Others disdain the usefulness of that which is protected. There are also those who believe that the Court's interest is in the fate of those whom the patent monopolist may have excluded from participation. But spurious and unarticulated motivations aside, the most frequently cited reason for prohibiting patentees from imposing various use-restrictive contracts upon licensees has been a finding that the proper scope of the patent monopoly has been exceeded.

In applying its scope test—a test which implicitly, at least, involves an economic appraisal of profit maximization under a valid patent as contrasted to monopoly extension into inappropriate areas—the Supreme Court has mostly been mistaken. And its mistakes come from getting the wrong answers to the right questions. No careful distinction between monopoly maximization and monopoly extension has been articulated and consistently applied. The Supreme Court's facility for finding a leveraging process by which one monopoly becomes two (or more) monopolies is particularly notable. Examples have been provided in case after case. In addition, under both patent-misuse law and antitrust law, there is an increasing propensity to apply a foreclosure text. Emphasis is thus focused on competitors rather than upon competition (or, more appropriately, the competitive process). Equating effect on competitors with effect on competition is a dubious hypothesis which the Court tends to adopt as an obvious conclusion. This persists even though there has been neither legislative nor judicial adoption of the proposition that inefficient competitors are to be favored over a consumer-benefiting competitive process.

The competitor-competition confusion has come to be based, both explicitly and implicitly, on a theory of how monopoly is or can be achieved—monopoly by aggression as contrasted to monopoly by consent. There is a close affinity between monopoly by aggression (again, more aptly, a dubious hypothesis rather than a theory) and patent misuse or abuse. It should not be surprising, therefore, as monopolization mythology has gained the upper hand in the antitrust arena, that what some viewed as intensified conflict between patent law and antitrust law turns out to be compatibility, albeit a compatibility in error. Neither should it be a cause for surprise that this development has called for cures from antitrust diseases, phantom and real, which are more harmful to the competitive process than the maladies themselves.

Antitrust law, including the Clayton Act, the Robinson-Patman Act, and the Miller-Tydings and McGuire Fair Trade acts, in addition to the Sherman Act, has become increasingly stringent with respect to vertical integrations and vertical contracts—contracts not between competitors but between suppliers and their customers or between buyers and their sources of supply. Many if not most patent licensing contracts are of this type. Included are the tie-in sales, exclusive licensing, territorial division, discriminating licensing and price-restrictive licenses analyzed in preceding chapters. These contractual arrangements are often means by which patentees are able to "efficiently" recover that value which is measured by customer evaluation of the competitive superiority afforded by the patent. Moreover, as chapters 5 and 6 attempted to demonstrate, these vertical contracts not only are "efficient" as profit-maximizing devices for those who employ them, but they also can be, and mostly are, efficient in the social sense. They can be means of getting more of what the community wants at lower overall cost than if their use were prohibited.

One's appraisal of relief in patent-misuse cases will of course depend upon one's appraisal of the law and the law process which occasion the violation. The problem of providing relief from use-restrictive contracts imposed by the patentees upon licensees is very limited under a competitive superiority test. If no leveraging to new monopoly can be exposed, no illegality should be found. This is so even when we accept the standards which courts proclaim they are applying. If this conclusion is correct, much if not most relief from patent misuse is analogous to an attempt by a doctor to cure health. But even if it were to be established that a use-restrictive licensing practice "may be substantially to lessen competition or tend to create a monopoly in any line of commerce," so that the aggressive activities complained of could be forecast to be *more* rather than *less* likely to restrain trade or create monopoly beyond that due to the competitive superiority of the patent, even then relief would seem to be appropriately applied by proscribing the activities which brought about this result.

Antitrust law, however, has another and better theory of how competition may be injured than a theory of aggressive action. This theory, unlike the leveraging or competitor-foreclosing theory typified by use-restrictive licensing, involves agreement among consenting rivals. It is typified by cartel agreements among competitors. Horizontal price agreements and agreements to divide markets or to allocate customers are of this output-restricting type. Horizontal mergers can have similar effects, even though efficiencies may be created. The pooling of competing patents is another example. Competition between patents, or between the patented and the unpatented, is not immune, nor should it be, from this aspect of antitrust law.

With price-fixing agreements concealment is often possible; and with merely injunctive relief there is small deterrence (much to gain and little to lose) from willful violation. There is therefore a strong case for imposing stronger penalty sanctions on those collusive activities which can be clearly and accurately identified and which unequivocally impair competition and efficiency.[1]

There is no reason for excluding patentees from this rule when it is properly applied. An agreement among *competing* patentees to fix royalty rates is no more to be sanctioned, for example, than is a price agreement among competing producers of unpatented products. But

---

1. The 1969 *President's Task Force Report on Productivity and Competition* (the *Stigler Report*) recommended more emphasis by enforcement agencies on "continued, vigilant, aggressive seeking-out and conviction of conventional price-fixers." Also recommended were substantially increased fines for such violations. This report has been reprinted in "Small Business and the Robinson-Patman Act, Hearings before the Special Subcommittee on Small Business," *H. Res.* 66, vol. 1 (7–9 Oct. 1969), pp. 271–89.

identifying *competing* patents is of central importance. And the relationship of pooled patents is often complex. Identifying by court decision the relationship of patents pooled or cross-licensed, often long after pooling has been accomplished, is difficult, time-consuming, and expensive. In addition, when private litigation is involved there is often strong incentive to submerge or to conceal pertinent information with respect to both the validity and the scope of the patent claims. There is also, between private litigants, incentive to stress *noncompeting* rather than *competing* patent characteristics.[2]

Relief in patent-pooling cases has not usually stressed distinguishing the valid or the competing patents from the invalid or the noncompeting patents in a pool. Courts, in attempting to fashion relief concerned with antitrust allegations, understandably avoid technically complicated issues of validity, scope, and the competitive character of claims. This perhaps explains why the remedial sanctions applied have been regulatory. Recreating competition is an infinitely more demanding task. Regulatory relief not only is characteristic of patent pooling cases, it is also characteristic of a wide variety of patent misuse cases.

Compulsory Licensing

In fashioning relief particular emphasis has been placed upon compulsory licensing, particularly compulsory licensing on "reasonable" terms. Thus the cure for the absence of competition which gives rise to the need for relief has come to be not the restoration of competition but rather its abandonment. And, because neither the antitrust enforcement agencies nor the courts are at all equipped to function as regulatory agencies, the common economic shortcomings of regulation are magnified. Compulsory licensing in the United States, unlike the compulsory licensing legislatively imposed in other countries, has not been adopted as a statutory requirement. Rather, its application in this country has been limited to relief. It has come to be widely applied in a variety of "misuse" situations.[3] Since 1877 attempts have been made to introduce compulsory licensing provisions into the American patent law through bills in Congress. These attempts have been fre-

---

2. See, for example, the contention of the defendants in the "Cracking" case analyzed by John S. McGee in chapter 10.
3. Refusal to grant licenses, it should be added, has been found to be misuse. See Leitch Manufacturing Co. v. Barber Asphalt Co., 302 U.S. 458 (1938).

quent and unsuccessful.[4] But the Supreme Court has held compulsory licensing at reasonable rates to be within the range of remedies when thought necessary to correct past or prevent future antitrust violations.

The final report of the Temporary National Economics Committee (TNEC) in 1941 had recommended legislation making "any future patent available for use by anyone who may desire its use and who is willing to pay a fair price for the privilege in order to eliminate the use of patents in ways inimical to the public policy inherent in the patent laws."[5] This recommendation, like earlier recommendations to the same effect, although not convincing to the legislature, had substantial support in the Department of Justice in the formation of consent decrees. The first compulsory licensing decree in a litigated case was entered in the *Hartford-Empire* case. And the focus of this case was directed to the same practices which had formed the subject matter of the Department of Justice presentation before the TNEC four years earlier.

Compulsory licensing is a vastly overrated remedy. In 1960 a staff report of the Senate Subcommittee on Patents, Trademarks and Copyrights summarized and evaluated the compulsory patent licensing provisions in the antitrust decrees which were entered during the years 1941–57.[6] This study was undertaken "to determine how effective compulsory licensing in antitrust judgments has been in opening industry to competition, and what practical problems have arisen in the administration of such compulsory licensing."[7] This assessment of compulsory licensing thus set as its principal goal the effect of compulsory licensing on entry into those industries in which compulsory licensing had been decreed. Primarily, the method of assessment utilized in this study was to question those who had availed themselves of the decree provisions. The central criterion for assessment was whether licensees, operating under licenses compulsorily imposed, obtained substantial benefit from them.

---

4. See Legislative Reference Service, *Compulsory Licensing of Patents: A Legislative History*, Senate Patent Study no. 12 (1958). See also *Compulsory Licensing of Patents under Some Non-American Systems*, the Senate Subcommittee on Patents, Trademarks and Copyrights Study no. 19 (1959).

5. TNEC, *Final Report and Recommendations*, S. Doc. no. 35, 77th Cong., 1st sess., p. 36 (1941).

6. *Staff Report, Compulsory Patent Licensing under Antitrust Judgments*, of the Subcommittee on Patents, Trademarks and Copyrights of the Committee on the Judiciary, U.S. Senate, 86th Cong. 2d sess. (1960).

7. Ibid., p. 1.

The primary purpose of a civil antitrust decree, although it often resembles criminal penalties designed for punishing wrongdoers and thus deterring future violations and is sometimes designed to deprive wrongdoers of undeserved "fruits" of their illegal actions, is generally supported as a means of restoring competition. This is to cure the *effects* of the unlawful conduct. Measuring the effect of a decree on the restoration of *competition* by testing its beneficial effects upon licensees might well seem of dubious evaluative significance—at least to those who view the patent system as designed to give patentees the benefit of the return measured by the competitive superiority of their inventions. Surely the right to exclude others from making, vending, or using, which gives rise to the temporary monopoly protection which is a patent, can hardly be expected not to be exclusionary. It would indeed be surprising if the licensee of a valuable patent would not benefit from a more "reasonable" (always lower?) royalty. Asking who benefits can be a sidetrack from the main line to useful relief. If emphasis is diverted to "licensee benefit," it can easily be found that even at zero royalty (royalty-free licensing) there would be licensees who could be expected to report that something undesirable was "doing them in." In some way or other, when licensees are questioned they judge themselves suppressed. Others rationalize compulsory licensing because of a conviction that patentees' interests are promoted by suppressing rather than promoting the use of patents.[8]

The *Compulsory Patent Licensing Report* provides useful information on the extent of the use of compulsory licensing and also infor-

---

8. Reading the general literature on compulsory licensing, especially the proposals of those who would amend patent law to make it obligatory (the TNEC recommendation provides an example), makes it apparent that a popular theory which supports it rests on a belief in "patent suppression." "Suppression" is a problem which can only be cured by making patent information widely available to all comers. Of course this end is achieved only if patentees set royalty rates bringing about wide use. Any rate suppresses to some degree. Compulsory licensing at reasonable royalties was *not* introduced as a means of redressing antitrust violation arising from collusive arrangements giving rise to monopoly in excess of that return arising from a patent's competitive superiority.

Opponents of a compulsory licensing amendment to patent law, on the other hand, point to the fact that there is neither evidence that patents are ever suppressed nor any theory which would explain why anyone owning an asset having net value in use would find it in his economic interest to suppress it. Rumors continually crop up concerning such things as power pills which are never used or disclosed because they would destroy the value of investment in the petroleum industry. As yet, however, no verified case has been uncovered.

mative data on the practical problems encountered in enforcing and complying with compulsory licensing provisions in decrees. The list of judgments containing "patent relief," of which the first was entered in August 1941 and the last (in the *Report*) in January 1959, covered 108 cases.[9] Of these only 13 were litigated cases. The rest were consent judgments.

In listing "cases in which compulsory licensing decrees have been effective"[10] the *Report* lists 8 case examples. The *Report's* criterion for effectiveness, as has been indicated, was licensee benefit. This was determined by questionnaire. Even in these limited case examples no attempt was made, except in the most general terms, to describe or explain the specific nature of the antitrust violations alleged or to relate the correction of these, in terms of alternative forms of relief or otherwise, to the compulsory licensing arrangement imposed. Principal emphasis, to repeat, was upon usefulness to licensees.

Of the 108 listed relief cases, 13 involving compulsory licensing were litigated; 81 of the 103 cases were specifically studied, and 12 of these were litigated. Of the studied consent judgments 69 called for compulsory licensing, and of these 7 provided compulsory licensing on a royalty-free basis. "If they were excluded," as the *Report* indicates, "more than half of all of the compulsory licensing judgments produced no license."[11] By the *Report's* own standard, therefore, it follows that more than one-third of all compulsory licensing relief judgments were ineffective.[12] Among the 12 litigated cases included in the study the proportionate amount of licensing was considerably greater, but even here the performance was by no means uniform. Three litigated cases, in each of which industrywide agreements involving pooled patents were used as a screen for industrywide control (cases in which there was substantial evidence that the monopoly exercised substantially exceeded that reasonably ascribable to the competitive superiority afforded by the separate patents), accounted for a very large proportion of the licensing. The *Report* notes the considerable licensing activity under the litigated judgments in *United States* v. *General Electric, United States* v. *Hartford-Empire,* and

9. *Staff Report, Compulsory Patent Licensing,* appendix.

10. Ibid., p. 6.

11. Ibid., p. 18, n. 16.

12. This conclusion assumes that even at "reasonable" royalties practicing the patented art is not attractive to prospective licensees. It ignores the possibility that royalties are set so low that infringement action is not worth pressing.

"scope extension" cases discussed in chapter 10, as well as in *United States* v. *Imperial Chemical Industries, Limited*,[13] a similar kind of case. In its discussion of the practical problems of administering compulsory licensing decrees, stress appropriately was placed by the *Staff Report* on the problem of determining reasonable royalties. The following involved provision was presented as typical of the procedure for determining reasonableness:

Upon receiving any application for a license in accordance with the provisions of this section IV, the defendant shall advise the applicant of the royalty it deems reasonable for the patent or patents to which the application pertains. If the parties are unable to agree upon what constitutes a reasonable royalty within 60 days from the date the application for the license was received by the defendant, the applicant therefor or the defendant may forthwith petition this Court for the determination of a reasonable royalty, and the said defendant shall, upon receipt of notice of filing such petition, promptly give notice thereof to the Attorney General. In any such proceeding the burden of proof shall be upon the defendant to establish the reasonableness of the royalty requested by it; and the reasonable royalty rates, if any, determined by the Court, shall apply to the applicant and to all other licensees under the same patent or patents. Pending the completion of negotiations or of any such Court proceedings, the applicant shall have the right to make, use, and vend under the patent or patents to which its application pertains, without payment of royalty or other compensation, but subject to the following provisions: The defendant may petition the Court to fix an interim royalty rate pending final determination of what constitutes a reasonable royalty, if any. If the Court fixes such interim royalty rate, the defendant shall then grant, and the applicant shall accept, a license providing for the periodic payment of royalties at such interim rates from the date of the making of such application by the applicant. If the applicant fails to accept such license or fails to pay the interim royalty therein provided, such action shall be grounds for the denial or dismissal of his application. Where an interim license has been issued pursuant to these provsions, reasonable royalty rates, if any, as finally determined by the Court shall be retroactive for the applicant and all other licensees under the same patent or patents to the date the applicant filed his application for a license.[14]

The *Report,* in commenting on this procedure, notes that "the licensor and the applicant in a vast number of judgments have reached a royalty agreement and neither the Justice Department nor the courts

13. 100 F. Supp. 504 (S.D.N.Y. 1951); 105 F. Supp. 215 (S.D.N.Y. 1952).
14. Staff Report, *Compulsory Patent Licensing*, pp. 22–23.

has had any part whatever in fixing the royalty rates."[15] Moreover, according to the *Report*, "In only six situations to date have the courts had occasion to determine the rate of royalty. In only three of these hearings did the Justice Department have an active role in the fixing of such a rate."[16] For the most part, then, the "reasonableness" of the rate under compulsory licensing is a negotiated rate between licensor and licensee under the supervision of and subject to court approval. Neither description nor appraisal of this bargaining method of royalty fixing was a part of the *Report*.[17] The position of the Department of Justice, a position apparently also reflecting considerable judicial opinion as well, places principal emphasis on protecting applicants. This is evidenced in the *Report* by a 1956 letter from the then assistant attorney general to Senator O'Mahoney:

> It is the policy of the Department not to participate in such proceedings to determine reasonable royalty rates. We feel that such matters are properly the concern only of the patentee and applicant for license so long as the applicant is afforded protection, by resort to the Court, against such arbitrary royalties as might amount to a refusal to license. Aside from this basic view, reasonable royalty proceedings would generally require assignment of personnel which, in our opinion, can be more fruitfully employed in other matters.[18]

The main conclusion of the *Staff Report* was negative as to the central question whether compulsory patent licensing relief, no matter how carefully administered, should have a prominent place in antitrust enforcement. Assessment of compulsory licensing was far from laudatory even on the narrow criterion of advantage to licensees. Although it was found "effective" in certain instances, when the judgments were viewed as a group it was concluded that "too much reliance may have been placed by the Department upon compulsory licensing relief to restore illegally suppressed competition."[19]

The validity of this conclusion would, it might be added, be supported more strongly and reinforced further were additional and more relevant criteria than "benefits to licensees" included in the assess-

---

15. Ibid., p. 23.
16. Ibid., p. 24.
17. Thus bilateral monopoly, a dubious substitute for competition as a means of achieving efficient resource allocation, went unchallenged.
18. Staff Report, *Compulsory Patent Licensing,* pp. 23–24.
19. Ibid., p. 52.

ment. Among the "effective" compulsory licensing decrees listed were
cases in which "suppressed competition" was erroneously found. Also
listed were cases in which "scope extension" criteria were applied
when there was no credible evidence that it existed. These cases, at
least according to the economic criteria which the foregoing analysis
has set forth, are not proper candidates for application of a misuse
doctrine, much less for compulsory licensing relief. Two cases are
especially notable among the examples included: The *Line Material*
case,[20] involving a cross-license among noncompeting patents under
which licensee prices were fixed, and *United States* v. *Eastman Kodak
Company*,[21] a case involving a vertical arrangement imposed by Eastman on its distributors, under which the films had to be finished by
Eastman, the film supplier.

A case for compulsory licensing, difficult and controversial as it
is as a patent-misuse corrective, might be used as a last resort, after
alternative remedies have been carefully assessed in situations clearly
calling for relief. It might, for example, as an application of least-
worse remedy, be applied to inextricably intermixed and unidentifiable
pools of competing and noncompeting patents. The *Report* suggests
that increasing attention be focused on patent divestiture as a remedy.
But a precondition to divestiture is the identification of *competing*
patents acquired by cross-license, acquisition, or merger. Were relief
problems limited to this patent analogue to antitrust's horizontal
merger, limited antitrust resources might well be diverted from less
urgent uses to the economically relevant problem concerning the competitive relationship among patents.

Particular Relief Problems Arising from Patent Pools

In 1950 Congress adopted a new amendment to the Clayton Act
to place greater inhibition on merger activity. Its applicability to
patent pooling has been suggested. The 1950 amendment changed
the first paragraph of section 7 of the Clayton Act in several ways.
It included the acquisition of assets, as well as the acquisition of stock
within the scope of the statute; it eliminated as a prerequisite for
illegal acquisition the existence of competition between the acquiring

---

20. Cited in *Staff Report*, ibid., p. 10, as Civil Action no. 1696, E.D. Wis.
21. Cited in *Staff Report*, ibid., p. 7, as Civil Action no. 6450, W.D. N.Y.

and the acquired corporation;[22] and, although retaining the older section 7 language, "[where] the effect of such acquisition may be substantially to lessen competition or tend to create monopoly," it made this more inclusive by adding the language "in any line of commerce in any section of the country."[23]

To some this Clayton Act amendment, the Celler-Kefauver amendment, makes it possible to provide not only preventative relief but also authority for divesting all forms of merged assets, including patent assets. Although the Supreme Court has not faced the question whether a patent is an asset for purposes of section 7 of the Clayton Act, there seems to be wide belief, "in view of the broad jurisdictional approach that the Court has taken with respect to the statute,"[24] that patent pooling would be covered. Not only is lower court precedent available,[25] but this conclusion is also confirmed by a long-time student of antitrust, Professor Donald Turner, former assistant attorney general in charge of the Antitrust Division. In 1965 he wrote:

> I assume, and I think it is a completely safe assumption, that both a patent and an exclusive license under a patent are "assets" within the meaning of Section 7. Consequently, to use the words of the statute, it is unlawful for a corporation to acquire a patent or an exclusive license under a patent from another corporation where the effect may be to substantially lessen competition or to tend to create a monopoly.[26]

Use of the amended Clayton Act to resolve the patent pooling problem should not be predicated solely on the grounds that the amendment plugged the "asset loophole" in the 1914 act. The amendment has done much more than create the possibility of preventing the purchase of competing patents or permitting the divestiture of

22. The ostensible purpose of the "acquiring and the acquired" language was not to obviate the need for showing a potential elimination of competition. Rather, the purpose was to cover potential anticompetitive effects wherever they might occur.

23. 64 Stat. 1125; 15 U.S.C. Sec. 18.

24. See Derald Kadish, "Patents and Antitrust: Guides and Caveats," 13 *Idea* 83 (Spring 1969), at p. 86.

25. See, for example, U.S. v. Columbia Pictures Corp., 189 F. Supp. 153 (S.D. N.Y. 1960), at pp. 181–82: "As used here [in section 7] the words 'acquire' and 'assets' are not terms of art or technical legal language. In the context of this statute, they are generic, imprecise terms encompassing a broad spectrum of transactions. . . . As used in this statute . . . 'assets' may mean anything of value."

26. Turner, "Patents and Antitrust Innovation," 26 *U. Pitt L. Rev.* 151 (1966), at p. 155.

competing patents so acquired. The amendment was designed by its framers, and has been interpreted by the courts, to apply to the acquisition of noncompeting assets as well as competing assets. This is evidenced by its widespread use against vertical and conglomerate mergers. The amended act has as least as great a potential for protecting competitors from aggressive rivals as it has for promoting competition. It has thus strengthened the applicability of antitrust law so as to restrain rather than to promote the competitive process. It has significantly enhanced the use of a misguided economic hypothesis concerning "incipient monopoly" and "foreclosure." Thus antitrust law and patent-misuse law, because of this amendment, may be said to have accelerated the trend *away* from the kind of consumer-oriented antitrust and patent law upon which the analysis of this book is based. The 1950 amendment is thus capable of being used, and has been used, to "Robinson-Patmanize"[27] antitrust law.

Potentially, however, both section 2 of the Sherman Act and section 7 of the Clayton Act, as amended, offer considerably more opportunity than prosecuting agencies have used to more diligently scrutinize patent acquisition with the aim of identifying the competitive relationship between owned patents and those acquired. And although this is a difficult, time-consuming, and costly task, often inconclusive even with substantial technical assistance, diversion of antitrust activity and resources in this direction and away from patent abuses arising from use restrictions by a patentee upon his licensees would line up practice with desirable policy under both antitrust law and patent law.

Invalidity and the Relief Question

Conceptually, one of the clearest cases of improper extension of scope, achieving monopoly reward when none is due, is the extraction of revenue from invalid patents (or invalid claims of otherwise valid patents). And again, as with the determination of the competing or noncompeting nature of patents acquired, this is not any easy problem or one which is cheaply resolved either through litigation before courts or initially in the Patent Office. Moreover, although

27. For an unequivocal example of how the Robinson-Patman Act has been used to restrain trade by use of the foreclosure theory see Bowman, "Restraint of Trade by the Supreme Court: The Utah Pie Case," 77 *Yale L. Rev.* 70 (Nov. 1967).

invalidity of the patent or invalidity of one of its claims is a possible outcome of interference proceedings among contesting parties attempting to establish the priority or the dominance of their claims over those of adversaries, there may be strong incentive for settlement so as to avoid an outcome which would be adverse to the interests of both parties—a holding that neither claim is valid.

Until very recently invalidity claims by licensees have not been a means by which the validity of patents could be tested in courts. Licensing contracts, typically containing provisions that validity would not be contested by licensees, were generally upheld. In 1969, however, in the case of *Lear, Incorporated* v. *Adkins,*[28] the Supreme Court overruled this long-standing precedent and made it possible for a licensee to challenge the validity of a patent even though he had expressly agreed that he would not. This right, although by no means guaranteeing that licensees will undertake such challenges even when they have substantial reason to doubt validity, has made it less likely that output will be restricted by the assessment of monopoly charges where none are appropriate.

An equally far-reaching decision with respect to validity claims by

---

28. 395 U.S. 653 (1969). In this case Lear had entered into a licensing arrangement with Adkins, under the terms of which Lear was obligated to pay agreed royalties to Adkins *regardless of the validity of the patent.* The supreme court of California had held that "one of the oldest doctrines in the field of patent law establishes that so long as a licensee is operating under a license agreement, he is estopped to deny the validity of his licensor's patent in a suit for royalties under the agreement." The Supreme Court's rationale overturning the California Supreme Court Opinion was, in sum, as follows (395 U.S. at p. 670):

A patent, in the last analysis, simply represents a legal conclusion reached by the Patent Office. Moreover, the legal conclusion is predicated on factors as to which reasonable men can differ widely. Yet the Patent Office is often obliged to reach its decision in an *ex parte* proceeding, without the aid of the arguments which could be advanced by parties interested in proving patent invalidity. Consequently, it does not seem to us to be unfair to require a patentee to defend the Patent Office's judgment when his licensee places the question in issue, especially since the licensor's case is buttressed by the presumption of validity which attaches to his patent. Thus, although licensee estopped may be consistent with the letter of contractual doctrine, we cannot say that it is compelled by the spirit of contract law, which seeks to balance the claims of promisor and promisee in accord with the requirements of good faith.

Surely the equities of the licensor do not weigh very heavily when they are balanced against the important public interest in permitting full and free competition in the use of ideas which are in reality a part of the public domain.

licensees was delivered by Justice White for a unanimous Court early in 1971 in the case of *Blonder-Tongue* v. *University of Illinois Foundation.*[29] Before this opinion, if a particular patent were held invalid upon challenge by a licensee in a court hearing, this was not determinative of this same issue when another licensee subsequently raised it. The question had to be retried. The *Blonder-Tongue* decision overruled the prior holdings. It appropriately stressed the high cost of successive trials, not only in terms of court time, but also and more important, in terms of societal costs of the kind stressed by Justice Harlan in the *Lear* case.

Even with these relaxed rules on challenges of validity by licensees, there are still effective deterrents to challenge. For example, substantial costs are involved in bringing suit. And licensees must overcome the presumption of validity found by the Patent Office. Moreover, under the *Blonder-Tongue* rule, there is the "free ride" problem. If one of a number of licensees undertakes a validity challenge and is successful, other licensees benefit without cost. If, on the other hand, the suit is unsuccessful, it is only the challenging litigant who pays. This may well induce a rivalry in waiting for others to bring suits.[30]

Another reason for licensees not to press invalidity suits exists when licensees and the patentee have the common goal of using the poten-

---

29. 402 U.S. 313 (1971). Section 282 of the Patent Code provides: "A patent shall be presumed valid. The burden of establishing invalidity shall rest on a party asserting it." Suppose, however, that in a previous case involving different parties that this burden had been borne and the patent had there been held invalid. Should that invalidity holding be determinative in a subsequent suit involving the same patent but different parties? Regarding this question in Triplett v. Lowell, 297 U.S. 638 at p. 642 (1936), the holding was: "Neither reason nor authority supports the contention that an adjudication adverse to any or all the claims of a patent precludes another suit upon the same claims against a different defendant. While the earlier decision may by comity be given great weight in a later litigation and thus persuade the court to render a like decree, it is not *res adjudicata* and may not be pleaded as a defense." In Blonder-Tongue the foregoing Triplett case was overruled to the extent that it foreclosed an estoppal plea by one facing a charge of infringement of a patent that had once been declared invalid.

30. This "free ride" aspect of a single licensee's bearing the full cost of a patent invalidity suit may be minimized by class action. In Dale Electronics, Inc. v. R. C. L. Electronics, Inc. (62 *Patent, Trade Mark and Copyright Journal*, A-1, 27 Jan. 1972) a federal district judge in New Hampshire held that a determination of patent validity may begin by class action. He wrote: "There is nothing in Blonder-Tongue holding that a patent class action cannot be instituted or that the determination that a patent is valid should not be held binding on all class defendants."

tially invalid patent or patents as a screen for an industry cartel. In such cases, if invalid patents are to be privately challenged it is up to noncartel participants, prospective infringers, to overcome the presumption of validity inhering in a granted patent. And once again, the "free ride" problem is involved in assessing the likelihood of a single infringer bringing a case. In either of the foregoing circumstances, if multiple patents are involved, and especially if they are licensed in blocks, this "validity" problem is likely to be magnified.

Insofar as there is merit to the proposition that private incentive for licensees to test patent validity is lacking, this adds importance to the suggestion that more careful and detailed consideration be given to original applications before they are approved by the Patent Office.[31] It also adds force to the contention that legislation would be desirable making it possible for the Department of Justice to bring action for patent cancellation on validity grounds. As Justice Harlan pointed out in *Lear* v. *Adkins* (a point supported by Justice White in *Blonder-Tongue*): "Surely the equities of the licensor do not weigh very heavily when they are balanced against the important public interest in permitting full and free competition in the use of ideas which are in reality a part of the public domain."[32]

Attempting to find means of confining a patentee's monopoly to valid claims not only is consistent with recent Supreme Court holdings but, more important, it is in line with that primary goal of both patent and antitrust law—the socially efficient allocation of scarce resources.

Fully Exploiting a Patent's Competitive Superiority

There has been, and continues to be, a widespread economic misconception about patent monopoly. This misconception has been judicially fostered and successively augmented for more than sixty

31. President Johnson's (Exec. Order no. 11215) Commission on the Patent System, established to evaluate the patent system and recommend ways it might be revised, viewed the problem of improving the quality of patents primarily as a Patent Office obligation. Its Recommendation XII provided that the Patent Office should continually evaluate the quality of patents being issued and should "furnish information for the publication of an annual rating of the overall quality of patents issued each year" (See Banner, "The Recent Proposal to Change the United States Patent System," 29 *Ohio S. L. J.* 873 [Fall 1968]).

32. 395 U.S. 653 (1969), at p. 670.

years, and shared by lawyers and nonlawyers alike: that restriction
on use by licensees creates a monopoly broader than the patent. This
is not indicative of a disposition to challenge the underlying rationale
of the patent system. There is substantial support, not greatly diminished by critics of the system itself, that an attempt to create things
which might otherwise not exist should be sponsored by allowing
defined and limited monopoly in the short run for expected greater
good in the long run. And the right of a patentee to achieve his full
reward is consistent with this. If it could be accepted, as a recent task
force report avers but nowhere supports,[33] that "a rational patent
owner can *exact the full monopoly reward* by setting appropriate
royalties, and that reward will be greatest if the invention is   exploited under competitive conditions,"[34] there would have been little
occasion for this extended exposition. If, however, the critical analysis detailed in the foregoing chapters deserves serious consideration, then most of the recommendations contained in this White
House report do not meet its self-imposed test: "full monopoly reward." Its questionable recommendations include: (1) "in general, a
patent owner who has granted a license with respect to his patent
must license all qualified applicants on equivalent terms";[35] (2) "the
grant of an exclusive license to a single licensee or a small group of
licensees generally puts the licensee or licensees in a position to exact
a monopoly profit. In effect, the patent owner is sharing his monopoly
profit with the licensees. This will generally be to the patent owner's
advantage *only if the patent is vulnerable or if the arrangement creates
a monopoly broader than the patent*";[36] but (3) "a patentee may decline to issue licenses at all, or he may issue licenses in some fields of
use and reserve to himself the practice of the patent in other fields."[37]

These unsupported task-force recommendations reflect the very
substantial acceptance, by both the legal and the economic professions,
of the increasingly proscriptive judicial opinions relating to licensor-

---

33. *White House Task Force Report on Antitrust Policy* (the *Neal Report*)
(released 21 May 1969 and reprinted in Hearings before the Special Subcommittee on Small Business, *H. Res.* 66, vol. 1, 1969 Oct. 7, 8, and 9), at p. 292.
34. Ibid., p. 305, part 5, The Patent Laws.
35. Ibid.
36. Ibid.
37. Ibid. But see its own n. 1 at p. 306: "We have not given detailed consideration to the desirability of permitting license restrictions on pricing, field of
use or territories." Neither, it should be stressed, was there any exposition of
the "detailed considerations" for the recommendations they did make.

licensee contracts under both patent law and antitrust law. Although
agreement is surprisingly widespread about the relevant questions, a
critical analysis in search of better answers deserves far more careful
work if useful and needed reform is to be accomplished. And in this
process I hope that undoing needless and often harmful regulatory
limitations on patentees—even though they are of long standing—
will be given as much consideration as adopting further restraints
upon how patent monopoly may be exercised.

Table of Cases

258

Table of Cases

Index

Accumulation of patents, 207n, 218, 224–25, 231, 236
Admission prices, 185–86, 190
Advertising, 130n, 132, 134–35
Agency agreements, 125–27, 131, 133, 136, 192–93, 194
Aggression, monopoly by, 241, 242
Allocation of resources. *See* Resource allocation
All-or-none offers, 116
Almost-simultaneous discovery, 21, 22
Ancillarity, doctrine of, 136, 137–38
Antitrust law: effectiveness of, 200, 239; fallacious, 57–58; goal of, 1–3, 4, 6–7, 9–14, 115, 254; standards of, 7–8, 51, 56n, 57–58, 241
Appropriability of information, 24–26, 27n
Arnold, Thurman, 185n
Arrow, Kenneth, 16, 23–27, 32, 37, 50, 118
Assets, patents as, 249–51
Assigning-back agreements, 228–30, 232
Automobile repairs, example of, 174–75
Autonomy, local, 133
Average cost, 67–68

"Bacon and eggs," example of, 65n–66n, 93

Baxter, William, 89, 90n, 91, 110
Bentham, Jeremy, 18
Black, Justice, 43, 181, 220n
Blocking, mutual, 51
Block licensing, 234–38, 254
Books, 156, 162n
Bork, Robert, 129–32, 135–36
Brandeis, Justice, 167, 172, 173–74, 175, 205–7, 214
Brown, James A., 219n–220n
Burstein, M. L., 116–18
Burton, Justice, 181n
Butler, Justice, 186
Button-fastener, example of, 103–4, 146–49, 150, 153

Cancellation. *See* Divestiture
Capital, need for, 76n
Cartels: illegality of, 7, 8, 138, 201, 242; and patent pooling, 196, 218–19, 227; and price maintenance, 123
Celler-Kefauver amendment, 250
Centralization of decision-making, 5, 26–27, 29, 33, 134
Checkout device, example of, 42–43, 47–48
Choice: consumer, 4, 11, 130n, 201; of investors, 23n
Clark, J. B., 18, 19–21, 23
Clark, Justice, 44–46, 157, 158
Class action, 253n
Clayton Act: and exclusionary techniques, 57, 59, 166, 167–69;

261

Ward S. Bowman, Jr., professor of law and economics at Yale Law School since 1956, has served as an economic consultant at the Antitrust Division and as a member of the President's Task Force on Productivity and Competition. For ten years, he was a research associate at the University of Chicago Law School. He has contributed numerous articles to scholarly publications.

1973